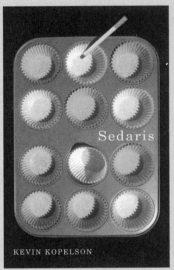
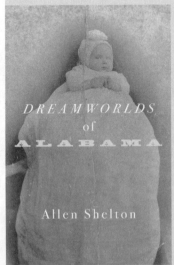

Martin Amis is the author of six books of non-fiction and ten novels, the most recent of which is *House of Meetings* (Vintage). Extracts from his novels *Money, London Fields, Time's Arrow* and *The Information* (Vintage) have appeared as works-in-progress in *Granta*. Amis became Professor of Creative Writing at Manchester University in 2007. His book about September 11, *The Second Plane*, will be published in January 2008 by Cape in the UK and Knopf in the US.

Tash Aw grew up in Malaysia and moved to Britain when he was eighteen. In 2005 his first novel, *The Harmony Silk Factory* (HaperPerennial/Penguin), won the Whitbread Award and the Commonwealth Writers' Prize for Best First Book. 'To The City' is an extract from his second novel, *Map of the Invisible World*, which will be published in 2009. He lives in London.

Julian Barnes is the author of ten novels and two collections of short stories. His first contribution to *Granta* was an excerpt from *Flaubert's Parrot* (Picador/Vintage) in *Granta* 7 'Best of Young British Novelists' in 1983. His next book, *Nothing to be Frightened Of*, will be published in spring 2008 by Cape in the UK and Knopf in the US.

William Boyd's most recent novel, *Restless*, is published by Bloomsbury in the UK and the US. He is the author of eight other novels and three collections of short stories—and is the screenwriter of thirteen films, one of which, *The Trench* (1999), he also directed.

Ashley Capps received her MFA from the Iowa Writers' Workshop. Her first collection of poems, *Mistaking the Sea for Green Fields* (University of Akron Press), was published in 2006. She is from Charlotte, North Carolina.

Lucy Eyre's novel about philosophy, *If Minds Had Toes*, is published by Bloomsbury in the UK and the US.

James Fenton has worked as political journalist, literary critic, war correspondent and columnist, most recently for the London *Guardian*. He was Oxford Professor of Poetry, 1994–99, and his *Selected Poems* was published in 2006 by Penguin in the UK and Farrar, Straus & Giroux in the US. A contributor to *Granta* since 1984, his pieces including 'The Fall of Saigon' in *Granta* 15, and 'The Snap Revolution' in *Granta* 18.

Bruce Frankel has been a journalist for French Television 1 (TF1) since 1981. In 2005, he completed an independent documentary, *CBI Sound Off*, about the veterans of the China–Burma–India theatre of operations in the Second World War. He is currently working on the second volume of his photo-manuscript, *The Edge of Seeing*.

NOTES ON CONTRIBUTORS

Lavinia Greenlaw has written three collections of poetry: *Night Photograph*, *A World Where News Travelled Slowly* and *Minsk* (Faber/Houghton Mifflin), and two novels. Her memoir, *The Importance of Music to Girls*, is published by Faber in the UK and will be published by Farrar, Straus & Giroux in the US in April 2008.

Isabel Hilton's book, *The Search for the Panchen Lama*, is published by Penguin in the UK and by W.W. Norton in the US. She is a columnist for the London *Guardian*, and the founder and editor of www.chinadialogue.net. She first appeared in the magazine with 'The General' in *Granta* 31.

David Hockney was born in Bradford in 1937 and is regarded as one of the world's most influential artists. His most recent book, *Hockney's Pictures*, is published by Thames and Hudson.

Michael Hofmann has translated books by Ernst Jünger, Franz Kafka, Wolfgang Koeppen and many others. His *Selected Poems* will be published by Faber in March 2008. His translations of the works of Joseph Roth are available from Granta Books.

Alan Hollinghurst is the author of four novels: *The Swimming-Pool Library* (Vintage), *The Folding Star* (Vintage/Bloomsbury), *The Spell* (Vintage/Penguin) and *The Line of Beauty* (Picador), which won the Man Booker Prize in 2004. He lives in London.

A. M. Homes is the author of two collections of short stories and five novels, most recently *This Book Will Save Your Life* (Granta/Penguin). An extract from her memoir, *The Mistress's Daughter* (Granta/Viking), appeared in *Granta* 98.

Ian Jack edited *Granta* from 1995 to 2007 and previously edited the *Independent on Sunday*. He has written for the magazine since 1987, when his piece 'Finished with Engines' was published in *Granta* 21. He has since written about the Titanic, Kathleen Ferrier, the Hatfield train crash and the three IRA men killed in Gibraltar. 'The Serampur Scotch' is taken from a book about the industrial revolution and India that he may never finish. He writes for the London *Guardian*.

Hanif Kureishi was chosen as one of *Granta*'s Best of Young British Novelists in 1993. His novels include *The Buddha of Suburbia* (Faber/Penguin), *The Black Album* (Faber/Scribner) and *Intimacy* (Faber/Simon & Schuster). 'Something to Tell You' is an extract from his forthcoming novel of the same title, which will be published in the UK by Faber in March 2008 and in the US by Scribner.

Doris Lessing was born in 1919 in Persia, now Iran, and grew up in Southern Rhodesia, now Zimbabwe, arriving in England in 1949. She is the author of more than twenty novels, most recently *The Cleft* (Fourth Estate/HarperCollins). In October 2007, she won the Nobel Prize in Literature. She last appeared in the magazine with 'The Death of a Chair' in *Granta* 90.

Mario Vargas Llosa was born in Peru in 1936. His most recent books in English include a novel, *The Bad Girl* (Faber/Farrar, Straus & Giroux), and *Touchstones*, a collection of essays on literature, art and politics (Faber). He first appeared in the magazine with 'La Orgia Perpetua' in *Granta* 4.

Derek Mahon was awarded the 2007 David Cohen Prize for Literature. His collections of poetry include *Harbour Lights*, *Collected Poems* and *Adaptations*, all published by The Gallery Press. 'Somewhere the Wave' is the title poem of an 'interim' collection published by Gallery in a limited edition. He was born in Belfast in 1941 and now lives in Kinsale, County Cork.

Ian McEwan has been shortlisted for the Man Booker Prize four times, winning the award for *Amsterdam* in 1998. His novel *Atonement* received the W. H. Smith Literary Award (2002), the National Book Critics' Circle Fiction Award (2003), the *Los Angeles Times* Prize for Fiction (2003), and the Santiago Prize for the European Novel (2004). His most recent novel is *On Chesil Beach*. All are published by Vintage and Anchor. He was chosen as one of *Granta*'s Best of Young British Novelists in 1983.

Jamie McKendrick's most recent collections of poetry are *Ink Stone* and *Crocodiles & Obelisks* (Faber). *The Embrace*, his translations of Valerio Magrelli's poems, will be published next year by Faber.

Alice Oswald is the author of three collections of poetry: *The Thing in the Gap Stone Stile* (Faber/Oxford University Press USA), which was a Poetry Book Society Choice; *Dart* (Faber), which won the T. S. Eliot Prize in 2002; and *The Thunder Mutters* (Faber). She lives in Devon and is married with three children.

Helen Oyeyemi was born in Nigeria in 1984 and moved to London when she was four. She is the author of two novels, *The Icarus Girl* and *The Opposite House* (Bloomsbury/Nan A. Talese), and two plays, *Juniper's Whitening* and *Victimese*. 'pie-kah' is taken from her novel of the same title, which will be published by Picador in the UK and by Nan A. Talese in the US.

Don Paterson works as a poetry editor and as a jazz guitarist, and lectures in creative writing at the University of St Andrews. In 2003 his poetry collection *Landing Light* (Faber/Graywolf) won the Whitbread Poetry Prize and the T. S. Eliot Prize. He is the author, most recently, of *The Blind Eye* (Faber).

Jayne Anne Phillips is the author of two short story collections, *Black Tickets* (Faber/Delta) and *Fast Lanes* (Faber/Vintage), and three novels, *Machine Dreams* (Faber/Vintage), *Shelter* (Faber/Delta) and *Motherkind* (Vintage), which was shortlisted for the Orange Prize in 2001. She directs the MFA Program at Rutgers-Newark, the State University of New Jersey. 'Solly and Lark' is taken from her novel *Termite*, which will be published by Cape in the UK and Knopf in the US. An earlier extract was published in *Granta* 82.

Harold Pinter was born in London in 1930 and is married to Antonia Fraser. He has written twenty-nine plays, twenty-one screenplays and directed twenty-seven theatre productions, including James Joyce's *Exiles*, David Mamet's *Oleanna* and seven plays by Simon Gray. His awards include the Companion of Honour for services to Literature and the Molière d'honneur for lifetime achievement. In 2005, he received the Nobel Prize in Literature.

Craig Raine's *Collected Poems 1978–1999* is published by Picador. His most recent book is a critical study, *T. S. Eliot*, published by Oxford University Press in the UK and the US. He is the editor of *Areté*, the arts tri-quarterly. 'How Snow Falls' is the title poem of his forthcoming collection.

Oliver Reynolds was born in Cardiff in 1957. He has published four books of poetry, including *Almost*, which was published by Faber in 1999.

Salman Rushdie has written three books of non-fiction, a collection of stories, and ten novels, the newest of which, *The Enchantress of Florence*, will be published in April 2008 by Cape in the UK and Random House in the US. In 1983, he was chosen as one *Granta*'s Best of Young British Novelists.

Ingo Schulze was born in Dresden in 1962. His first collection of short stories, *33 Moments of Happiness* (Picador/Vintage), won Germany's prestigious Döblin Prize. 'Estonia, Out in the Country' is taken from his most recent collection of short stories, *Handy* (Berlin Verlag). He lives in Berlin.

Carolin Seeliger is a freelance photographer.

Nicholas Shakespeare was one of *Granta*'s Best of Young British Novelists in 1993. He has written for *Granta* on Abimael Guzman, Martha Gellhorn and Tasmania, the background to his most recent novel, *Secrets of the Sea* (Harvill Secker). He is also the author of a biography, *Bruce Chatwin* (Cape/Anchor), and is currently preparing an edition of Chatwin's letters.

Helen Simpson is the author of four collections of short stories including *Hey Yeah Right Get a Life* (Vintage), published as *Getting a Life* by Vintage in the US, and *Constitutional* (Jonathan Cape), published as *In the Driving Seat* by Knopf in the US. In 1993 she was chosen as one of *Granta*'s Best of Young British Novelists. She lives in London.

Tobias Wenzel was born in 1974 and lives in Berlin where he works as a freelance journalist. 'My Question For Myself' is taken from his forthcoming book of the same title. More information and photographs can be found at www.questionformyself.com.

NOW IS THE WINTER OF YOUR CONTENT

"Combines the ambition of a 19th-century social novel with a cops-and-Bhais detective thriller…As sprawling as the heat-drenched city it richly portrays."
— *New York Times*

"One of the oddest innocents ever to creep through American literature.... Much of *Kockroach* is classic gangster parody.... But there's plenty of rueful, Kafkaesque reflection on what it means to be human, too.... Pick up this witty, unsettling book."
—*Washington Post Book World*

The story of a man's descent into savagery during what he intends to be his last week on earth.

"Brilliant, monumentally horrible and truly disturbing."
—*Arena* (UK)

A provocative anthology of short stories, centered around the theme of sex and politics from some of the best fiction writers at work today.

When a drug-addicted man and his mother kidnap a teenage boy they are forced to reexamine what it means to love and be a family.

"One of the funniest, strangest and most revolting memoirs ever written."
— *The Sunday Times*

"This is not a book for the faint of heart, Franklin's vivid prose is spilling all over the pages…[it's] very good storytelling, with a purpose that belies its graphic nature."
—*Pittsburgh Tribune*

"A brilliant, insightful, and intriguing literary voyage… an exciting, frenetic read… the story lines dig into you and leave their mark."
—*Boston Herald*

100

CONGRATULATIONS TO GRANTA ON THE OCCASION OF ITS 100TH ISSUE

Sight & Sound is offering all Granta readers the choice of a free BFI Screen Guide with every 12-issue subscription. Both 100 *European Horror Films* and 100 *Road Movies* are enlightening, entertaining and invaluable guides to two film-genres with deep literary roots.

SUBSCRIBE TODAY
UK: £41 for 12 issues (or £38 if paying by Direct Debit) – saving you £7 on the shop price.
Overseas: £61 for 12 issues

And choose your free BFI Screen Guide:

RRP
£12

TO ORDER
Call our subscription hotline on +44 (0)1858 438848 and quote reference GRTA or visit www.subscription.co.uk/sightandsound/GRTA

This offer expires 29th Feb 2008

Sight & Sound is the international film magazine offering a unique insight into the very best of film culture – for more information visit www.bfi.org.uk/sightandsound

INTRODUCTION

I possess a complete run of *Granta* except for issue number one. *Granta* 1 is forever unobtainable, I've decided. It's gone, it's vanished. I've been trying for years to find it in antiquarian booksellers, and more lately on the Web, but in vain (I have the 1989 limited-edition reprint, of course, but it's not the same, not the genuine article). And my search is fuelled by the bitterly enduring knowledge that, once, I did actually have *Granta* 1. I bought it in Oxford in 1979 and owned it for a while and then lost it. I have the original numbers two to six, also extremely rare, the issues that appeared before *Granta*'s association with Penguin began with the celebrated *Granta* 7—the first 'Best of Young British Novelists'—but having them and the rest and not having number one still irritates and frustrates.

I cite this as evidence of the longevity of my connection with the magazine, but in fact the link goes back even further, pre-dating the acquisition of the missing *Granta* 1. In 1979 I was living in Oxford trying to finish a doctoral thesis and teaching in various Oxford colleges as a jobbing lecturer. I had just had my first novel accepted by a London publisher, but I was going to have to wait until January 1981 to see it published. I was reviewing books, writing short stories, and was seized with a sense of being engaged with literary life in a way that I haven't fully replicated since. I read everything. I bought all the little magazines. Nothing stirred in the undergrowth of the literary world that didn't attract my beady-eyed attention. At the same time, Susan, my wife, was working at Oxford University Press, running the publicity and marketing for the English Literature and Oxford Poetry lists. One night she came home from work with news of a new literary magazine that was starting up: she had met the editor, some American guy, who was looking for advertising, and she had decided to take a page in support.

What magazine? I asked, cultural antennae quivering. The old Cambridge University magazine, *Granta*, she said. This American, Bill

13

Buford, is reviving it. My scoff was audible. Bad idea, I remember saying—a *university* magazine? As well revive *Isis* (Oxford's equivalent to *Granta*, to which I had been a regular contributor) and try to remarket it as a literary journal. Moreover, *Granta* was a terrible name—as bad as *Isis* (another river). What does it say to potential readers? Nothing. Misguided idea all round, hasn't a hope, no legs.

I enjoy it when naysayers get their comeuppance and I happily castigate myself for my condescension and lack of prescience on this occasion. But it was this early whiff of *Granta* that made me buy *Granta* 1, when I saw it on sale in a little shop in Broad Street, opposite Balliol, that seemed to sell every literary magazine in the world. My scepticism fell from me immediately. This wasn't a magazine: it was like a paperback book. It had a title: 'New American Writing'. Writers such as William Gass, Joyce Carol Oates, Donald Barthelme and Susan Sontag were listed on the contents' page. This was indeed the old Cambridge University magazine, but fearlessly reinvented. It looked very impressive. And there was the editor's name—William Buford—the American who'd come to Oxford University Press looking for advertising. The serendipitous connection made me buy it and made me buy the next issue also, with its blazing red cover and its publication of George Steiner's entire novella, *The Portage to San Cristobal of A. H.*. And then I bought *Granta* 3, with its provocative title, 'The End of the English Novel'. As someone whose English novel was about to appear, I read its grim prognostications and faint glimmerings of hope for the moribund form with appalled fascination. Here was a new writer called Salman Rushdie with an extract from a novel called *Midnight's Children*; here were Angela Carter and Russell Hoban, Lorna Sage and Christine Brooke-Rose. How did one join this gang?

The fact was that *Granta* had arrived in its first year of publication fully formed and fighting fit, establishing itself very quickly as something entirely different from its peers and competitors. Indeed, the ambitions it set out for itself in its first year of publication haven't changed that much in its subsequent vivacious life. By *Granta* 2 it was already bullishly advertising itself in this way:

> With issues of two, three and four hundred pages, the literary
> quarterly we now publish is unlike anything you'll find in Britain.

It is part magazine, part journal, part paperback book, an
anthology dealing not just in fiction but in writing of all kinds—
short stories, essays, autobiographies, histories, poetry, even whole
novels—but always writing which is vital and challenging.

Granta's young, brash and audacious boast has been more than
lived up to. Its claims to fame—the invention of 'Dirty Realism' in
new American writing, its intriguingly themed numbers, its eye-
catching covers (with David Hockney's wonderful artwork for this
issue acting as a centennial apotheosis), its photo essays, its
reinvigoration of the travel writing genre, and its encouragement of
its own brand of reportage (highly personal, often very intrepid,
always well written)—have always been leavened over the nearly
thirty years of its life by the fiction it has published. For a writer of
fiction, the great appeal of *Granta* has been that you could write at
almost any length and without censorship. Anything genuinely goes.
It's surprising how few magazines offer these literary freedoms.

My own move from paying customer to contributor came in
1983, with the publication of *Granta* 7 and the first selection of the
'Best of Young British Novelists'. All twenty of us contributed a work
of fiction, and that first *Granta* story of mine was called 'Extracts
from the Journal of Flying Officer J', a reworking (with illustrations
by the author) of 'As You Like It', seen through the distorting lens
of W. H. Auden's *The Orators*. Its publication was a forceful example
of *Granta*'s generous latitude to its writers.

Over the years, under Bill Buford's and then Ian Jack's editorship,
seven stories of mine have appeared in the magazine, more than in
any other individual publication. So perhaps it is oddly fitting that
the journey of my own *Granta* life to date should have progressed
in this way: from supercilious sceptic to regular contributor to
enthusiastic guest editor. My objective for *Granta* 100 has been very
simple: to ask a selection of writers associated with the magazine to
provide something as yet unpublished for this milestone edition.
Almost all the writers in this issue (poets apart) have been published
by *Granta* before—and some many times. Poetry pretty much died
out after the first few issues of the magazine, but the inclusion of
ten poets here is in the hope it won't be neglected in the future.
Fulfilling another *Granta* tradition of blazing a trail, there are four

William Boyd

'new voices'—Tash Aw, Lucy Eyre, Helen Oyeyemi and Ingo Schulze—who haven't previously appeared in its pages.

Granta 3 floated the idea of 'The End of the English Novel'. Over the many years of its existence *Granta*'s own example and practice have disproved this notion. The baleful note was unfounded: not only the English novel, but also other forms of writing that Granta has championed show robust and dynamic signs of life—something underlined by the appearance of this hundredth issue of the magazine. Those gathered together here are all part of *Granta*'s past, present and future history and they form a small selection of *Granta*'s wider community of writers, the hundreds who have contributed to the magazine over its long life: *Granta*'s *tertulia*, if you like. The Spanish word is richer and more nuanced than the English equivalent, 'circle of friends', implying as it does that the links between the members of the *tertulia* are particularly strong, the intellectual bonds more firm, the shared cultural values all important. I hope that *Granta* 100 shows that spirit to be secure and thriving.

William Boyd

GRANTA

SOLLY AND LARK

Winfield, West Virginia, 1965

Jayne Anne Phillips

Rain falling across the alley and the backyards looks green as grass against washed brush and soaked trees. You see through it like it might rain forever, and you forget how hard it's pouring until you stand out in it. Nonie said the rain drummed all night, and she went to work early in case they have any water to mop up at the restaurant. The backyard looks thick and spongy. Dimpled water stands in the tracks of the alley, and I'm staring out the screen door, feeling the rush of breath falling water makes. Termite likes the sound and he likes it if I shut the back door, open it, shut it again, like I'm changing the weather in the room. He's nine this year, and he might not walk or talk, but he loves rain. He listens like it's music. I shut the door and think about the water coming up, how it's moving up the slant in the basement floor. I butter the toast, and when I turn to open the door again Solly is there, up close in a dull black slicker, water running off his face in the billed hood.

'Lark, you okay?' He's nearly shouting in the sluice of the water. 'My dad said to drop off these water jugs. He said to fill them, while the tap water is still safe.'

I move back to let him in and the hood falls back off his wet hair. I realize I haven't seen him close since before I left school, since I'd pass him in the halls and he'd look at me, some girl or other trailing after him. It got around that we were cousins, to explain the looks between us and the growing up together, our houses like two shambling arms of the same building, except Solly's is bigger. Cousins because people think of Nonie and Nick Tucci as weirdly related, both raising kids alone and living off the alley, like we're all a tribe down here, not quite across the tracks but almost. Nick Tucci's got three boys, Joey and Solly and Zeke, and a good factory job. Nonie helps Charlie run the restaurant, and she's got Termite and me. She's our aunt, and she doesn't talk about our mother. Solly's mother took off a long time ago. We've both got these missing persons, like old mysteries.

'You want some toast?' I ask Solly.

He looks at the hot bread in my hands, and then he's at the sink with the plastic jugs. 'No thanks,' he says.

He steps out of his boots and I see the shine of blond whiskers along his jaw, on his cheeks that look hollowed out. He's got such long bones, Solly does, and a bruisy mouth, like his lips are a little swollen. Most people wouldn't say he's handsome though, his face is too mismatched, the square chin and straight nose, the deep-set eyes. He stands there dripping on the linoleum by the shelves of cans and bottles, filling the plastic jugs and capping them, and a steam nearly rises off him. The rain is cool and warm at once.

'Seems strange to put water by with so much of it pouring down,' I tell him.

'Yeah, well, if you end up on the roof you could catch it in your hands and drink it. May not come to that, but the river is rising fast. They don't expect the crest until tonight. Lumber Street will flood for sure and they've closed the bridge. Nonie go to work today?'

'Sure. She and Charlie? You kidding? They'd go to work unless the town closed down.'

'It just might. Lark, the Armory is open. They've got food, cots, a generator. I could take you and Termite there now, just in case. No need for boats.'

'He'd like a boat ride.' I smile, but Solly doesn't. I fold Termite's toast in a four-square and put it in his hand; that way he can hold it himself. 'Solly, you know the Armory will scare him, all those people, all that noise. We need to stay here unless we really have to leave. Even if Nonie can't get home tonight, I can manage.'

'How will you manage?'

'We have a bed in the attic, and room for groceries and blankets and water. I've stacked up some of the furniture down here. Maybe you can help me get some things upstairs. The rest will have to fend for itself.' I'm standing behind Termite's chair, and I look at Solly. It feels hard to walk over near him, cross a few squares of linoleum flooring, but I do. We stand at the kitchen window, inches apart, nearest the pour of the rain. 'If it gets bad enough, you'll come and get us.'

'Yeah,' he says, 'I will.' He's not going to argue. He looks at me with that mix of hard and soft in his eyes, and he won't look away.

I open the refrigerator and reach into it like there's something I need. 'We'll be fine,' I say.

There's a beat of silence, like he's waiting for me. 'All right, Lark.'

Termite stays completely still. I can feel him, tuned in to us, to the spaces between our words, and I rattle the loose metal shelf in the fridge, shift jars and milk bottles, before I shut the big door.

Solly is moving the water jugs, lining them up beside the wall. 'You got plenty of bottled water now, anyway,' he says. 'Noon on, just to be safe, stop using the tap.' Then he moves past me and crouches by Termite's chair. 'Hey, Termite,' he says, 'you like rain? It's raining. No wagon today.' He puts his hand on Termite's shoulder. 'That wagon would fill up and float,' he says softly, then he looks up at me. 'He used to talk to me. He doesn't answer me any more. I know he knows me.'

'Of course he does. Just not so used to you as he was.'

'Yeah. That wagon. I see you pulling him in it, up the alley. He still likes it. A couple more years though, he won't even fit. Anyway, I brought you something, Termite. Music you might like. Better than radio, Termite. You can listen through these.' Solly pulls a portable tape player out of the pocket of the big coat, and headphones. He goes to put them on Termite's head. Termite pulls away. And I know he won't eat. It's too different that Solly's here. I'll have to make him food later.

'He'll listen another time,' I tell Solly. 'It's just he hasn't used headphones much, and they might remind him of school. He's listening to the rain. Like he thinks he can hear when the sound of it is going to change.'

'Change? He's a weatherman now? Maybe he could stop it raining. Some day it'll stop. Things do stop.' Solly stands. 'You need me to go to the store for you? Anything like that?'

'Nonie brings milk or whatever from the restaurant. But there's water coming up in the basement. I wonder if you could help me move some boxes. I don't want to ask Nonie, and I can't lift them by myself.'

'Lights working down there?'

'By the workbench. But I'll get a flashlight.' I go into the drawer for the flashlight and I feel Termite start to nod and rock in his chair, like he does if there's a new hum of energy, anything strung out.

'Yeah, Termite, it's me.' Solly touches Termite's back, a man's touch, quiet and still, and Termite stops.

I turn away from them and start down the basement steps. 'Termite is all right up there,' I call back. 'He'll let me know if he gets bored.' I hear Solly on the stairs behind me in his boots and I feel a shudder inside, like he's come back and we're both much smaller, together all day like we used to be. I pull the chain over the workbench and the light goes on over words we carved in the wood, our names, a little family of stick figures, and the requisite bad words, s-words and f-words. We wrote prayer words too. We wrote 'Jesus'. Angled into a corner, small, like a flower almost, is Joey's faint drawing of a cock.

Solly runs his hand over the scarred wood, over Joey's little hieroglyph. 'Joey,' he says. 'Always such a father figure, wasn't he?'

I shine the light where the dark is darker, and I hear the slip of water. I see it's higher than it was two hours ago. 'There are eight boxes,' I tell Solly. 'Big ones, stacked up.'

'She used to have a bedspread over these,' Solly says.

'How do you know?'

'I remember a big shape in the corner, and the cloth of the spread was red checks. Don't you remember? We bounced balls against it. We climbed on it.' He looks at me, unsmiling. 'What is it with you? Holes in your head?'

'I never paid much attention, I guess. But there's no cloth now, and I've been home with Termite, and I noticed the boxes, the return addresses. Florida. I opened one, and I think they belonged to my mother. I can't imagine why else Nonie would be keeping them.'

'You ask her?'

'I'm not ready to ask. I want to go through them.'

'For clues.'

'Maybe.'

Now he smiles. 'Don't you ever think our mothers might be drifting around a swimming pool together on one of those blow-up floats, sipping cool drinks under palm trees?'

'They didn't know one another, did they?'

'No, they didn't, but it doesn't seem like that, does it? My dad, he knew them both, and they both left, and left their kids. Remember that next time Nick gives you the eye.'

'You think it was all about Nick?' I smile, to show him it's a joke.

'No. He's just another link between them. But doesn't it seem sometimes like they were sisters under the skin, or maybe even the same person?' He pulls the slicker hood off, unzips the front of the jacket. 'After she was gone awhile, I started pretending that. It made you and me more the same.'

He looks at me so hard I step back. But he's already grabbed me, without ever moving. It's because of the room. Now I remember the red-checked cloth, with lawn chairs leaning up against it, and a couple of old cot mattresses thrown over the top. Nonie kept the storm cellar doors open in the summer, and we came in and out that way, under the branches of bushy lilacs that hung over both sides. They're gone now. 'You think you need me to help you with those boxes?' I ask him. 'They're pretty heavy.'

'I think I can manage, Lark,' he says, with an edge. 'You want them in the attic?'

'It's the only second floor we've got.'

'Don't worry. The water won't get that high unless half the town floods. Which might not be a bad idea. We could all float away.'

I hear the bell on Termite's chair. He rings it once. 'He wants something. I'll go up.'

'Yeah, go on up with him.' Solly pulls off the slicker and he's wearing a flannel shirt with the arms cut out. His arms are tight. For so many years, even though he was a year older, he was my size. I'm always surprised at how tall he is, muscular and lean, like I turned around and he changed. He does all the sports with the dumb jocks and he gets what the dumb jocks get—the blonde girls with their flipped hair and a job at the gas station the summer after graduation. I suppose now he pretends he's like those girls, with their sweater sets and college funds, like he lives in that second-hand convertible of Joey's that he keeps so clean, driving girls here and there. Probably a good plan. Even if their Mommies and Daddies figure it's high school stuff. They'll ship their girls off now, get them away from Saul Tucci. Solly is not what they want.

'You going off to school, Solly?' I can't help asking him.

'Like the rest of the sheep? Go play some football fifty miles from here? Nah, I don't think so. There was one letter I answered—Fort Lauderdale. Lure of the sea. My own palm tree.' He rakes his fingers through his wet hair and I see the darkish roots at his hairline. One of those girls streaked his hair like hers, playing at twosies. My twin. He looks straight across at me. 'Shot in the dark. We're only a double-A team. Wasn't like I had endless offers.'

Solly in Florida, I think. Solly in Florida.

'Don't know about that one yet,' he says. 'I haven't told Nick about it, or anyone.'

'Well. Let me know, when you hear.'

'Yeah?'

I want to get away from him. 'Sorry it's so close down here. Gets hot, with the windows shut against the rain.' I turn and start up the stairs and he stands there like he's watching me walk out of a story. For a weird moment I think I hear his heart beating but it's my own head pounding, a thud I only notice when I get up the steps and back into the kitchen. Things stop, Solly said. I think about living here on and on, and he wouldn't. I think about going away myself, living a whole different life, like I could exist on a different planet and this life wouldn't know about me, and I wouldn't know about it. I sit down in a kitchen chair close beside Termite and I see his toast on the table where he dropped it. 'You hungry yet?' I ask him, but my voice has a dead, automatic sound and he puts his arms across my knees. He smells of the baby powder Nonie and I still dust across his shoulders after baths. I realize I'm never going to leave him, not in this life. He's so quiet, listening. His open hands in my lap barely move, so faintly, like his thin fingers touch a current of air I'm too thick and gross to feel. The undersides of his fingers are white as alabaster, unlined between the knuckles, like he's always just born. There's a faint pink blush under his skin. When he has a fever, his skin gets dappled.

We hear Solly coming up the stairs with the boxes. I feel him look in at us. He turns in the little hallway, walks into Termite's room and on up, into the attic through the pull-down steps in Termite's ceiling. Termite hears Solly in his room. He likes the attic steps, the creak they make pulling down, how they sound under someone's weight. It's like the air in the attic falls down those stairs in moted streaks cast through the dormer window above. Termite can smell it and feel it, but he doesn't stir now.

'I want you to have a real breakfast,' I tell him. 'I'll make you and Solly something.' He lets me talk.

I peel some peaches and start the toast again. All the time I'm cooking the eggs, Termite is holding Solly's tape player, like he holds the radio, but he leans away when I move to turn it on. I get the food on the plates and I hear Solly, up and down the basement steps. Then he's in the kitchen.

'I lined up the boxes along the wall by the attic window,' he says. 'You'll have enough light to sift through the evidence. May as well leave

23

them up there. Safer. Nonie's basement takes in water, any big rain.'

'Thanks, Solly. I made you some food.' I'm washing out the cast-iron skillet in the sink and Solly comes over near me and puts his hands on me, up under my hair, on my neck, just for a second, as though to move me aside. He's taken his shirt off and tied it around his waist, and he leans in to splash his face in the stream of water.

'Those boxes were dirty,' he says. 'I kept wondering why. Like mud splashed up on them. Then I realized the backs were covered with crumbled hornets' nests. Old ones. Muddy dust.' He unties the shirt and wipes his face with it. Then he sits down by Termite, puts the spoon in Termite's hand, starts helping him. The water is running but I can hear Solly talking. 'We used to go down by the railyard, Lark and me and you, or down under the bridge by the river, and we'd take bottles of Fresca and those pop-top cans of ravioli Joey heated up for Tucci dinners when the old man wasn't home. I'd feed you and we'd wait for trains. Bet you don't know that. Bet you don't know that any more.'

By the time I'm finished cleaning up, Termite has eaten and Solly's plate is just sitting there.

'What's in the tape player?' I ask him.

'A tape Joey sent me. Jazz piano, and someone singing scat vocals. That's sounds, no real words. Termite might like it, especially through the headphones. If he wants to listen.' Solly's talking to me, but looking at Termite. He wipes Termite's mouth with his fingers, touches his face. I see Termite lean so slightly, rest his jaw on Solly's palm, and stay quiet. Like he's reading something he remembers. Someone he lost.

I never even thought, all this time. I lost Solly, but Termite lost him too.

I see Solly realize. His face changes and he puts his hands flat on the table, like someone's punched him and he needs a moment. It's something else between us, all we've done and all we didn't know. He looks over at me, but he keeps his voice smooth. 'Joey's down at Camp Lejeune, getting an education. Left last month. You knew he was going down there, didn't you, Lark?'

I nod. Termite turns his head to listen, hear our voices, but we're not talking. I move to pick up the headphones.

Solly stops me. 'Here, let me. Listen to these voices, Termite. They sing like you talk.' He stands and puts the headphones on Termite and turns on the tape. Termite sits up, then leans back, touches his wrists to the sides of his head, as though to press the music closer.

'He likes it.' I look at Solly. We're by ourselves now.

'Anybody would. I'll leave it. You should listen.'

'You better go, Solly.'

'I was going to. As soon as I finished with the boxes. But I kept thinking about what was in them. I never saw a picture of your mother except this one that you keep in the kitchen, her as a kid with Nonie. When she looks like you. I get you confused with her.' He steps around the table, stands there, touches the back of Termite's head. 'Then when I can't picture your mother, I get to not quite picturing mine.'

I don't answer.

'We used to get in bed with my mother.'

'You told me that. I don't remember her at all.'

'You were three. I was four. It must have been soon after you came here. Probably with those boxes.'

'I don't know when the boxes came. Maybe they came with Termite.' I look past Solly, out the kitchen window into the rain. But he keeps talking.

'She'd have Zeke asleep in the crib beside us and we'd get in bed with her and she'd let us nurse what was left. She was in your mouth and she was in my mouth. It kept us quiet and it calmed her down. We'd fall asleep, and she would.'

'How could you remember that?'

'Because I know I crawled over her to get to you. That's where I slept, next to you.'

I look at him. Then I can't look away again.

'Do something to me,' Solly says.

'You've got girls to do that.'

'I want you to. Do what you used to do.'

'Not any more. That was a long time ago.'

'I'm like your brother, even if I'm not. I'm like Termite except I can talk to you. I can touch you back. I remember things.' He comes close to me behind Termite's chair. I see Termite relax his shoulders and lean his head to listen, and I can hear something like clicks and sweeps through the headphones. Solly's got it up loud, the way Termite likes it. I look at Solly. He's so familiar, like he's me, he's mine, like he's my child, but he's a stranger, the cold, hot look he gets, like any of them. If I let him do what he wants I'll get that look too, that cancels everything. It's like a pit I could fall into. I need to keep out of it.

'Let me,' he says.

Solly could talk me into things because in my mind he still wore the face he used to have, behind the older face I saw. I forgot and I thought doing things with him was like doing things to myself. I got my period early and he was drawn to me then. I was eleven and kept myself so clean, but it was like he could tell. He would come and tease me and talk at me. It wasn't just looking. He would try to get me to want to be touched, he would show me things. I liked it, thinking about it, liked watching his body work, how he delivered himself into it so quickly, so easily, what he could do to me, how my not letting him do what he wanted just extended everything, how he'd find some other way to get around what I wouldn't let him do. He'd hold on to my wrists and mouth the backs of my legs, I'd be blue on that soft skin behind my knees. He'd get to me, talking without words, with sounds. I'd have that achy, crampy feeling in my belly and he'd say he knew it hurt, he'd pull me across him and stroke the bones of my hips, those socket bones the belly sinks between, until the pain turned syrupy. I lay there feeling him harden under me and I thought about his hands, about bleeding into them, filling them. He wanted me to, he said. And other things. Lots of things.

He's looking at me and his eyes are tawny and gold, flecked with green. His lashes look wet. 'Lark,' he says.

I shake my head. 'Solly, it's not true.'

'What's not true?'

'We don't have the same mother. You know we don't. But it's like you said: Nick knew them both. And Nick says things, about my mother.' I'm looking at Solly like he can tell me. 'Suppose it's Nick. Suppose Nick is my father, and he's the reason your mother left, and mine did.'

'No,' Solly says. He steps closer. I can feel the tension in his shoulders and chest, his clenched hands. 'If that were true, and he looks at you the way he does sometimes, I'd want to kill him.'

'If we're related by blood—'

'It's not true, Lark.' He closes his eyes, opens them. 'But if it were, it wouldn't matter. What they did, any of them, doesn't matter.'

'It matters what we did, Solly. Why we wanted to.'

We must have stopped when he was fourteen or so, when it wasn't kids any more. There was that one time, the last time. I told him so. After that I stayed away from him. Then he got angry and stayed away from me. Or not away, but we were never alone any more, or trying to be. I'd left him, so he left me. He had this one and that one. I'm sure he got to a lot of them. He was too young, but that's how he was; I guess it's how I was, but only with him. It was like we ruined each other. I'd see him and I'd look away, but I always knew if he was in a room, or across a street or in a hallway at school, or tackling sandbags at a football practice, outside some classroom window. I'd sense him lunging and hitting, pounding at all the anonymous smeared bodies in their pads and helmets.

'Lark,' he says, in a whisper.

He reaches across and puts his finger in the centre of my chest like a hard little point, and moves it down like he's writing a line on me. It's the storm, I think, the storm has closed us off here, the rain has drowned everything out. I can hear the rain, pouring.

'Don't put your hands on me, or your mouth,' I tell him.

He knows this game. It's an old game. His lips look almost swollen and he opens his mouth slightly and breathes, like he's filled with some horrible relief. I feel like something has got us, just swallowed us.

'Okay.' He mouths the word like he can't talk, not even a whisper. Just the shape of a sound on his lips and he clinches his teeth. Now that he knows I'll do it I can see the feeling come on him full-blown, into his eyes, into his breathing and the tawny flush of his face.

'Don't touch me with your hands,' I tell him, but he doesn't have to. Just the force of him moving toward me backs us into the little hallway, then into my room and against the wall. I can see the flecks of dirt across his chest. A gleam of blond hairs and sweat fills the space my eyes can see and his nipples are hard and tiny. It's so long since I've been this close to the smell and feel of him. He flattens his palms on either side of the wall at my head and keeps his hands still to promise he will. I put my mouth on him and the brown nub of his nipple fits between my teeth like a little stone. I pull on the other and touch and roll it under my fingers, and the sounds he makes seem to start inside me. There's a measure of time we have before he can't hear me or listen to me any more. He reaches down to pull the laundry basket and all the piled clothes over behind me and his face moves down my chest and belly, along the bone of my hip, and he nudges me back on to the basket. He arches over me and I get my shirt off and push my forehead hard against him through his jeans, then I put my hand inside the button and feel for the zipper, pull his pants down, close my eyes. I feel him hard and silken in my mouth, and in my hands, and against my face and in my hair. He's pushing and pushing at me, all over me, not fast, just on and on. I hold him at the hollow of my neck and then I raise my arms all along the line of his torso. The blunt head of him moves its tear of wet across my ribs and my breasts and finds the hollow under my arm, and that's how he comes, and on my neck and my chest, with me holding him so I feel the pulsing as it moves through him.

'Do that to me,' he says, 'Lark, do that to me.' He sinks to his knees and lies across me and we slide down on the towels and T-shirts and sheets that have spilled. It's easy now, like no time has gone by without this, and I put my hand on the cleft of his buttocks and touch the secret fur, push my finger just inside, like I own his body, like he would own mine if he ever got inside me. If he got inside me I would never get away. □

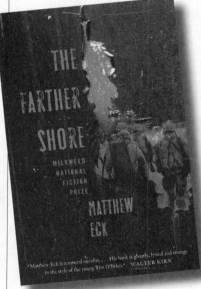

Poem
(To A)

I shall miss you so much when I'm dead
The loveliest of smiles
The softness of your body in our bed

My everlasting bride
Remember that when I am dead
You are forever alive in my heart and my head

Harold Pinter

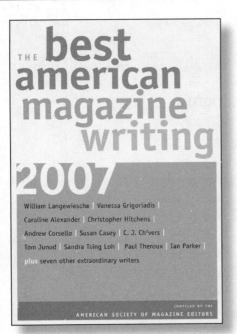

GRANTA

ON BUYING
A CLAVICHORD

James Fenton

James Fenton

Nothing about this business park, this new address, suggests early instruments, but the owner of the agency has two firms under one roof. So, as he completes the tuning of my prospective clavichord, we are surrounded by factory safetywear catalogues. I've been here before to buy humidifiers, which was when I saw the clavichord that stuck in my mind: a simple, modern instrument built by John Morley. Shut, the case looks as if it could contain, say, a pair of sporting rifles.

The owner is halfway through the tuning when I arrive. As he works through the fifths, he inserts a small rubber wedge, to damp the adjacent strings. He gives the lever a gentle turn. Men in overalls drop in to buy boxes of thick gloves. The building seems to expand and contract rhythmically, as if adjusted by some faint automatic mechanism. A periodic bleep, as of a faulty smoke alarm, jars a little, and when a mobile phone goes off the owner remarks: 'That was nearly in tune.'

I study photographs of work boots.

I am listening to one of the softest sounds in Western music. The clavichord itself was often said to be no match for any other instrument, or even for the voice. It seems it could hold its own, in sixteenth-century Spain, against the harp or the *vihuela*, the early guitar. But for the most part it was loved for its solo quietness and unmatched expressivity. The 'dumb spinet', it was sometimes called, unable to be heard at any considerable distance, 'whence it comes to be particularly used among nuns, who learn to play, and are unwilling to disturb the dormitory'.[1]

Isabella d'Este, ordering her first clavichord in 1496, flatters the instrument-maker, Lorenzo Gusnasco, by giving him freedom to design it as he likes, while insisting on only one stipulation: 'that you make it easy to play because we have such a light touch that we are unable to play when it is necessary to force because of the stiffness of the keys'.[2] And Gusnasco flatters Isabella in turn when he assures her that her clavichord 'is extremely delicate to play, and the keys are slightly narrower than usual, apt thus for your delicate hands'.[3]

Those palaces kept two sorts of musicians in attendance. There were players for the road, for the hunt, for the battlefield, for public spaces. They made a great noise with trumpets, pipes and drums. They slept beyond the palace gates, with the majority of the lesser

1. *The New Bach Reader* ed. Hans T. David and Arthur Mendel, revised ed. Christoph Wolff, W. W. Norton, 1998, p 436, citing James Grassineau's *Musical Dictionary* (1740).
2. *The Clavichord* by Bernard Brauchli, Cambridge University Press, 1998, p 48.
3. Ibid.

courtiers. Then there were the house musicians. They played soft instruments such as lutes and clavichords, and they sang *sotto voce*. Always to hand, they lived and slept under the palace roof, and the music they made was made in small rooms.[4]

An optical illusion of a clavichord sits on a shelf in the Studiolo of the Palace of Urbino to this day. It is executed in *intarsia*. The artist has suspended the rules of perspective, in order to supply the most accurate information about its construction and qualities. It has three octaves and a semitone, and is tuned according to the Pythagorean system. So careful is this representation that a working instrument has been reconstructed from the data supplied by this image in inlaid wood.

The clavichord died out because no way could be found to turn the volume up, and it remains dead to the concert hall now, when it could easily be amplified, since amplification would destroy the point. The thing to hear is the sound itself, unmediated, the sound of the struck (as opposed to plucked) wire.

This soft sound is at its softest when the instrument is being tuned. For the struck note is not of a constant pitch. Stronger pressure increases the volume and may also be used to create a vibrato. The tuner must establish the softly struck note as the norm, from which the player may then depart at will, pressing on the held key to vary the pitch. When the modern pianoforte came to life and the clavichord died, nothing replaced this keyboard's ability to yield a vibrato tone.

The piano, which revelled in its new dynamic range, is remembered for killing the harpsichord and the other plucked instruments. These had begun to seem inferior, having no volume control for the single plucked note, and thus no means for varying the dynamics of the phrase. But the clavichord, the forgotten victim of this technology, had offered the player variation of both volume and pitch. The piano could not do this, and no subsequent keyboard instrument—that is, no acoustic instrument—has supplied that loss.

Something else unique. The clavichord player can actually feel the tension of the strings. He presses the key, which is simply the accessible part of the lever. The lever works the tangent, the tangent (the touching-rod) hits the string and remains pressed against it until the finger releases it. For as long as this contact lasts, or until the

4. See the 'Ordine et Officij de Casa de lo Illustrissimo Signor Duca de Urbino' (ed Sabine Eiche, Urbino 1999), where the lutenists, the organist and the singers who sing *sotto voce* and preferably in the Castilian style are listed together as in-house musicians, while other singers, and the majority of courtiers, are expected to live outside the palace.

James Fenton

sound of the struck string decays, the player's finger can feel the string, and can manipulate the sound.

The piano, by contrast, offers no direct contact with the string. Charles Rosen tells us that 'there is nothing one can do with a piano except play louder and softer, faster and slower. A single note on the piano cannot be played more or less beautifully, only more or less *forte* or *piano* and longer or shorter. In spite of the beliefs of many generations of piano teachers, there is no way of pushing down a key more gracefully that will make the slightest difference to the resulting sound.'

He goes on: 'Inside the piano, the elaborate arrangements of joints and springs will only cause the hammer to hit the strings with greater or lesser force. The graceful or dramatic movements of the arms or wrists of the performer are simply a form of choreography that has no practical effect on the mechanism of the instrument, although if it looks more graceful, it may sound more exquisite, not only to the public but to the pianist convinced by his own gestures.'[5]

And later in the same book: 'Claudio Arrau's habit...of simulating a vibrato on the more expressive long notes had no effect on the mechanism inside the instrument, but it was a psychological aid to interpretation that perhaps even convinced members of the audience that the note had extra resonance.' Such a habit, in a pianist, contains a memory of what was, in the days of the clavichord, a virtuosic achievement.

Charles Burney describes C. P. E. Bach in Hamburg in 1772 playing on his Silbermann clavichord (his favourite instrument) three or four of his 'choicest and most difficult compositions'. 'In the pathetic and slow movements, whenever he had a long note to express, he absolutely contrived to produce, from his instrument, a cry of sorrow and complaint, such as can only be effected upon the clavichord, and perhaps by himself.' That cry of sorrow and complaint would have been produced by manipulating the key up and down, to vary the tension on the wire.

The performance was resumed after dinner. Now Bach 'grew so animated and possessed, that he not only played, but looked like one inspired. His eyes were fixed, his underlip fell, and drops of effervescence distilled from his countenance. He said, if he were to be set to work frequently in this manner, he should grow young

5. *Piano Notes* by Charles Rosen, New York, Free Press, 2002, p 24.

again.' But this animation seems to have been confined to the face. Nothing is said about great movements of the body, or of a clavichordist 'convinced by his own gestures'. No doubt there was nothing of this kind to see, just as, when his father, Johann Sebastian Bach, had played, there was nothing to see.

'I have always had great admiration,' says Rosen, 'for an artist who appears to do nothing while achieving everything.'[6] That was how the elder Bach appeared, playing his favoured instrument, the clavichord. He was said to have performed 'with so easy and small a motion of the fingers that it was hardly perceptible. Only the first joints of the fingers were in motion; the hand retained even in the most difficult passages its rounded form; the fingers rose very little from the keys, hardly more than in a shake [trill], and when one was employed, the other remained quietly at its position. Still less did the other parts of his body take any share in his play, as happens with many whose hand is not light enough.'[7]

'When he wished to express strong emotions,' says Forkel, Bach 'did not do it, as many do, by striking the keys with great force, but by melodical and harmonical figures, that is, by the internal resources of art. In this he certainly felt very justly. How can it be the expression of violent passion when a person so beats upon his instrument that, with all the hammering and rattling, you cannot hear any note distinctly, much less distinguish one from another?'

With the son, Carl Philipp Emanuel, we enter the era of early Romanticism, of *Sturm und Drang*. The fixed eyes, the fallen underlip, the drops of effervescence distilled from the countenance—all these symptoms belong to the cult of sensibility. The player at the clavichord, alone perhaps or in some small company of friends, sets out to express his deepest feelings, the turmoil in his soul, in fantasias and improvisations. And it is this aspect of the small instrument which comes most unexpectedly, at least to an English sense of things.

For two reasons. The clavichord was not particularly common in England. It was imported, but it was not generally made here, and only one dubious English eighteenth-century instrument survives. Secondly, our romantic poets, however great the turmoil in their souls, were not, for the most part, particularly given to music-making. They sometimes thought about music, and how music might once have been. Blake, exceptionally, sang his own primitive songs,

6. *Piano Notes*, p 197.
7. Forkel in *The New Bach Reader*, p 433.

whose music was never written down. Byron gave music everywhere its great themes, and he wrote the song lyrics for *Hebrew Melodies*. Of the English Romantic poets, much the most musically gifted was John Clare, who played the fiddle and could write down a tune.

Our poets liked the *idea* of music, of primitive music in particular. They liked the thought of a harpist, an extinct, an exotic, musician. But perhaps they liked words more than the thing itself.

> A damsel with a dulcimer
> In a vision once I saw:
> It was an Abyssinian maid
> And on her Dulcimer she play'd,
> Singing of Mount Abora.

How specific do you suppose this vision to have been? Did Coleridge imagine his Abyssinian maid as a black girl with a light hammer in either hand, hitting the strings in rapid succession, as one would with most dulcimers?[8] Sitting in the dust, perhaps, with her dulcimer on the ground? Or standing at some kind of table? For she could not conveniently have held the dulcimer as she played it—though I suspect that this was the vision Coleridge had in mind, a dusky maiden vaguely striking an indistinct harp-like device.

An instrument with no performer but the wind, the Aeolian harp, suited an English Romantic sense of music very well. Coleridge is so vague about this kind of harp as to call it a lute:

> And that simplest Lute,
> Placed length-ways in the clasping casement, hark!
> How by the desultory breeze caressed,
> Like some coy maid half yielding to her lover,
> It pours such sweet upbraiding, as must needs
> Tempt to repeat the wrong! And now, its strings
> Boldlier swept, the long sequacious notes
> Over delicious surges sink and rise,
> Such a soft floating witchery of sound
> As twilight Elfins make, when they at eve
> Voyage on gentle gales from Fairy-Land,
> Where Melodies round honey-dropping flowers,

---

8. The Appalachian plucked dulcimer is an exception.

Footless and wild, like birds of Paradise,
Nor pause, nor perch, hovering on untamed wing!
Oh the one life within us and abroad,
Which meets all motion and becomes its soul,
A light in sound, a sound-like power in light,
Methinks, it should have been impossible
Not to love all things in a world so filled;
Where the breeze warbles, and the mute still air,
Is Music slumbering on her instrument.

Coleridge got this idea from James Thomson, who brings the Harp of Aeolus into his *Castle of Indolence* (1748) as a novelty whose actual existence has to be explained in a footnote[9]:

Ah me! what Hand can touch the Strings so fine?
Who up the lofty Diapasan roll
Such sweet, such sad, such solemn airs divine,
Then let them down again into the Soul?
Now rising love they fan'd; now pleasing Dole
They breath'd, in tender Musings, through the Heart;
And now a graver sacred Strain they stole,
As when Seraphic Hands an Hymn impart:
Wild warbling Nature all, above the Reach of Art!

This, we can see, is an imaginary music, and in the next stanza Thomson takes us to 'Bagdat', where the Arabian Caliphs had poets to sing to them when they could not sleep.

One cannot help just wondering if Coleridge really had an Aeolian harp, in 1796, in Clevedon in Somersetshire, as the eventual title of his poem informs us, or whether it, like Thomson's, was something imagined.[10]

It might be considered, and rejected, as a metaphor: 'The mind,' Coleridge wrote, 'does not resemble an Eolian Harp, nor even a barrel-organ turned by a stream of water, conceive as many tunes mechanized in it as you like—but rather, as far as Objects are concerned, a violin, or other instrument of few strings yet vast compass, played on by a musician of Genius.' Such ideas he plays with, and backs away from:

9. The note reads: '*This is not an Imagination of the Author; there being in fact such an instrument, called Aeolus's Harp, which, when placed against a little Rushing or Current of Air, produces the effect here described.*'
10. The answer is that he certainly did six years later, when Charles Lamb saw it at Greta Hall, according to Geoffrey Grigson, *The Harp of Aeolus*, 1948. What make of instrument it was, when and where he had acquired it, do not seem to be known.

James Fenton

> And what if all of animated nature
> Be but organic harps diversely framed,
> That tremble into thought, as o'er them sweeps
> Plastic and vast one intellectual breeze,
> At once the Soul of each, and God of All?

Then the reproof in his beloved's eye returns him to the thought of God.

The metaphor is heretical, but the notion of a changing music, varying from sweet to sad as the wind picks up and dies down—this almost theoretical notion in Thomson and Coleridge, for which they would have known no counterpart in English music as actually written—this is the actual music of the German Romantic clavichord:

> Schiller knew how to employ the long autumn evenings for his reflections in a way which was fruitful for the latter [his friend Andreas Streicher], and agreeable to himself. It had already been observed in Stuttgart, that listening to sad or lively music brought him out of himself, and no great artistry on the clavichord was required to rouse him effectively by playing the appropriate music. Engaged on a new work at that time (Kabale und Liebe) which aroused his feeling most painfully, nothing could have been more desirable than to have had in his own home the means of sustaining his inspiration and easing the turbulent flow of his thoughts. Usually he raised the question as early as midday dinner, asking Streicher with unassuming affability: 'Will you be playing the clavichord again today?'—And when dusk came on his wish would be fulfilled, while he would stride for hours up and down in the room, often lit only by the moon, not infrequently breaking into unintelligible cries of enthusiasm.

In the same source, we read that Jean Paul devoted 'many hours to an old out-of-tune clavichord, whose only tuning lever and tuning master was the weather'. He wrote: 'When I want to express a particular feeling that seizes me, it strives to find not words but sounds, and I crave to express it on my clavichord. As soon as I shed tears at the clavichord over my invention, the creative process is over and feeling takes command. Nothing exhausts me as much, nothing soothes me more than improvising at the clavichord. I could improvise myself to death.'[11]

But this is to take something that could only ever have been very soft, and make it expressive of a vastness we would associate with large orchestras, or with the virtuoso pianist storming the keyboard. The reason why, as I wait for my clavichord to be tuned, I am made so alive to the tiniest noises in the warehouse, is that my attention has been entirely focused on this minute sound. Occasionally I wonder whether, as I lose a little of my hearing, it is sensible to think of a clavichord anyway. Perhaps in due course I will not be able to hear myself play.

I am learning the piano, and the clavichord is certainly a distraction from that pursuit. Perhaps even it could be thought detrimental. An old remark comes back to me, something heard in childhood, to the effect that it is bad for a pianist to play the organ, because of the different techniques involved: the pressure of the fingers on the keys is everything, for the pianist, and nothing for the organist, for whom the note sounds the same whatever the pressure.

Then I think: that old saw about organ-playing being bad for the pianist—why didn't I throw that out of my mind years ago? How could it possibly be true? The keyboard player must always learn to adapt. My old piano, my teacher's piano, the substitute piano I bought because the contrast between my teacher's piano and mine was too great, my friend's piano on which we play four-hands, and then the examination room piano on which I have taken my tests— I've been playing on five contrasting keyboards in the last two years. And it cannot be that learning the piano means learning only to play one individual instrument. It must mean learning adaptability.

Yet it turns out that this old worry, implanted in childhood, is of some antiquity, like so many early worries:

> If it happens by chance that players of dances play on an organ,
> they are never, or at least very rarely, able to play musically, for
> they are unable to refrain from beating on the keys (nothing worse
> could be heard). Likewise, organists will never play dances well on
> plucked instruments because it is done in a different way...

11. *The Clavichord*, p 51.

James Fenton

This warns the sixteenth-century musician not to mix harpsichord or spinet with organ-playing:

> ...the organist who wants to play dances must observe these rules except for the prohibition of jumping and striking with the fingers, which he is allowed to do for two reasons. First, because plucked keyboard instruments need to be struck, because the jacks and plectra work better this way. Secondly, in order to give grace to the dances. Thus the organist who wants to play dances is allowed to strike with the fingers like any other player, but the player of dances who wants to play music on the organ is not allowed to strike with the fingers.[12]

The offence is one of creating short staccato notes, instead of respecting the organ's natural legato. (And there is also the offence of playing dance music on the church organ—an abuse discouraged by the Council of Trent.)

It turns out that organists like Johann Sebastian Bach were not always able to practise in church. The building would normally be unheated, and an assistant, or perhaps more than one, would be required to man the pump. So the alternative was to practise, to improvise (as organists do) and to compose upon the clavichord, and, to this end, a pedal-clavichord was constructed for Bach, which would most likely have had a separate set of bass strings to be played by the feet. Bach liked best, Forkel says, to play upon the clavichord—the harpsichord 'had not soul enough for him', while the piano was 'still too much in its infancy and still much too coarse to satisfy him'.[13] And Mozart—if further permission for this musical adventure were needed—played the clavichord, both as a practice instrument while travelling, and to compose on. A label on an instrument in the Mozart birthplace, written in his wife Constanze's hand, asserts that in five months in 1791 Mozart composed The Magic Flute, La Clemenza di Tito, his Requiem and a Masonic cantata on this clavichord. Haydn wrote the greater part of The Creation on one, which survives in London at the Royal College of Music.

*

12. Brauchli, p 258, quoting Il Transilvano by Girolamo Diruta, 1593.
13. Forkel, p 436.

On Buying a Clavichord

*Three things I've been promising myself for twenty years that I
would do before I die:*
            —climb the Matterhorn
            —learn to play the harpsichord
            —study Chinese
                    (Susan Sontag, 'Project for a Trip to China')

The next line reads: 'Perhaps it's not too late to climb the
Matterhorn.' But the implicit pessimism about learning to play
a keyboard instrument—even one so mildly recherché as the
harpsichord—needs a little explaining. Sontag was in her forties when
she published these lines. It was by no means too late to take
instruction in music. She had been thinking of doing so most of her
adult life.

But a mixture of horrors holds us back. Some—a surprising
number—associate music with early punishment. We see, not a
beloved instructor but a teacher's screaming face, and we feel the
ruler across the knuckles. A larger number perhaps are inhibited by
being heard at a disadvantage. The nun at her dumb spinet might
be horrified not at the thought of waking the dormitory so much as
being heard behaving like a child. Our loved ones inhibit us, if not
by the anticipation of their impatience then with the thought of their
necessary indulgence. How could we put them through all of this
palaver of scales, arpeggios and endlessly reiterated tunes?

It is going to be a small humiliation, this learning of the keyboard—
there's no doubt about it; and who knows if we will be able doggedly
to make our way through to a point, at least, when sitting down to
practise or to play seems like something better than an act of infantile
regression? Or an attempt to atone for the shortcomings of our
childhood?

We try out an electric keyboard with a decently weighted action,
imitating the resistance of a piano key. The demonstrator is a
showman, a barnstormer in the arpeggio department, smirking
through the octaves. Doubtless he puts on a white tux and performs
in hotel foyers in the evening. He demonstrates the harpsichord stop
and the two contrasting piano sounds, based upon aural samples of
the finest Steinway models. We are impressed by the technology, but
distressed on his behalf. What a disappointment to be deferring to

James Fenton

us, in a department store, instead of thrilling us from the platform. What on earth could have gone wrong with his life?

Something, anyway, about this plan to compromise with an electronic keyboard, seems deeply wrong. The perfectly weighted keys, the sampled sound, the headphones to spare our neighbours: this was the world from which we wanted to escape. And really we are only putting off that moment when we are heard playing, if we confine ourselves to the electronic route, like my friend who plays with headphones because he cannot bear the prospect of the disapproval of his daughters. One day he will have to face those daughters down.

Vanity comes into it as well. When the Scottish ambassador, Sir James Melville, was sent by Mary Queen of Scots to the court of Elizabeth I, he was questioned by the Virgin Queen as to what kind of exercises her rival used. Melville spoke of the Queen's hunting in the Highlands, and how, when more serious affairs permitted, she was taken up with the reading of histories, and that sometimes she played upon the lute and the virginals. Elizabeth asked if Mary played well. The diplomat replied: 'Reasonably for a Queen.'

'That same day after dinner,' Melville continues,

> my Lord of Hunsdean drew me up to a quiet gallery, that I might hear some music (but he said he durst not avow it), where I might hear the Queen play upon the virginals. After I had hearkened awhile, I took by the tapestry that hung before the door, I entred within the chamber, and stood a pretty space hearing her play excellently well. But she left off immediately, so soon as she turned her about and saw me. She appeared to be surprised to see me and came forward, seeming to strike me with her hand; alledging she used not to play before men, but when she was solitary, to shun melancholy. She asked how I came there. I answered, As I was walking with my lord of Hunsdean, as we passed by the chamber door, I heard such melody as ravished me, whereby I was drawn in ere I knew how... She enquired whether my Queen or she played best. In that I found myself obliged to give her the praise.[14]

One could hardly not praise her, having so rashly intruded upon her.

14. *The Harpsichord and Clavichord* by Raymond Russell, 2nd edition, Faber & Faber, 1973, p 67.

Bloody Mary played the clavichord, and surprised the best performers both by the rapidity of her hand and by her style of playing.[15]

To climb the Matterhorn interests me not at all, and I have lived long enough in the East, and acquired a good enough smattering of its languages, to know that Chinese is well beyond my scope of useful study. To learn to play the harpsichord, the organ, or any of the great keyboard instruments, whether to ward off melancholy or sustain inspiration and ease the turbulent flow of one's thoughts—that seems like a project. 'Start with the harpsichord,' says Christian Friedrich Daniel Schubart; 'Crown your career with the clavichord.' The poet-musician, Bernard Brauchli calls him, 'one of the most ardent and romantic defenders of the clavichord'. An enemy of Absolutism, he suffered in prison for his convictions, and wrote in his confinement about the aesthetics of music.

> You cannot, I admit, play concerts with big ensembles, since it does not thunder and roar like the fortepiano; neither can you, surrounded by a large audience, sound above their shouts of bravo and make their cheers seem like the babbling of a brook. However, on a clavichord by Stein, Fritz, Silbermann or Späth—soft and responsive to every breath of the soul—you shall find the soundboard of your heart. He who, sitting at the clavichord, pines for the harpsichord, has no heart, is a bungler, stands in front of the Rhine and longs for a crayfish brook.

And again:

> Have no regrets when alone under the moonlight you improvise, or when you cool yourself on a summer night, or when you celebrate a spring evening. Ah! Do not lament the thundering of the harpsichord. Look, your clavichord breathes as sweetly as your heart.[16]

□

---

15. See the report of the Venetian ambassador, Giovanni Michiel, 1557, Calendar of State Papers Vol 6 pt II, p1043
16. Brauchli, p 174, quoting *Musikalische Rhapsodien*, Stuttgart 1786, vol 3.

MY QUESTION FOR MYSELF

'I have never been asked by a journalist what my favourite colour is,' Frank McCourt told me once, with a tinge of irony and some disappointment. His statement made a link to a problem that I have experienced for a long time as a literary journalist: the doubt that I might forget a question, a question that could be crucial to the person I was interviewing. So, two years ago, I decided to turn my anxiety into a game. At the end of each interview, I asked the writer to adopt the role of interviewer, asking him- or herself a question and then supplying the answer.

Most writers accepted this challenge, some with bemusement, others with a willing smile. There were questions such as: "Your time is running out, are you satisfied?" "What is evil?" "Is it really safe to put orange and banana peels on the compost heap?" Many were questions I would never have thought of asking, or wouldn't have wanted to risk asking. They were questions that only one person could ask: the individual himself.

These little soliloquies encouraged me and drove me forward. I began to work with the photographer Carolin Seeliger, who decided to take exclusively black-and-white photo portraits of the writers. She uses a large-format camera and tends to focus on the eyes, giving them a brilliance that attracts the onlooker's gaze. In the selection of questions and responses that appear at intervals throughout this issue, her portraits perfectly complement the writers' monologues.

Tobias Wenzel

Zadie Smith

'Zadie, what do all three of your books have in common?'

'Well, at the end of all of them they celebrate ambivalence.'

How Snow Falls

Craig Raine

Like the unshaven prickle
of a sharpened razor,

this new coldness in the air,
the pang

of something intangible.
Filling our eyes,

the sinusitis of perfume
without the perfume.

And then love's vertigo,
love's exactitude,

this snow, this transfiguration
we never quite get over.

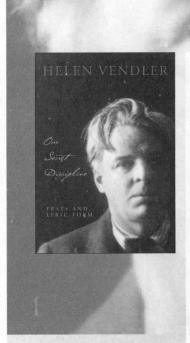
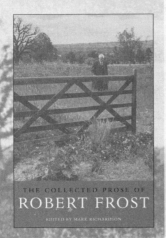

GRANTA

SOMETHING TO TELL YOU

Hanif Kureishi

The plane must have touched down around three in the morning. I had to slap and shake Miriam awake. She'd been living in a squat in Brixton and was eager to get away. The area had recently been torn apart by anti-police riots. Miriam had been up for a week throwing bricks and helping out at the Law Centre. The contemporary graffiti advised: 'Help the police—beat yourself up.'

Inevitably, Miriam had taken something to calm her nerves on the flight, cough syrup I think, one of her favourites, which had pole-axed her. I helped her throw her stuff into her various hippie bags and shoved her out into the Third World. Lucky them.

It was still dark but warming up. In the chaos outside the airport, scores of raggedy beggars pressed menacingly at us; the women fell at, and kissed, Miriam's red Dr Martens.

Wanting to escape, we got into the first car that offered a ride. I was nervous, not knowing how we'd find our way around this place, but Miriam closed her eyes again, refusing to take responsibility for anything. I'd have dumped her if it wouldn't have caused more problems than it solved.

We can't have been in Pakistan, the land of our forefathers, for more than an hour when the taxi driver pulled a gun on us. He and his companion, who looked about fourteen and was wrapped in a grim blanket against the night cold, had been friendly until then, saying—as we took off from the airport to Papa's place with Bollywood music rattling the car windows—'Good cassette? Good seat, comfortable, eh? You try some *paan*? You want cushion?'

'Groovy,' murmured Miriam, shutting her eyes. 'I think I'm already on a cushion.'

This was the early Eighties; I had graduated, Lennon had been murdered, and the revolution had come at last: Margaret Thatcher was its figurehead. Miriam and I were in an ancient Morris Minor with beads and bells strung across it. She must have thought we were approaching some sort of head idyll and would soon run into Mia Farrow, Donovan and George Harrison meditating in front of a murmuring Indian.

The driver had taken a sharp left off the road, through some trees and across a lot of dirt, where we came to a standstill. He dragged us out of the car and told us to follow him. We did. He was waving a gun at our faces. It was not Dad's house; it was the end. A sudden, violent death early in the morning for me—on day one in the fatherland. I wondered whether we'd be in the newspapers back home, and if Mum would give them photographs of us.

Not that Miriam and I were alone. I could see people in the vicinity, living in tents and shacks, some of them squatting to watch us, others, skinny children and adults, just standing there. It looked like some kind of permanent pop festival: rotting ripped canvas and busted corrugated metal, fires, dogs, kids running about, the heat and light beginning to come up. No one was going to help us.

We considered the shooter. Oh, did we take it in! Sister and I were shouting, indeed jumping up and down and wildly yelling like crazies, which made the robber confused. He appeared to get the message that we didn't have any money. Then Miriam, who was accustomed to intense situations, had the stunning idea of giving him the corned beef.

She said, 'It's not sacred to them, is it?'

'Corned beef? I don't think so.'

She became very enthusiastic about it. She seemed to believe they should want corned beef, perhaps she thought they'd had a famine recently. They did indeed want corned beef. The robber grabbed the heavy bag and kept it without looking inside. Then he and the other man drove us back to the road, and then to Papa's place. Even robberies by taxi drivers are eccentric in Karachi.

'Papa won't be getting a brand-new bag then,' I said as we hit the main road. Miriam groaned as we swerved past donkey carts, BMWs, camels, a tank with Chinese markings, and crazy coloured buses with people hanging from the roofs like beads from a curtain.

Luckily, along with the reggae records Dad had requested, I'd put an extra couple of cans of corned beef in my own bag. Papa wasn't disappointed. Although, apparently, he had told Miriam that corned beef was the thing he missed most about Britain, I can't believe he'd have wanted a suitcase full of it. He was partial to the stuff though, sitting at his typewriter eating it from the can, helped down with vodka obtained from a police friend.

'It could be worse,' he'd say. 'The only other thing to eat is curried goat brain.'

Mother had wanted us to come here. She was sick of worrying about Miriam when she wasn't at home, and arguing with her when she went there to crash. Mother was also, at times, bitterly angry with Father. She had found us hell to cope with, and she had no support. It would benefit all of us to spend time with him, getting to know how he lived and how he really felt about things. Even Miriam agreed.

Long before we got to Pakistan, like a lot of other 'ethnics', she'd been getting into the roots thing. She was a Pakistani, a minority in Britain, but there was this other place, where she had a deep connection, which was spiritual, even Sufic. To prepare for the trip, she'd joined a group of whirling dervishes in Notting Hill. When she demonstrated the 'whirling' to me, at Heathrow, it was pretty gentle, a tea dance version. Still, we'd see just how spiritual the place was. So far we'd had a gun at our heads.

Soon Papa's servant was making us tea and toast. Papa, not only thin but as fragile as a Giacometti, yet dignified in his white salwar-kamiz and sandals, informed us we would not be staying with him, but with our uncle, his older brother Yasir. To be honest, it was a relief.

'What the fuck is this, a squat?' Miriam said, when we were alone.

It turned out that Father, an aristocrat to those he left behind, was living in a crumbling flat, the walls peeling, the wires exposed, the busted furniture seeming to have been distributed at random, as though a place would be found for it later. Dust blew in through the windows, settling among the ragged piles of newspaper rustling on the floor and the packets of unused white paper, already curling in the heat.

Later that morning, saying he had to write his column, Papa got his servant to drive us to Yasir's. It was a broad one-storey house that looked like a mansion in movies set in Beverly Hills, an empty swimming pool full of leaves in the front, and rats rushing through them.

Miriam was annoyed we weren't staying with Dad, but I went along with the adventure. For a suburban kid with not very much, I like my luxuries, and luxuries there were at Yasir's.

It was a house of doe-eyed beauties. There were at least four. The Raj Quartet I called them. I was still mourning Ajita, of course, as well as assuming we could get back together when she eventually returned to London. I had never given up on her. We would be closer than before; we would marry and have children.

Meanwhile, it occurred to me that this quartet of dark-skinned, long-haired women staring at us from a doorway, Uncle Yasir's daughters, might help me bear my pain.

I was looking at the girls, confronting the anguish of choice, not unlike a cat being offered a box of captive mice, when there was a commotion. Apparently there was a rabid dog on the roof. We rushed out to see it being chased by servants with long sticks. The servants got a few good cracks in, and the dog lay injured in the road outside, making god-awful noises. When we went out later, it was dead. 'You like our country?' said the house guard.

Miriam was told that she not only had to share a room with two of her cousins, but with a servant, too, a couple of children and our grandmother, who was, apparently, a princess. This old woman spoke little English and washed her hands and clothes continuously; the rest of the time she spent either praying or studying the Koran.

It was a large house, but the women kept to their side of it and they were very close with one another. So Miriam and I were separated, and each day we did different things, as we always had at home. I liked to read the books I'd brought with me, while Miriam would go to the market with the women and then cook with them. In the evenings dad and his friends would come over, or I'd go with him to their houses.

When Papa was writing his column, which he began early in the morning, I'd sit in his flat listening to the heroes of ska and bluebeat, while being shaved by his servant. Papa was working on a piece ostensibly about families called 'The Son-in-Law Also Rises'. It was giving him difficulty because, having written it straightforwardly, he then had to obscure it, turning it into a kind of poetic code, so the reader would understand it but not the authorities.

Dad's weekly column was on diverse subjects, all obliquely political. Why were there not more flowers bordering the main roads in Karachi? Surely the more colour there was—colour representing democracy—the more lively everything would be? His essay on the fact that people wash too often, and would have more personality if they were dirtier—thus expressing themselves more honestly—was about the water shortages. An essay ostensibly about the subtle beauty of darkness and the velvet folds of the night was about the daily electricity breakdowns. He'd hand them to me for my suggestions, and

I even wrote a couple of paragraphs, my first published works.

After this was done, at lunchtime we'd tour the city, visiting Dad's friends, mostly old men who'd lived through the history of Pakistan, ending up at my father's club.

In the evening we'd go to parties where the men wore ties and jackets, and the women jewellery and pretty sandals. There were good manners, heavy drinking, and much competitive talk of favours, status and material possessions: cars, houses, clothes.

Far from being 'spiritual', as Miriam understood it, Karachi was the most materialistic place we had been. Deprivation was the spur. However, I might have considered my father's friends to be vulgar and shallow, but it was I who was made to feel shabby, like someone who'd stupidly missed a good opportunity in Britain. I was gently mocked by these provincial bourgeois, with my father watching me carefully to see how I coped. What sort of man, half here and half there, had I turned out to be? I was an oddity again, as I had been at school.

All the same, my father was educating me, telling me about the country, talking all the time about partition, Islam, liberalism, colonialism. I may have been a feisty little British kid with Trot acquaintances and a liking for The Jam, but I began to see how much Dad needed his liberal companions who approved of Reagan and Thatcher. This was anathema to me, but represented 'freedom' in this increasingly Islamized land. Dad's friends were, like him, already alienated in this relatively new country, and he believed their condition would get worse as the country became more theocratic. As Dad said, 'There are few honest men here. In fact, I may be the only one! No wonder there are those who wish to establish a republic of virtue.'

Many of my father's friends tried to impress on me that I, as a member of the 'coming up' generation, had to do my best to keep freedom alive in Pakistan. 'We are dying out here, yaar. Please, you must help us.' The British had gone, there'd been a vacuum, and now the barbarians were taking over. Look what had happened in Iran: the 'spiritual' politics of the revolution had ended in a vicious God-kissed dictatorship with widespread amputations, stonings and executions. If the people there could remove a man as powerful as the Shah, what might happen in other Muslim countries?

I learned that Father was an impressive man: articulate, amusing and much admired for his writing. He'd almost gone to jail; only his 'connections' had kept him out. He had been defiant but never stupid. I read his pieces, collected at last, in a book published only in Pakistan. In such a corrupt place he represented some kind of independence, authority and integrity.

If he seemed to have the measure of life, it wasn't long before I had to put to him the question I was most afraid of. Why hadn't he stayed with us? What made him come here? Why had we never been a proper family?

He didn't shirk the question but went at it head on, as if he'd been expecting it for years. Apart from the 'difficulties' he had with mother—the usual stuff between a man and a woman, at which I nodded gravely, as though I understood—there had been an insult, he said. He had liked Mum. He still respected her, he said. It was odd to hear him speaking about her as a girlfriend he'd had years ago, but now, clearly, was indifferent to.

I learned, though, that he had had, briefly, at the same time as Mum, another girlfriend, whose parents had invited him to dinner at their house in Surrey. They were eating when the mother said, 'Oh, you can eat with a knife and fork? I thought you people normally ate with your fingers.'

This was to a man who'd been brought up in a wealthy liberal Indian family in colonial Bombay. Among the many children, Father was the prince of the family, inheritor of the family talent. 'Isn't he a magnificent man?' Yasir had said to me. 'Your grandfather told me to look after him always.'

Dad had been educated in California, where he'd established himself on the college circuit as a champion debater and skilful seducer of women. He believed he had the talent and class to become a minister in the Indian government, ambassador to Paris or New York, a newspaper editor or a university chancellor. Dad told me he couldn't face more of this prejudice, as it was called then. He had 'got out', gone home to the country he had never known, to be part of its birth, to experience the adventure of being a 'pioneer'.

As we drove around Karachi—him tiny behind the wheel of the car—he began to weep, this clean man in his white salwar-kamiz and sandals, with an alcohol smell that I got used to, and even came to like. He regretted it, he said, the fact that we as a family weren't together and he couldn't do his duty as a father. Mother wouldn't live in Pakistan and he was unable to live in England.

If he had left us in Britain, it was, he added, as much for our sake as for his. It was obvious we would have more of a chance there. What should have happened, he said, was that his family should never have left India for Pakistan. India was where his heart was, where he'd belonged, where he and Yasir and his sisters and brothers had grown up, in Bombay and Delhi.

He now realized that Bombay, rather than Karachi, was the place where his ideals could have been met, crazy though it might be there. In Pakistan they had made a mess of things. He admitted it could have been predicted by a cursory reading of history. Any state based on a religious idea—on one god—was going to be a dictatorship. 'Voltaire could have foretold, boy. You only have to read anywhere there to realize.'

He went on, 'Liberals like me are marginal here. We are called the 'high and dry' generation. We are, indeed, frequently high, but rarely dry. We wander around the city, looking for one another to talk to. The younger, bright ones all leave. Your cousins will never have a home, but will wander the world forever. Meanwhile, the mullahs will take over. That is why I'm making the library.'

Packages of books from Britain and the US arrived at Papa's flat a couple of times a week. He didn't unpack them all, and, when he did, I noticed that some of them were volumes he already had, in new editions. With Yasir's money, Papa was building a library in the house of a wealthy lawyer. Such a darkness had fallen upon the country that the preservation of any kind of critical culture was crucial. A student or woman, as he put it, might want access to the little library, where he knew the books would be protected after his death.

Dad insisted I go to meet his older sister, a poet and university lecturer. She was in bed when we arrived, having had arthritis for the last ten years. 'I've been expecting you,' she said, pinching my cheek. 'This will be difficult, but there's something you need to see.'

We got her up and on to her walking frame and accompanied her to the university, which she was determined to show me, though it was closed due to 'disturbances'. She, Dad and I shuffled and banged our way through the corridors and open rooms, looking at the rows of wooden benches and undecorated, crumbling walls.

She taught English literature, Shakespeare, Austen, the Romantics. However, the place had been attacked frequently by radical Islamists, and no one had returned to classes. The books she taught were considered '*haram*', forbidden. Meanwhile madrassas or 'bomb schools' were being established by President Zia. This was where many poor families sent their kids, the only places they would receive education, and food.

When I wondered what it meant for my aunt to teach English literature in such a place, to people who had never been to England, she said, 'They've gone, the British. Colonialism restrained radical Islam, and the British at least left us their literature and their language. A language doesn't belong to anyone. Like the air, everyone can use it. But they left a political hole which others fill with stones. The Americans, the CIA, supported the Islamic revival to keep the Communists out of the Middle East. That is what we English teachers call an irony.' She went on, 'It is the women I fear for, the young women growing up here. No ideology hates women more than this one. These fanatics will undo all the good work done by women in the Sixties and Seventies.'

She would return to the university when the time was right, though she doubted that she'd live to see it. 'A student said to me, "We will kill ten thousand people, which will destroy this country's institutions and create a revolution. Then we could attack Afghanistan and go upwards... There will be the believers and there will be the dead. The West will defeat Communism but not Islam— because the people believe in Islam."'

Meanwhile my aunt was content to remain in her room and write poetry. She had published five volumes, paying for the printing costs herself, the Urdu on one page, the English on the other. She adored the Trinidad poet Derek Walcott, who was her light. 'His father, I'm sure, was a clerk in the colonial administration, like so many of our educated.' He had taught her that she could write from her position— 'cross-cultural', she called it—and make sense. Other local poets met at her house, to read their work and talk. They wouldn't be the first poets, nor the last, to have to work 'underground'.

'I envy the birds,' she said. 'They can sing. No one shuts their mouths or imprisons them. Only they are free here.'

Language; poetry; speaking; freedom. The country was wretched but some of the people were magnificent, forced into seriousness. Dad would have known the effect this would have on me.

Our lives had been separate. Dad had never visited our schools or even our house when he was in Britain; there'd been no everyday affection. But as he drove about Karachi he did ask me, What is it you really do? As though he needed to know the secret I'd been keeping from the anxious enquirers at the dinner parties.

I didn't have much of a reply. I said I was going to do a PhD on the later work of Wittgenstein. I'd say this to anyone who enquired about my choice of career, and I did so to Papa. He could show me off or at least shut the questioners up; I had, after all, graduated with honours—whatever they are—in Philosophy.

This was, though, only for the benefit of others and Dad knew it. When, in private, he called me a 'bum', which he did from time to time, often appending other words like 'useless' or 'lazy' or, when he was particularly drunk, 'fucking useless lazy stupid', I tried to defend myself. I was not bringing shame on the family. I did want to do some kind of intellectual work and had even considered doing an MA. But really I only considered Philosophy as the basis of intellectual engagement, a critical tool, rather than anything that seemed worth pursing for itself. Who can name a living British philosopher of distinction? Later, psychoanalysis came to interest me more, being closer to the human.

This was all too vague for Papa, and the 'bum' taunts didn't stop. He'd say, 'Your other cousins, what are they doing? They're training to be doctors, lawyers, engineers. They'll be able to work anywhere in the world. Who the fuck wants a Philosophy PhD? Yasir was like you, doing nothing, sitting in pubs. Then our father, who was in Britain, kicked his arse and he opened factories and hotels. So, you can consider your arse to be kicked!'

How could I put pleasure before duty? What could be more infuriatingly enviable than that? Papa had kicked my arse. Where had he kicked it to? I felt worthless, and glad he hadn't been around in London: one of us might have killed the other.

As I considered the serious side of Papa's attack, I drifted around Yasir's house, wondering what to do with myself. I'd already learned how difficult it was to find solitude in this country. The price of an extended and strong family was that everyone scrutinized and overlooked one another continuously; every word or act was discussed, usually with disapproval.

One day I discovered that my uncle also had a library. Or at least there was a room called 'the library', which contained a wall of books, and a long table and several chairs. The room was musty but clean. No one ever used it, like front parlours in the suburbs.

I took in the books, which were hardbacks. Poetry, literature, a lot of left-wing politics, many published by Victor Gollancz. They'd been bought in London by one of my uncles and shipped to Pakistan. The uncle, who lived in Yasir's house but now 'roamed around all day', had developed schizophrenia. In his early twenties he'd been a brilliant student, but his mind had deteriorated.

I sat at the library table and opened the first book, the contents crumbling and falling on the floor, as though I had opened a packet of flour upside down. I tried other volumes. In the end my reading schedule was determined by the digestion of the local worms. As it happened, there was one book less fancied by the worms than others. It was the Hogarth edition of *Civilization and Its Discontents*, which I had never read before. It occurred to me, as I went at it, that it was more relevant to the society in which I was presently situated than to Britain. Whatever: I was gripped from the first sentence, which referred to 'what is truly valuable in life...'

What was truly valuable in life? Who wouldn't have wanted to know that? I could have ripped at those pages with my fingernails in order to get all of the material inside me. Of course, I was maddened by the fact that whole sentences had been devoured by the local wildlife. Indeed, one of the reasons I wanted to return to London was that I wanted to read it properly. In the end, the only way to satisfy my habit—if I didn't want to ask my father for books, which I didn't—was to read the same pages over and over.

Often, my only companion was my schizophrenic uncle, who would sit at the end of the table, babbling, often entertainingly, with a Joycean flow. The meaning, of course, was opaque to me, but I loved him, and wanted to know him. There was no way in. I was as 'in' as I was going to get.

While I settled into a daily routine of carefully turning the medieval parchment pages of old books, I noticed a movement at the door. I said nothing but could see Najma, at twenty-one the youngest female cousin, watching me. She waited for me to finish, smiling and then hiding her face whenever I looked at her. I had played with her in London as a kid. We had met at least once a year, and I felt we had a connection.

'Take me to a hotel, please,' she said. 'This evening.'

I was mad with excitement. The bum also rises.

This advent of heterosexuality surprised me a little. I had already been made aware of the broad sensuality of Muslim societies: the women, for instance, who slept in the same room, were forever caressing and working one another's hair and bodies; and the boys always holding hands, dancing and giggling together in someone's bedroom, playing homoerotically. They talked of how lecherous the older men were, particularly teachers of the Koran, and how, where possible, you had to mind your arse in their presence. Of course, many of my favourite writers had gone to Muslim countries to get laid. I recalled Flaubert's letters from Egypt. 'Those shaved cunts make a strange effect—the flesh is hard as bronze and my girl had a splendid arse.' 'At Esna in one day I fired five times and sucked three.' As for the boys, 'We have considered it our duty to indulge in this form of ejaculation.'

I had been introduced to young men of my age, and went out with them a few times, standing around brightly decorated hamburger and kebab stalls, talking about girls. But compared to these boys, after Ajita, I had little hope; they seemed too young, I was alienated, and had no idea where I belonged, if anywhere now. I would have to make a place. Or find someone to talk to.

It took Najma three hours to get ready. I'd never waited so long for a girl before and hope to never again. I was reminded, unfortunately, once more of Ajita, who was inevitably late for classes, giving the excellent excuse that she didn't want the lecturer to see her with bad hair.

Najma turned up, aflame with colour, in a glittering salwar-kamiz with gold embroidery. On her wrists she had silver bangles; on her hands there was some sort of brown writing; her hair resembled a swinging black carpet, and she wore more make-up than I'd seen on anyone aside from a junkie transvestite friend of Miriam's. Najma didn't need the slap; she was young and her skin was like the surface of a good cup of coffee.

I assumed we were going to the hotel to fuck. I didn't realize that the Karachi hotels were the smartest places in town, where all the aspiring courting couples went. The radical Muslims were always threatening to bomb these hotels—and did occasionally—but as there were no bars and few restaurants in the city, there was nowhere else to go apart from private houses.

Sitting there in my ragged black suit—I could scratch my crack through the gash in the behind—drinking nothing stronger than a salted lassi, all I did was worry about the size of the bill and feel as out of place as I did on the street. But in the car on the way home she asked if I'd let her suck me off. It sounded like a good idea, particularly as I doubted whether I'd be able to find my way through the complicated layers of clothes she seemed to be wearing. She pulled over somewhere. As I ran my fingers through Najma's black hair I thought it could have been Ajita—in a neighbouring country—who was satisfying me. At the end she said, 'I love you, my husband.'

Husband? I put this down to the poetic exaggerations of passion. Najma and I had a lot of time together and after our first lovemaking she made it clear she was in love with me. I liked that about her. I fall in love too easily myself. You see a face and the fantasies start, like tapping on the magic lantern.

She liked to deride the West for its 'corruption' and 'excess'. It was a dirty place, and she couldn't wait to move there, to escape the cul-de-sac which was Pakistan, the increasing violence, the power of the mullahs, and the bent politicians. I would be her ticket.

I'd read and she'd lie with her head in my lap, talking. Other women who came to the house were training as doctors and airline pilots, but the Chekhovian women in my family only wanted to get away, to America or Britain—Inglestan it was called—except that they couldn't do it without a sufficiently ambitious husband. The ones left behind, or waiting to leave, watched videos of Bollywood movies, visited friends and aunties, gossiped, went out for kebabs, but otherwise were forced into indolence, though their imaginations remained lush and hot.

I didn't want the sucking to stop. I liked it a lot, along with the spanking and other stuff I hadn't yet got round to. She liked—she was very fond of—the economics, too. Not a Merc, darling, I'd say, when she seemed to think that that was what we'd move around London in. I'd prefer a Jag. I've had Jags, even a Roller, a Bentley for a week, but I sent it back. I've had a lot of trouble with Mercs, they're always breaking down, the big ends go, Jesus.

Then I'd tell her New York wasn't enough for her. We would have to go out to LA, to Hollywood, where the swimming pools were top class and maybe she could become an actress, she had the looks.

'Next week?' she said.

'Maybe,' I said, hastening to add that though I might seem a bit short of money at the moment, I'd had it before and soon would again, once I started back at work. It wouldn't take someone as smart as me long to make real money.

I have to say I didn't begin by wanting to deceive Najma with these spidery nonsense nets. She had taken it for granted that I was already wealthy, and would become even wealthier in the near future, like her male cousins. She'd been to Britain often, but had little idea of what it was really like. Most people, in fact, seemed to think that Miriam and I were rich. If we weren't we must have been stupid, or mentally weak. One time I saw a young servant of Yasir's wearing my shoes, then a pair of my suit trousers. When I remonstrated with him he just grinned.

'But you are rich,' he said in strange English.

'Get that stuff off,' I said, 'I'm going to tell Yasir.'

He acted like I'd hit him. 'Please, I beg you, no, no,' he pleaded. 'He sack me.'

Off he went in my gear. What could I do? He earned almost nothing. Miriam, being generous and ingenious, found a way to fund him while benefiting us. She got him to bring us joints which we'd smoke on the roof. Not long after, I discovered from Najma that Papa was referring to us as 'les enfants terribles'. His own children!

Not that we weren't looking into him too, eager to get the low-down. I knew little about his romantic life, whether he had anyone or not. It seemed unlikely. He had his routine, his worries and his books.

There was, though, his second wife, Miriam, and I went to her office, where she was the editor of a woman's magazine. She was very cool, small with fine features, polite, curious and intelligent. She had an English upper-class accent with the head-wagging Indian lilt I'd liked since meeting Ajita. I could see Miriam getting a crush on her. But she wasn't for a moment emotionally engaged with us. She didn't talk about Papa or our lives without him. After our visit, Miriam phoned a couple of times but was told she was away.

Things began to go bad. One time I was in the library and Najma was waiting outside as she always did. I went to her, checked for prying eyes, and kissed her shiny lips a little and began to touch her, but she was cold and pushed me away. She was silent for a while, letting me take in her hurt, before beginning to abuse me in Urdu. Her father, in a rage, came in. They talked a lot in Urdu too. I got out of there. It was breaking down.

It turned out that Najma had gone to Miriam and confessed to her. We were in love, we were going to marry, we were off to London, New York, Hollywood, in a Merc, or was it a Jag?

Miriam calmly told her to forget it, Jamal was marrying no one. He's not even a student; he's got the degree but so does every bum and semi-fool in London Town. Forget the Jag, the fucker might be able to drive but he hasn't taken his test, they wouldn't let him on the road in England. If he's intending to marry, she finished off, he hasn't mentioned it to me, and he mentions everything to me, otherwise I slap him.

I was in a rage with Miriam. Why did she do this? She liked the girl, she said. She felt sorry for her being subjected to my lies and stupid stories. But what was she doing herself?

It was taken for granted I'd accompany Papa during the day (I was learning a lot), just as he took it for granted that Miriam would stay at the house with the other women. They would discuss 'women's things'. But, apparently, she had stopped doing this. Instead, she had taken to driving off in Uncle Yasir's car, often with her head uncovered. When asked where she'd been, she'd reply, 'Sightseeing.' I had some idea of what these sights might be when she told me that her favourite thing in Karachi was to go to the beach and there, under a palm tree, split open a coconut and pour half a bottle of gin into it.

Most of the sightseeing she did was from within the arms of one of our cousin's fiancés, an airline pilot, who had a beach hut. He and our cousin were to be married later that year, but the pilot was taking the opportunity to get to know the further reaches of the family. He and Miriam had also been meeting in rooms in the hotel I'd visited with Najma, where he knew the manager.

They'd been spotted. Gossip was one of the few things that moved urgently in Karachi. He'd taken it for granted that English girls were easy, and when he ran into Miriam he knew he was right. I'd been wondering how she knew so many little things about the country. Of course our cousin went crazy, and threatened to stab Miriam. Miriam was outnumbered. I refused to help her.

Miriam had thought we could live in Pakistan a while, get a job, save a bit, hang out on the beach and deal hash, and so on. But in a little less than a month the whole thing had become impossible. We were too alien; there was no way we could fit in. There were American and British wives living there, but they had gone native, wearing the clothes, doing the accent, trying to learn the language in order to speak to the servants.

Outside, if Miriam wasn't covered, she was jeered and hissed at. They even pinched her. She picked up fruit from stalls and threw it at people. I was terrified she'd get into a fist fight or worse. I kept my head down, but Miriam, being a modern woman of the most extreme kind, fucked them all up. Our grandmother, the Princess, had already gone to her, placed her hand on her forehead and said, 'I'm going to recite a small prayer which will drive out the devil and the evil spirits which possess you. Satan, be off! Give us victory over those who disbelieve!' The following morning she had two sheep slaughtered. The meat was distributed among the poor, who were asked to pray for Miriam's quick recovery.

It all blew up at Papa's flat one morning when I heard a commotion in the sitting room. There were raised voices. Then I heard what sounded like a large object being thrown across the floor. I guessed the large object might be Papa. When I ran in, followed by the servant, Miriam was sitting on Papa, rather as she used to sit on me, screaming at him. He was trying to protect his face as well as trying to strike her. She was strong and difficult to pull off. There was something she wanted to tell him.

'He's been abusing me!' she said, as we held her, trying to pin her arms behind her back.

Papa was dusting himself down. Then I saw she had spat at him, that her spittle was on his face. He took his handkerchief and cleaned himself.

She said, 'He says I kiss the arse of whitey! He calls me "a rotten girl" and a dirty slut who can't behave! Yet he left us there in London! He abandoned us! What could be worse than that!'

'Get out,' cried Papa in a weak voice. He went into another room and shut the door.

It was the last time we saw him.

Dad must have spoken to Yasir. When we got back to his house we were informed that we were leaving later, around one in the morning. We were not given any choice. The servants were already packing our bags. No one said goodbye or waved. We weren't allowed to say goodbye to the girls.

The funny thing was, we spotted Miriam's lover, the pilot, going through the 'crew lane' in the airport. Later, during the flight, he came to collect her. Apparently she 'guided the plane'. A packed 747 with Miriam at the wheel, sitting on the pilot's knee, with, no doubt, her hand in his fly.

Mother had wanted us to see father 'in his own environment'. She thought it would be informative. It was. We could no longer idealize him. In most ways he was worse off than us. He couldn't save us, nor we him. He couldn't be the father we had wanted him to be. If I wanted a father, I'd have to find a better one.

By the time we returned to London, Miriam and I weren't speaking. I hated her and didn't want to see her again. I didn't want to be the little brother any more. Usually I'm quite passive, if not evasive; I go along with things, to see what's happening, not wanting to make things worse by tossing my chillies into the stew. But I had said to Miriam, as we left Papa's, that she had ruined the whole trip.

'No wonder Papa thinks you're an idiot and a bitch,' I explained. 'You can't control yourself for five minutes! These people have their own way of life and you just pissed all over it! There can be few people in this world who are more selfish than you!'

She was so sullen and freaked, traumatized, I supposed, she couldn't even hit me. It occurred to me that she'd either damage herself in some way or go back on the smack.

We rode back into London on the Tube. The little houses and neat gardens sitting there in the cold looked staid, cute, prim. Saying nothing, hating everything, we both had furious eyes. This was our land and it was where we had to live. All we could do now was get on with our lives—or not. At Victoria Station the two us parted without speaking. I went home to Mum and Miriam went to stay with someone who had a council flat in North Kensington.

I knew that whatever happened, I needed to get a job. Luckily, I had a friend from university who was working in the British Library, and he said he could get me something there.

The one person I didn't expect to see again was Najma, but she turned up a year later in Britain and rang Mother, asking for me. For a moment, in my confusion and with Mum's lack of clarity— 'an Indian girl phoned'—I thought it was Ajita. I began to cry with relief. She hadn't forgotten me. She was coming back.

Najma had married a Pakistani who came here to study engineering, and the two of them were living in Watford, with twins. I went out to see them a few times.

One kid had a fever, the other was perhaps a little backward. The couple had been racially harassed, knew no one, and the husband was out all day. Najma would cook for me; she knew I loved her food, and we'd sit together, chastely, while she talked of everything she missed 'back home'. Exiled, she continued to curse the West for its immorality, while blaming it for failing to dispense its wealth to her family with the alacrity her fantasies demanded.

I took the husband out for a drink, and had to listen to him complaining about the excessive price of prostitutes in Britain.

I could only say that Britain might turn out to be more expensive than he thought. ☐

GRANTA

THREE CHARACTER SKETCHES

Mario Vargas Llosa

TRANSLATED FROM THE SPANISH
BY ROMY SUTHERLAND AND JOHN KING

Mario Vargas Llosa

1. My Arequipeña

I'm thinking of a girl: the youngest daughter of the great-great-grandmother of my great-grandmother.

She was born in a house made of white stone blocks with balconies and studded doors, in Real Street, which at the time had a gutter running through it to carry Arequipa's waste into the River Chilí. It had been quite some time since the hundred or so Spaniards returning from war had founded this city which would see so many priests, lawyers, revolts and conspiracies come and go. It was a city of straight paved roads, intimate squares, elegant houses and innumerable churches. They already called it 'the white city', as it had been built from the fire of volcanoes that cools into that docile stone in which every nuance of white is trapped, and which is used as the building blocks of the city's homes and monuments. It was already the city it would later more fully become: Arequipa, beautiful, pious, unruly.

She had been brought up cosseted by a swarm of women—mother, grandmothers, aunts, neighbours, servants—and her most vivid memories of the years when she could barely utter a word were the family summer trips on the back of a mule—her own mule, like her mother's and sisters', had parasols—to a farm in Camaná. She had been a happy girl, with her round face and curious eyes peeping out from behind her bibs, blouses and knitted jackets festooned with woollen pompoms (one of which she once swallowed, to the consternation of the local physician, poet and orator, Dr Don Juan Gonzalo de Somocurcio y Ureta, who did his best to treat her indigestion and fever with a skilful blood-letting).

She had been a cheeky, vivacious girl forever running around, jumping up and down, hollering. She knew how to slip away from her two maids, Loreta and Dominga, when they played hide-and-seek. On feast days after eleven o'clock mass they would take her to watch the comedians in San Juan de Dios Square.

She knew her prayers, how to curtsy to grown-ups and give orders to the domestics, but had still not learned how to read or write when one afternoon, after a family celebration with cakes, caramel desserts topped with cream, pastries with sacrilegious names, and vanilla chocolate, they took her away to the convent, to become a bride of Christ. Ten servants carried her dowry through streets teeming with curiosity: the women of the neighbourhood came out to stare, bid their farewells and shed a tear. At the door of the monastery of Santa Catalina, a flurry of maids carried her chests into a small house built especially for her, in which, from that day, she would dwell for the rest of her life.

Loreta and Dominga remained with her in Santa Catalina, along with María Locumba, her cook's young daughter, who would be her playmate in the first stages of her novitiate (while she was still considered a child).

She was never to leave Santa Catalina; she spent her life behind those thick walls. She was twelve on entering the convent, and she died three years short of her ninetieth birthday.

She was an exemplary nun: pious, hard-working, sweet and obliging. When the earthquake took place, a cornice from the famous 'patio of oranges' fell on her and broke her leg. From then on she walked with a limp. When the war filled the city with the wounded, the nuns and their servants spent three days between the refectory and the basement, amid the stench of gunpowder and a hellish singe. One could make out the red tongues of fire licking the sky, and hear the moans and curses of the victims, some of whom pounded the convent doors, pleading for assistance or food. My Arequipeña was the most courageous of them all. She encouraged the elderly, consoled the crying, and returned to their senses the bewildered who had been screaming, 'They are coming to kill us!' She was the one who most forcefully opposed the Bishop's recommendation that the nuns evacuate the monastery until the conflict was over.

These two historical events—the earthquake and the war—were the extent of her civic life. The rest of her seventy-five cloistered years were spent praying, embroidering, hearing mass, confessing, making aprons for the poor and some of those sacrilegiously named pastries for the rich; and—of course—eating and sleeping (both of which she undertook avariciously). During the first ten years of monastery life she received family visits. Once every two months, one hour at a time, she spoke with her mother and sisters from behind the bars of the locutory. Each time they informed her of the family's countless births and deaths. But after her mother died—how she regretted not having been able to attend her funeral, how she prayed that God would keep her with him—her sisters spread out the visits to only twice a year, then to once, until eventually they never returned. By then Loreta had died. Dominga held out a while longer, but she never got used to the enclosed existence and spent the last years of her life in silence. María Locumba's daughter, the poor wretch, escaped before her twentieth birthday. One nun insisted that she had seen her jump over the walls of the vegetable patch, just as the sun was setting. Another—more than a touch troubled—swore that Satan had turned her into a frog and carried her away through the gutters.

Being alone with no one left to serve her didn't bother Arequipeña. For the love of God some of her fellow nuns flagellated themselves and slept in scratchy cilices. She preferred to work hard, to use her hands, and to sweat from her toil. Exerting herself physically to the point of panting freed her from thinking, from being mired in the mundane, and from evoking the past.

She died from the paralysing stabs of pain in her back and lower belly that woke her, howling, in the middle of the night and kept her prostrate for fourteen days. The Mother Superior sent a novice with alabaster hands and coal-coloured eyes to keep her company day and night, to feed her soup and to clean her ca-ca. She was lucid until the end, and received the last sacrament laughing.

The same day she died an artist came, in accordance with the customs of Santa Catalina, to paint her portrait. Revolted by the stench of the already reeking body, he did a sloppy job and left as fast as he could. The portrait is still there, hanging on the wall of the southern-most house of the Santa Catalina monastery, that city within my city of Arequipa. Yes, this skeleton dressed in a nun's habit, with blind eyes, lipless mouth, unsightly nose, and sorceress fingers, is my beloved Arequipeña, the youngest daughter of the great-great-grandmother of my great-grandmother. Each time I visit Santa Catalina, whose cemetery remains enclosed, I fling flowers over the adobe wall in the hope that they will fall near the earth once nourished by her worms.

2. P'tit Pierre

He had been born in a small town in Brittany and (naturally) he must have had a mother and father, but I am sure that he did not know them or never remembered them. At some point he began to see himself as self-generated, a child of chance, like certain wild flowers that seem resistant to all adversity and yet are fragile. Although the translation of his name—P'tit Pierre—is Little Peter, in his case it should have been little stone (without the capital letters). Because when I knew him in Paris, that is what P'tit Pierre had been all his life: a pebble, a rolling, wandering stone, without a surname, a history or any ambition.

He had always lived around the Latin Quarter, with no known address, virtually at the mercy of the elements, earning his living as a *bricoleur*. The word fitted him perfectly: a man for any job, a one-man band who could clean out pipes and chimneys, tile halls, repair roofs, mend old things and turn dilapidated attics into elegant *garçonnières*. But he was also unpredictable and very much his own man. He fixed the price of his services according to whether or not he liked his customers, and would think nothing of disappearing without warning in the middle of a job if he got bored with what he was doing. He didn't know the value of money, and never had any because everything he earned disappeared immediately, paying off the bills of his friends in a kind of potlatch. Getting rid of everything he had as quickly as possible was, for him, something of a religion.

I came to know him through my friend Nicole, a neighbour of mine. The built-in shower in my garret was falling to pieces, and in order to bathe I had to perform all manner of gymnastics and contortions every morning. Nicole said, 'P'tit Pierre is the answer.' She had met him recently and was delighted with his work. With extraordinary skill and ingenuity, P'tit Pierre had begun to transform her small bathroom magically into a sumptuous palace for ablutions and diverse pleasures. P'tit Pierre came to my garret, examined my shower and humanized it with a sentence that summed him up completely: 'I'll cure her.'

We became friends. He was thin, shabby, with long curly hair that had never seen a comb, and roving blue eyes. Nicole lived with a Spanish boy who was in the cinema world, as she was, and P'tit Pierre would wake them in the morning with crisp croissants fresh from the *boulangerie* around the corner. After working on their playful bathroom he would come to wake me up. We'd go down to Le Tournon for a sandwich, and I'd begin to learn about his carefree lifestyle, which consisted of sleeping wherever the night found him: on the landings, couches and cushions of his innumerable friends, in whose houses he also left strewn around the few clothes and tools which were his capital.

While I wrote, he resuscitated my shower or rummaged through my things quite unselfconsciously, or started doing sketches, which he'd then tear up. He'd sometimes disappear for many days or weeks, and when he reappeared, the same as ever, smiling and warm, I'd hear about his strange adventures, which he took for granted as the mere rituals of normal life. I found out that he had lived in a gypsy camp and that, on another occasion, he was locked up for swimming naked with a group of boys and girls who had formed a commune. But he was too much of an individualist for such promiscuous experiments, and did not stay with the group for long.

He sometimes had charitable affairs with the owners of the houses that he painted, ladies whose maternal instincts, it seemed, were kindled by his absent-minded nature. He went to bed with them out of sympathy or pity and not in any self-interested way, since, as I said earlier, P'tit Pierre was a curious mortal, completely devoid of greed or calculation. One day he appeared with a girl who looked fresh out of nursery. She was an old flame, so when P'tit Pierre seduced her, she must have been in nappies (I exaggerate a little). They had lived together for a while until she ran off with a Vietnamese boy. Now she was back with her parents, finishing school. P'tit Pierre took her out from time to time to get some air.

When, after several months, my shower was finally repaired, P'tit Pierre refused to charge me for the work. We continued to run into each other in the bistros of the Latin Quarter, sometimes with long gaps between meetings. One afternoon I bumped into Nicole in the street. She blushed on giving me her news: 'Did you know that I am living with P'tit Pierre?'

I was not as surprised as others were, since I had always suspected that P'tit Pierre was in love with the magnificent Nicole. How had this change come about? How had P'tit Pierre moved from being the bearer of croissants to Nicole and her Spanish lover to becoming the lover himself? My theory was that the decisive factor had not been the buttery croissants but the bathroom, that marvel of marvels, a space of scarcely five square yards into which the imagination (and the love) of P'tit Pierre had concentrated mirrors, carpet squares, adornments, porcelain receptacles and cabinets, all with Babylonian refinement and Cartesian balance. My friends in the *quartier* were sure that the relationship between that cultured, bourgeois, prosperous woman and the semi-literate, dreamy artisan would not last long. With my incorrigible romantic imagination, I bet that it would.

I was wrong only in part, since I was correct in assuming that this love affair would be unexpected and dramatic rather than conventional. I heard news of them in snippets and, after a time, through hearsay, because I left Paris soon after Nicole and P'tit Pierre began to live together. I went back some years later, and it was when I was catching up with a friend that I found out that they were in the throes of tumultuous passion: they separated then made up, only to split up again. Someone, somewhere, sometime asked me, 'Do you remember P'tit Pierre? Did you know that he'd gone mad? He's been locked up for some time now in an asylum in Brittany.'

It was the part about being locked up—and his supposed violence—that didn't ring true to me. Because if madness is a break with normality, P'tit Pierre had never been a sane man. Since before he'd reached the age of reason—like his ancestor, the urchin Gavroche in *Les Misérables*—he had not conformed with accepted behaviour, the dominant morality, dishonest values or probably even the law. But I could not conceive of him showing any trace of physical aggression towards another person. I had never known anyone more gentle, unselfish, helpful and kind-hearted than P'tit Pierre. No one would convince me that this man, for whom the lyrical Spanish word *nefelibata*—someone lost in the clouds—seemed to have been invented, could become a furious madman.

Several more years had passed without news of him when, in a stopover between flights at Madrid airport, a shadow blocked my path, spreading its arms wide. 'Don't you recognize me? I'm your neighbour from the Latin Quarter.' It was the Spanish cineaste who had lived with Nicole. He was so rotund and greying that I found it difficult to equate him with the weedy boy from León who, fifteen years back, would explode like a Spanish chauvinist whenever his French girlfriend gestured to pay the bill. We embraced and went for a coffee.

He visited Paris from time to time, but wouldn't live there again for anything in the world, because the city was now a shadow of its former self. And did he see Nicole? Yes, sometimes, they were still good friends. And how was she? Much better now, fully recovered. Had Nicole been ill? What, didn't I know what had happened? No, I didn't know a thing. It had been years since I'd heard any news of Nicole.

So he gave me the news of her and P'tit Pierre, against whom, he said, he had never harboured a grudge for taking his woman away. The story about the asylum was true, and also the rage. But not against others—P'tit Pierre was not capable of hurting anyone. But he was capable of hurting himself. He'd been locked up for some time in Brittany when Nicole was told that he'd got hold of an electric saw and had mutilated himself horribly with it. Nicole's visits disturbed him and for that reason, until there was a marked improvement in him, the doctors forbade her to see him.

Weeks, months or years later, the clinic told Nicole that P'tit Pierre had disappeared. He could not be found. About that time, I suppose, Nicole had—as they say—got on with her life, found a better job, taken a new lover. I imagine that the day she decided to sell her flat in the Latin Quarter, P'tit Pierre would have been a distant memory. What happened was that one of the potential buyers decided to poke around in the huge attic above the bedroom, bathroom and kitchen of the apartment. Was it Nicole who saw it first? Was it the potential buyer? The body of P'tit Pierre was swaying among the spider's webs and the dust, hanging from a beam. How did he manage to slip in without being seen? How long had he been dead? Hadn't there been perhaps some smell that would have given the location of the body away?

The plane was about to leave, and I couldn't ask the Spanish cineaste any of the questions that were pounding in my head. If I meet him again in some airport, I won't ask him then, either. I don't want to hear another word about P'tit Pierre, that little stone from the Latin Quarter who mended my shower. I am writing this story to see if, by doing so, I can free myself from the wretched shadow of a hanging man that sometimes wakes me in the night, sweating.

3. Fataumata's Feet

I don't know this woman, but her exotic name, Fataumata Touray, her country of origin, Gambia, and her current status as a resident of the Catalan city of Banyoles provide me with the elements necessary to reconstruct her story. It is, regrettably, the most common of stories, comparable to that of millions of women like Fataumata, who were born into poverty and will almost certainly die in poverty. It would be misleading to call what has happened to her tragic. Is there anything in this woman's life that does not merit this dramatic designation? For Fataumata, and others like her, dying tragically is dying naturally.

I don't need to go to the Josep Trueta Hospital in Girona—where they are now mending the ribs, wrists, bones and teeth she broke when jumping out of the second-floor window of her apartment building—to make out her dark, wrinkled skin; her snub nose; her thick lips; her teeth that would have been pearly white before they were broken; her ageless eyes; and her great gnarled feet, swollen from so much walking.

It is these enormous feet, which together form a creviced lunar landscape of hardened calluses, purplish nails, scabbed insteps and sturdy toes, that I find most worthy of admiration and respect in Fataumata Touray. They have been walking ever since she was born in far-off Gambia, a country that few people can locate on the map— because who in the world is interested, and what possible use could it be to know where Gambia is? It is thanks to the perpetual motion of these feet that Fataumata Touray is still alive, though it is difficult to gauge the extent to which she has benefited from such resilience. Out there, in Africa, even if she could run as a little girl, her feet would not have saved her from the practice of female circumcision performed so often by Muslim families on their adolescent girls, but they must have saved her from some beast or plague, or from a tattooed enemy intent on crushing anyone belonging to a different tribe for speaking different languages, worshipping other divinities, or practising different customs.

Here, in so-called 'civilized' Spain, in ancient Catalonia, these astute feet saved her from the flames in which other enemies, skin-heads probably also sporting tattoos, wanted to burn her to a crisp along with other Gambian immigrants, convinced, like her African enemies, that Fataumata and her tribe have no right to exist, that 'the world'—meaning Europe, Spain, Catalonia—would be better off without their black presence. I am certain that in the hand-to-mouth existence she has lived since birth, Fataumata has not once wondered what horrendous crime her minuscule tribe, now on the verge of extinction, had ever committed to warrant such antagonism, to have provoked such homicidal ferocity.

I am also convinced that the journey of these formidable feet from Gambia to Banyoles is one as unusual and bold as Odysseus's voyage from Troy to Ithaca (and perhaps more human). And what stirred this woman, whose peripatetic feet led her across forests, rivers and mountains, and crammed her into canoes, leaky boats and rat-infested shelters, was her desire to escape not from arrows, bullets or disease, but from hunger. Those lacerated feet have been fleeing from hunger ever since Fataumata was born (in a hammock, in a forest clearing or by the banks of a river), fleeing from hunger's dizziness and cramps, from the anguish and rage at her want of food with which to nourish herself and those wide-eyed skin-and-bone creatures she gave birth to at some godforsaken moment.

Hunger engenders miracles, stimulates the imagination and emboldens men and women to launch, barefoot, into audacious endeavours. Thousands of Spaniards, who five centuries ago were as hungry as Fataumata, escaped from Extremadura, Andalusia, Galicia and Castile, and embarked on the violent epic of the conquest and colonization of the Americas. A foolhardy enterprise, no doubt. One which, along with so many others, my paternal ancestors, the starving Vargas from the dignified and famished lands of Trujillo, took part in. If they had eaten and drunk well, lived without worrying where tomorrow's meal was coming from, they would not have crossed the Atlantic in toy boats, invaded massive empires, crossed the Andes, sacked a thousand temples and travelled the rivers of the Amazon; they would have stayed at home growing portly, wallowing in a life of plenty. Although it is perhaps not immediately obvious, Fataumata Touray—who some wanted to burn alive in Banyoles for having invaded other territories and for having a different skin colour, language and religion—is analogous to my own Spanish ancestors, and I feel an affinity with her.

Only forty years ago, another wave of thousands upon thousands of Spaniards—and it would not be stretching a point to imagine that these included some uncles, grandparents or even parents of the firebrands who torched Fataumata's apartment building—spread out over half of Europe, hoping to find work, a better standard of living, some source of income that an impoverished Spain at that time (like Fataumata's Gambia today) couldn't offer. In Germany, Switzerland, France and Britain, they worked hard and sweated through endless humiliation, discrimination and contempt for being different—the blacks of whiter Europe. That's now an old story. Spaniards no longer have to break their backs in a wealthier corner of Europe so that their families in Murcia or Andalusia can survive. They now cross the Pyrenees for tourism or business, to learn languages or take courses, and see themselves as decidedly European and modern. Spain has prospered considerably since those years when they exported human beings, as Gambia does today. And memory is so short, or perhaps so base, that a large number of Spaniards have already forgotten what it is to be hungry, and how respectable and admirable it is to want to escape it, crossing borders and travelling to other countries where it might be possible to find work. And they have the audacity to despise, or to discriminate against (or even to harm), the black immigrants whom they see as contaminating their urban landscape.

It requires no leap of the imagination to understand what Fataumata Touray did in Banyoles. She wasn't there holidaying, enjoying the soft breezes of the Mediterranean or tasting the delicacies of Catalan cuisine. She was—and I repeat that this is the most worthy and just of all human aspirations—trying to feed herself by the sweat of her brow. That is, by cleaning floors, collecting rubbish, taking care of dogs, washing nappies or selling hairpins, brooches and pendants on street corners, offering her services from door to door, sometimes not even for money, but simply for a meal. This is what immigrants do when they lack education and do not know the language: the stultifying, badly paid jobs the locals refuse to take. It could not have been going so badly for Fataumata in Banyoles, when, like a number of other Gambians, she settled in that quaint place and rested her large feet. Did she think, perhaps, that her time of stillness had finally arrived?

A vain illusion. One early July morning she awoke to flames and fumes in her immigrants' quarters on Pere Alsius Street. Her swift feet jumped out of bed to find the blaze had consumed the staircase—the arsonists knew what they were doing—and then propelled her out of a window into the void. Those feet saved her from a terrible death. What do the injuries, which have impaired the use of her hands and feet and impede her mouth from chewing, matter if the alternative was to be burned at the stake? In some senses one could even say that Fataumata is a lucky woman.

Unfortunately, this story is not exceptional. Attempts to burn alive immigrants of dark skin colour, of non-Western cultures or religions—Turks, blacks, gypsies, Arabs—are becoming a perverse sport of sorts, one practised in many European countries. To decry this outrage is seen by some as an expression of bad taste, paranoia, or as a politically motivated ploy.

It would be outrageous to follow the example of Mr Pere Bosch, the mayor of Banyoles, or of Mr Xavier Pomés, another prominent Catalonian politician. Both, with disquieting calm, have denied that what occurred was a racist attack. Mr Pomés has added, emphatically and in a somewhat injured tone, 'We cannot talk of xenophobia in the capital of Pla de l'Estany.' That's fine, the prestige of this civilized place remains unblemished. But, if this were the case, how do we explain the fact that certain people, with premeditated gusto, set fire to the house where Fataumata and her compatriots were sleeping? The gentlemen insist that we are dealing here with an unfortunate prank, an act of hooliganism which was not racially motivated.

All right then. The young people who wanted to turn Fataumata Touray into a human torch are not racists or xenophobes. They are just bad-mannered, ill-bred louts. They got bored on a peaceful night in Pla de l'Estany and wanted to have a bit of fun, to try something new and exciting. Isn't that what young people do, break the rules? They went too far, nobody can justify what they did, of course. But we should not blow the incident out of proportion. No one died, after all. This explanation, doubtless inspired by noble patriotism, has one flaw. Why didn't these bored, non-racist young people organize a raid, with their petrol cans, on Mr Pomés's house? Why did they choose Fataumata's poor quarters? Perhaps it was pure chance, or because the immigrant houses are not made of stone but of cheaper, more flammable materials.

Will Fataumata Touray be reassured by such explanations? Will she bear her injuries and scarring with greater understanding, now that she knows the people who burned her are not racist or xenophobes but simply loutish kids? Everything is possible in this world, even that. But what I am sure of is that she will not want to live with her unknown arsonists in the capital of Pla de l'Estany. As soon as she leaves the hospital, her wise feet will set off again, without any clear destination, along the dangerous, fire-strewn roads of Europe, that cradle and model of Western civilization. □

Jonathan Franzen

'Mr Franzen, you're at a point in your life and in your career where you really don't have to pose for photographs anymore. You've been photographed hundreds of times. You could just say: no more. Why don't you do that? Why are you so agreeable when people ask to take your picture?'

'Well, Mr Franzen, that's a very good question. I think I do it because it would be even more costly of energy to try to say no. I do it because it's the path of least resistance. I do it because sometimes it's easier just to be nice. It's a way of preserving privacy paradoxically to put yourself out there and smile for the camera. When you say yes, you're controlling something which by saying no you might be not in control of. The more you show of yourself the more protected you are. I don't know how that works. But that's the way it feels.'

From the Flood Plain

Jamie McKendrick

No flood as parched as this—a mere foot
or two of gilded bilge—will turf us out
from the lands of the frog and the newt
who for the best part of a century
have bided our time in the tall grass.
We've stood their ground, and stand it still,
though our legs are cased in long green boots
and the sofa's propped on a tower of bricks.

Unmoved, we see fish swim in the back yard
and a swan sneer from the vicar's garden,
though the cold waters still keep rising,
working away at the silicone seals,
unpicking the doors we've turned into dykes
and days may pass before our power's restored.

Après

Jamie McKendrick

When the flood waters left they left
the pine boards cupped; the plaster blistered
with salts; the cheap chipboard
bursting out of its laminate jacket
in all the kitchen units; the electrics wrecked
with the wires firing in the sockets;
the polyfilled cracks in the buckled doors
once more agape; the iron grate sporting
a hem of rust and the ash it contained
arranged in a scum-line above the skirting;
dampness, months-deep, fattening the pores
of the brickwork; a question-mark over the slate floor;
the oven fouled; the fridge unsafe; the whole place
humming with marsh rot and fetor
but the garden, the garden good, and greener
for an alien crop of hogweed higher
than us, hardy, sturdy, hirsute, armed
with a poison sap against expulsion.

GRANTA

IN-FLIGHT ENTERTAINMENT

Helen Simpson

Helen Simpson

After all that nonsense at Heathrow, it came as particularly welcome to find himself upgraded to first class. This hadn't happened to Alan before, and he looked around him with beady pleasure. Business class he was used to, club class and premium economy and what have you, the extra eight inches was a life-saver when you were six foot plus; but not first, until now.

His champagne was in a real glass rather than a plastic facsimile. It made a difference. He had way more room to stretch his legs, and on a nine-hour trip to Chicago that counted for something, especially after a four-hour delay. The big armchairs were ranged in curved couples, like Victorian love seats; his own faced forward, while the old guy opposite had the window seat of this pair, its back to the cockpit. They were near enough to converse if they chose, but thus far hadn't done so, which suited Alan just fine.

The other first-class passengers were mainly business types like himself, or much older men. No women, unless you counted the air stewardesses. His own stopped and smiled at him fondly, so he took another sparkle-filled glass from her tray. He could get used to this. Yes, really quite old; the passenger just across the aisle from him, for example, he must be eighty if he was a day, and not looking too good on it either. Cabin crew had already had to help him totter down the aisle to the toilet, first one in after the seat belt signs went off, and even now he couldn't seem to settle; he'd just pressed the button for more attention, Alan couldn't help but notice.

Yes, he was going to enjoy this flight, he decided, inspecting the menu and the list of films on offer. He was a bit of a film buff. Something retro to start with, something easy to eat by; here it was, just the thing, *North by Northwest* with Cary Grant and Eva Marie Saint. King prawns on a bed of wild rice with star anise. Already he was aware of his tightening facial skin and sore red eyes, but this could hardly be called an ordeal. It's being up in the clouds, he thought, as the champagne kicked in; it's being in transit. I'm where it's at.

All you needed for the modern world was to know how to work a remote control—when to fast-forward, when to double-click—which was something these older guys simply couldn't get the hang of. The screen on the swivel arm in front of him showed a shrunken globe with a jewel of an aeroplane—the one he was on—just clear of the tiny triangle which represented the UK, at the start of its journey across the pond. He felt unaccountably moved. The end of the world was nigh, that's what the Heathrow nutters had been shouting, basically. Global warming, he was sick of the sound of it, he only had to see those words and a wave of boredom engulfed him.

Even his parents had jumped on the bandwagon, wittering on about their carbon footprints the last time he went to see them, complaining about how the lawn needed mowing right through winter now, showing off their new wiggly light bulbs. His mother had sneaked a sticker on to the windscreen of his new Merc SUV—COSTING THE EARTH. He hadn't noticed, but Penny had been furious when she saw it.

'Your mother,' she'd hissed. 'She'd like us all to go back to saving little bits of string just like *her* mother did in the war. That does it, I'm not having her over here being holier than thou about our patio heaters.'

The old guy across the aisle was making quite a fuss now; Alan watched his freckled baldy head jerking around and his hands fluttering spasmodically as the air stewardess leaned down to ask him what he wanted. She was nice, that girl, a nice smile and nice teeth; though she wasn't smiling now, right enough. What a job! You had to hand it to them.

The thing was, as he'd tried to explain to his parents, the science behind these new reports could be quite shaky. There were two sides to every coin, and anyway Planet Earth has a self-regulating mechanism, rather like the economy, and we should leave it to right itself. Mother Nature knows a thing or two, he'd told them, tapping his nose; don't you worry. And if it does get too hot, America's going to send giant mirrors into space to deflect some of the sun's rays back off into the darkness.

'What about the polar bears?' his mother had persisted. She'd always preferred animals to humans, as she proudly announced from time to time.

'Yes, it's a shame about the polar bears,' Alan had said, growing exasperated. 'And the three-toed Amazonian tree frogs. But there you go. It's the survival of the fittest out there, Mum.'

'Last time we came to meet you at the airport,' his father had butted in, apropos of nothing in particular that Alan could see, 'there was this American family and the kids were all in T-shirts saying DARWIN WAS WRONG.'

Where was the food? He was going to go for the *boeuf en croûte* rather than the Indonesian fish curry. More of the cabin crew seemed to have converged now on the old man with his fluttering hands. The nice stewardess flashed Alan a smile when he caught her eye, then went back to looking worried. An announcement came out over the sound system for any doctor on board to please come forward. Now, for the first time, Alan's opposite number in the curving double seat leaned across and spoke to him.

'I can't see what's going on from here,' he rasped.

'It's the old guy in the next seat along,' hissed Alan. 'He seems to be in some sort of trouble. Oh, look, here's someone. Must be a doctor. He's obviously not best pleased. Now they're making the seat recline. They've got him lying down flat.'

Other heads too were craning to get a look at the drama. The cabin crew stuck determined smiles on their faces and started to do the rounds, taking orders for dinner.

'Four hours' delay,' volunteered Alan, 'thanks to those jokers at Heathrow. Alan Barr, by the way.'

'And I'm Jeremy Lees. Yes, those anti-flying protesters. A waste of time.'

'Complete time-wasters.'

'I suppose so,' said Jeremy. 'What I meant, though, was it was a waste of their time. They're not going to change anything.'

'Exactly. It's nonsense, isn't it, this global warming stuff. Trying to turn the wheel back. Half the scientists don't agree with it anyway.'

'Actually I think you'll find they do. Ah, red please,' said Jeremy as the air stewardess offered him wine. 'What have you got? Merlot or Zinfandel? I'll try the Zinfandel. Thank you. No, they do agree now, they've reached a consensus. I ought to know, I was one of them. No, it's not nonsense, I'm afraid. The world really is warming up.'

'Merlot,' said Alan, rather annoyed. These finger-wagging types were getting everywhere. Even his own firm had been pressured into signing up for some carbon-offsetting scheme recently. £19.50 extra it had cost for this trip to Chicago. Plant a bloody tree. All a big con trick. 'So how long have we got?' he demanded with a tinge of belligerence. 'Cheers.'

'Your health,' replied Jeremy, raising his glass in a courtly manner.

'Well. They *were* saying thirty years but now it's looking more like twenty, or even fifteen. Still, that should see me out.'

Old bugger, thought Alan; how self-centred can you get? The children'll be in their twenties.

'The thing is, the nearer you get to a mountain, the less of it you see,' said Jeremy obscurely. 'Like old people and death.'

Enough of you, thought Alan, nodding at him and donning his headphones. Cary Grant was waiting at a bus stop in the Midwest and in the distance was the little crop-spraying plane buzzing towards him. He hadn't really noticed it yet. This was the best bit of the film; Alan couldn't help losing concentration, though, when he noticed from the corner of his eye that his favourite air stewardess was holding a plastic bag of liquid aloft. She was standing just ahead of him in the aisle, while a man who was presumably the passenger-doctor had started to fit a drip. A second stewardess held a torch. Wow, thought Alan; it must be serious. He looked around him again, uneasy. He could see a man playing sudoku, and another forking food into his mouth like there was no tomorrow.

Nobody else seemed bothered.

'It's getting serious over there,' he said, pulling off his headphones and addressing Jeremy in a low voice. From the corner of his eye he could see Cary Grant running for his life.

'Oh?' said Jeremy.

'They've rigged up a drip,' said Alan. 'It all looks a bit DIY. One of them's shining a torch. You don't think they'll try to, uh, operate?'

'Extremely unlikely,' said Jeremy. 'Not the right conditions for that, really. Think of the litigation, too—it would take a brave doctor these days to operate, particularly in first class to America.'

Alan looked back at the furtive drama playing itself out across the aisle, at the hot, unhappy faces of the participating cabin crew. The doctor pushed down rhythmically, with pauses, straight-armed and grim. CPR, thought Alan, recognizing the process from countless episodes of *Casualty* and *ER*.

'This is your captain speaking,' came the aircraft sound system. 'Unfortunately, as some of you are already aware, one of our passengers has been taken ill and needs more help than we can provide on board. Accordingly we have arranged to land at the next available opportunity in order to provide this passenger with the medical attention he needs. We will be landing at Goose Bay in approximately two hours.'

'Goose Bay!' said Alan. 'Where the hell's that?'

There was a murmur of discomfiture all around him, a general raising of eyebrows, and a barrage of discreet but questioning looks directed at the ongoing life-and-death spectacle.

'It's in Labrador,' said Jeremy.

'How far is that from Quebec?' asked Alan. 'Montreal?'

'Oh, hundreds of miles,' said Jeremy. 'It's north of Newfoundland. We'll be up near Greenland, or what's left of it.'

Alan swore softly to himself. Four hours' delay at Heathrow, now this. He had to give his presentation in exactly thirteen hours' time. Great.

'Anyway, I'll tell you why there's no point in us trying to cut back on carbon emissions and all the rest of it,' he snapped at Jeremy, aware that he was allowing himself to slide into a rage. 'In a word, pal—China!'

'China,' said Jeremy, mildly amused. 'Yes, yes, the Yellow Peril.'

'If everyone in China gets on a plane, we're stuffed,' said Alan.

'Agreed. Though do remember they've only got four hundred or so airports at the moment, as opposed to five thousand plus in America.' He turned to the air stewardess at his side. 'I'll have the Swiss white chocolate pavé please, with the Tayside raspberry coulis.'

There was a flurry across the aisle and Alan craned his neck to make out the doctor arming himself with some sort of box-like machine. Whump, it went; whump, whump. Pause. Alan saw the old man's hands fly up in the air and come down again.

'What's that?' he asked the air stewardess with a jerk of his head.

Her eyes were suspiciously watery despite her professional smile. She shook her head and moved away.

'That'll be the defibrillator,' said Jeremy.

Alan realized she had failed to take his pudding order and wondered if he could call her back. Probably not a good idea under the circumstances. Now Cary Grant was climbing up the president's stone nose. Pudding was the best part of the meal for him. He allowed himself to be distracted by the Mount Rushmore chase sequence for a few minutes and the next time he looked up he saw the doctor shaking his head and rolling down his sleeves. Did that mean…? Apparently it did, because a tartan blanket was being pulled up over what must now be the corpse.

Jeez. It made you think.

'Jeremy,' he said after a few seconds, leaning across, 'er, something's *happened* over there I think.'

Jeremy looked up from his book, sharp eyes greatly intensified for a moment by the lenses of his glasses. He peered at Alan.

'He's gone, then?' he said.

'Incredible,' said Alan. 'I don't believe it. Right beside us.'

'Oh, I've seen it before on aeroplanes,' said Jeremy. 'It happens more than you might think, particularly in first class. If they're taken ill in economy, they're brought through here because there's more space. Quite a cause of bad feeling sometimes.'

'How so?' asked Alan, shocked.

'Well, people don't want to pay out several thousand for a ticket and then find they have to sit beside a dead body all the way to Hong Kong.'

Alan glanced involuntarily at the shape beneath the blanket. Put like that. Hardly ideal. Still, the poor guy.

'The poor guy,' he said reprovingly. 'Looks like he was on his own, too. Far from home and family. Poor guy!'

'Maybe,' said Jeremy. 'Or maybe it was as good a way to go as any, quick, up in the clouds, helped on his way by kind cabin crew. Certainly better than a hospice or a geriatric ward or at home alone in front of *Countdown*.'

Weirdo, thought Alan. He drew back into his broad-winged chair. It was unsettling, all this. Next thing he felt a tap on his shoulder, and turned round to the enquiring face of the sudoku man sitting across the aisle behind him.

'Do you think,' asked the man, 'do you think we'll still have to land at Goose Bay now that, er?'

'That's a point,' said Alan.

'We're six hours behind schedule as it is,' said the man, tapping his watch.

'You're right.'

'Because there's nothing they'll be able to do for him in Goose Bay.'

'No,' said Alan. 'With the best will in the world.'

'Exactly.'

When they asked the air stewardess about this a little later, however, she told them that they still *would* have to land there, as the request had been acted upon by Air Traffic Control: it was all logged in and un-deprogrammable.

Once stationary on Goose Bay's landing strip, it became apparent that they would be stuck there for quite some while. A coroner had to be found before the body could be taken off the plane, and tracking down a coroner in Goose Bay in the middle of the night was proving difficult.

'No,' said Jeremy when Alan enquired, 'this hasn't happened to me before. The other deaths took less time, I suppose, and the flights carried on to their destinations. No, I haven't had to make an unscheduled landing like this before.'

Great, thought Alan, staring furiously through the little aeroplane window. Outside were a desolate runway and a couple of hangars with corrugated-iron roofs. It was snowing heavily.

'Think of the problems for his next of kin,' said Jeremy. 'Having to fly here and identify the body. Repatriation won't be the easiest thing to organize from Goose Bay, one imagines.'

'We're in the middle of nowhere,' snapped Alan. 'Ridiculous. Look at that weather. Don't tell me you still believe in global warming. It's fucking freezing out there.'

'It's not a question of belief,' said Jeremy. 'It's happened. It's happening.'

'Not out there,' snorted Alan. 'Not from what I can see.'

'In fact, someone really should declare a global state of emergency, given the evidence. The scientists are quaking in their boots.'

'There's your so-called evidence,' said Alan, now in an evil temper. 'Look at that snow. If we hang around here for much longer they'll find it impossible to take off.'

'Don't worry,' soothed Jeremy. 'I won't preach. I used to try and explain it to everyone I met, but last year I could see that was futile so I gave up. After all, it's quite an unpleasant chunk of information to absorb.'

'So what *do* you think will happen?'

'No, no, I don't want to bore you.'

'I'm asking, pal.'

'Oh, in *that* case. Well, it'll all get very nasty.'

'We'll be swimming round the Statue of Liberty's torch,' sneered

Alan. 'I saw that film.'

'No, no,' said Jeremy. 'Crops will fail first. Food shortages will kill off four-fifths of the population, along with malaria and bird flu and so on. There'll be warlords and fighting in the streets. By the time you're my age you'll be beating them off your vegetable patch and your last tins of tuna.'

'Super,' said Alan.

'And don't think you'll be able to escape by moving to Canada,' Jeremy continued playfully. 'That's where the Americans will go. It's the same continent after all and lots of them are buying up real estate in this sort of area even now. No, you'll probably have to make your way back to bonny Scotland and hope for the best.'

'Oh, cheers,' said Alan. 'And what about you? You don't seem too worried yourself, I can't help noticing.'

'No,' agreed Jeremy. 'I think you'll find most people over seventy are the same—at some level we're banking on current fuel stocks to see us out. By the time rationing comes in, it'll all be someone else's problem.'

'So you're all right Jack!' snorted Alan.

'I'll tell you when I stopped trying to change things. It was when I realized that nothing was going to stop people flying.'

'Are you saying I shouldn't *fly* now?'

'I don't care what you do,' said Jeremy peaceably. 'I don't care about you. You don't care about me. We don't care about *him*.' He indicated in the direction of the dead man. 'We all know how to put ourselves first and that's what makes the world go round.'

'Because I'm a frequent flyer,' insisted Alan. 'My job requires me to fly in excess of fifty thousand miles a year.'

'I wouldn't boast about that when the floods come,' said Jeremy, 'or you'll find yourself strung up from the nearest lamp post. No, self-interest is usually the most efficient form of insurance, but it doesn't seem to be working here. You and nearly everybody else are such scientific ignoramuses that you can't take on board what's about to wipe you out.'

'You seem very sure that you're right about everything,' said Alan nastily.

'Not really,' said Jeremy. 'But I am about this.'

Just my luck, thought Alan, to get stuck with a moralizing old wise guy in the middle of nowhere.

'We need heat and light and food for survival,' continued Jeremy. 'We don't *need* to fly. But nobody's going to give up flying, because it's the biggest perk of modern life—so cheap and fast and easy.'

'You'd rather,' said Alan loudly, 'you'd rather keep it only for the *rich*, eh? You're just being elitist.'

'Elitist!' laughed Jeremy. 'You're the elitist, Alan. Even if you were dragged up on the meanest of shoestrings through your recent gadget-ridden childhood, you're still one of the world's rich. It's us rich ones that jet around the globe, guzzling untaxed kerosene and ploughing up the stratosphere like there's no tomorrow.'

'I took my family snorkelling in the Maldives last year,' said Alan, 'and all the people we met there were one hundred per cent dependent on our holidays for their livelihood. *Lovely* people they were. What about them? Tourism employs almost one in ten people worldwide, did you know that? Do you want them to starve?'

'Ha! The Maldives are about to go under, literally, and how will their people live then?'

'That's nothing to do with flying. Aeroplanes are a drop in the ocean compared to all the other stuff.'

'I'm afraid you're labouring under a misapprehension there, Alan. Flying is far and away the fastest-growing source of man-made greenhouse gases.'

'Yeah, yeah.'

'Over two billion people flew last year even though ninety-five per cent of the world's population has never been on a plane,' continued Jeremy, imperturbable. 'So a few people are flying a *lot*. But it's the non-flyers who are first in line to pay the price.'

'*We're* getting floods too,' said Alan, aggressive, defensive.

'And it doesn't look like we'll be voting for constraints on our flying until there's mass death at home. First to go under will be Bangladesh, but until Miami and Sydney join it we're not only not going to stop flying, we're not going to fly less either. In fact, quite the opposite, we're all set to fly more. Much more.'

'You're right there at least,' said Alan, yawning and stretching.

'Listen, you can turn off your mobile phone charger and drive an electric car and all the rest of it, but if you take just one flight a year you'll cancel out all the savings you've made. Flying is *incredibly* harmful to the atmosphere. Haven't you even heard of contrails?'

'You're on a hiding to nowhere,' smiled Alan. 'The aircraft industry is where it's at. Mega growth predicted. It's set to treble in the next twenty years; it's going through the roof.'

'Yes. I know.'

'Heathrow will get its third runway any time now.'

'Good for you. Nowhere else on the planet are the skies as crowded as over London and the South-East. That must make you very happy. Now, I wonder where this coroner can be? By my calculation we've been in Goose Bay for nearly three hours.'

'Unbelievable,' said Alan with a seismic yawn. 'I cannot believe this journey. We're going to be stuck here forever, frozen to the tarmac.'

'They'll discover us in a million years' time, the archaeologists,' said Jeremy. 'A perfectly preserved fossil from the late carboniverous period.'

At this point the coroner arrived, scowling and dishevelled, trailed by four big, sullen stretcher-bearers in plaid shirts.

'He looks like they had to drag him out of a bar,' said Alan, watching as this man was led to the shape beneath the blanket. 'He looks well over the limit.'

'The limit is probably higher in Goose Bay,' said Jeremy, surveying the cheerless scene outside. 'And who can wonder?'

Red-eyed, dehydrated and exhausted, Alan declined the next glass of champagne and ordered a black coffee. They were up in the air again. About bloody time. Less than two hours until he set foot on American soil. He couldn't wait. He missed its lavish confidence and grandeur, the twelve-lane highways of gigantic cars, the insouciance with which his friends there used planes like buses. Hell, loads of them commuted by plane every day, Burbank to LA, that sort of thing. They just got on and did things; they were always coming up with something new. Think of last year and the heated pavements in that ski resort in Colorado.

It was a real problem these days, finding a decent skiing holiday. Europe was useless. Penny was suggesting Dubai for next year. She'd heard it had guaranteed metre-deep snow everywhere, real snow topped up every night; and the shopping there was amazing, the Mall of the Emirates was right next door to the ski dome. It occurred to him that Jeremy would probably disapprove of this too, which made him angry again.

'What I can't understand,' he said unpleasantly, leaning over the seat divide, 'with all due respect, Jeremy, is why are you even on this plane? If you think flying's so bad, why are you *here*?'

'Might as well be,' shrugged Jeremy. 'Once I realized the world's going to hell in a handcart, or rather in a Boeing 747, or on an Airbus or a Dreamliner, I thought, Might as well. Haven't you noticed the old people at airports? All those beeping cartloads of us with our replacement hips and knees? It gets us out of the house, and we don't care about the delays because it makes the time we've got left seem longer.'

'Oh,' said Alan, taken aback.

'Plus,' said Jeremy slowly, 'I wouldn't mind joining the other Mile High club. Eventually.'

'The other *what*?'

'Well, I am already a member of the original Mile High club. Believe it or not. I was enrolled a few decades ago under a blanket in business class with the girl next door, so to speak. It's not humanly possible in economy, you'd have to go off for a tryst in the toilet ,and call me an old romantic but that never appealed. Business class is fine, though, if you're good at keeping quiet.'

'What do you mean, the *other* Mile High club?' said Alan, gawping at him.

'The one our friend's just joined,' said Jeremy.

'What friend?'

'You know. The one we left behind in Goose Bay.'

'You mean…?'

'Yes. A more distinguished way to go, don't you think? Nearer to heaven, and so on.'

'Oh,' said Alan. He couldn't believe his ears. He couldn't think of anything to say. He stretched his eyes at Jeremy, then gave a weak smile and feigned sleep behind a padded-satin eye mask.

Sleep would not come to him, however. Pictures of Scotland danced behind his eyelids. Raspberry canes in the rain. Gloom and doom. Tatties and neeps. Penny and the kids were turning their noses up. Barbed wire round his allotment, right enough. A big solid house near the Cairngorms, with a view of Ben Macdhui or Braeriach. He'd better buy a dinghy. A gun. That should hold them off for a while, until... Until *what*? A cataclysmic snort from his own nasal cavity shocked him awake.

'Coffee, sir?'

He took a cup before he was quite *compos mentis*, then sipped as he stared, sore-eyed, at their on-screen progress. The aeroplane-jewel was nearly at the gold dot marked Chicago. The Atlantic had been left behind, along with the frozen wastes of Goose Bay. They were high above the earth, zooming along at five hundred miles an hour. Of course he accepted this on a superficial level, but deep down he did not believe it. It was like when the physics teacher had tried to explain about magnetism, or when he'd told them that everything was really bundles of atoms holding hands. Pull the other one!

All the alarmist crap that old creep Jeremy had been coming out with, it just seemed like a fairy story now. He wasn't a six-year-old to believe in magic. Nothing but hot air. He drained his coffee cup and handed it back to the air stewardess.

It was a relief when the announcement was made that they were approaching their destination. At last, he thought. This journey had been a nightmare. When all was said and done, though, they'd made it, and he was still in time to give his presentation, even if there wouldn't be any chance to drop his bags off first at the hotel.

He tended to look forward to the seat-belts-on preparations for landing; he approved of how, flight's end in sight, the cabin crew became newly purposeful and bright-eyed. In quite a childish way he liked the tiny, brightly wrapped bonbons, he liked yawning to pop his ears. Yes, his spirits usually lifted during the descent, and he would have expected to feel extra jubilant towards the close of this particular protracted crossing. Right now, though, as they made their approach to O'Hare, he noticed that his spirits were not in fact responding with their usual ebullience. No. Instead, he felt somehow unnerved, he had a weight around his heart, a nasty sinking feeling; which was not like him at all. □

Hans Magnus Enzensberger

'Mr Enzensberger, why are you not unhappy?'

'The time I have left is too precious for that.'

Eel Tail

Alice Oswald

sometimes you see mudfish,
those short lead lengths of eels
that hide at low tide
those roping and wagging,
preliminary, pre-world creatures, cousins of the moon,
who love blackness, aloofness,
always move under cover of the unmoon
and then as soon as you see them
                    gone
untranslatable hissed interruptions
unspeakable wide chapped lips
it's the wind again
cursing the water and when it clears

you keep looking and looking for those
underlurkers, uncontrolled little eddies,
when you lever their rooves up
they lie limbless hairless
like the bends of some huge plumbing system
sucking and sucking the marshes and
sometimes its just a smirk of ripples
and then as soon as you see them
                    gone
untranslatable hissed interruptions
unspeakable wide chapped lips
it's the wind again
bothering the reeds and when it clears

you keep looking and looking for those
backlashes waterwicks
you keep finding those sea-veins still
flowing, little cables of shadow, vanishing
dream-lines long roots of the penumbra
but they just drill down into gravel and
dwindle as quick as drips
and then as soon as you see them
                    gone
untranslatable hissed interruptions
unspeakable wide chapped lips
it's the wind again
pushing on your ears and when it clears

sometimes you see that whip-thin
tail of a waning moon start
burrowing back into blackness
and then as soon as you see her
and then as soon as you say so
                    gone

GRANTA

THE SERAMPUR SCOTCH
Ian Jack

In Serampur I had an awful dream. I dreamed of my mother and brother. They stood on the slopes of a public park. Behind them lay a Victorian bandstand—octagonal with a curved roof like an onion—and behind that a line of trees. The landscape was in shades of green. The rich green of grass that has thrived on a summer's rain, the pale green of copper mould on the bandstand roof, the dark green foliage of oaks and elms. And all of this green under a sky of grey clouds which held the last of the evening's light. It looked like the end of an August day in Scotland, around nine o'clock, just before the street lamps string the towns with rosaries of bright orange and old people begin to mourn the passing of another summer, telling one another: 'Aye, the nights are fairly drawin' in.'

But this, the visual element, was only a dream within a dream. The larger dream had no pictures. It was simply a kind of soundtrack which said: 'These people and this scene are dead.' And so it was a cunning dream, a dream that told you that you were only dreaming, that the scene was not a real scene, and that the reality was that you would wake and never again see and hear the people in it.

I woke up in tears. I had lost my childhood, the people I loved, the kind of country I came from—there would be nobody else who knew me as these people had done, memories could no longer be exchanged, the sense of isolation from the past would be permanent and absolute. Only slowly did my surroundings penetrate and diminish this self-pity. First, the fan racing and creaking from its pivot on the ceiling, and then the chants of the Krishna worshippers who had set up camp a few hundred yards away on the banks of the Hooghly. Life began to fall into place. I looked at the luminous hands of my watch. It was two in the morning, a warm April night in Bengal, the year 1989. My mother and brother were alive, though my mother was old. By subtracting the time difference it seemed possible that they were settled in front of their gas fires and televisions in Fife and Edinburgh and watching the evening news. I crawled out from under the mosquito net and felt the coal smuts and tiny cinders on the floor scratch under my feet on the way to the bathroom, where I bathed in scoops of cold water from the bucket and, remembering my tears, thought ruefully: this was a dream of the middle-aged and homesick.

For the rest of the night there were no more memorable dreams. When I woke again at seven the Krishnaites were still chanting—they worked in relays—but now their shouts mingled with the sounds of Christianity from the chapel opposite my bathroom window. There a sparse congregation drawn from the Christian students and teachers of Serampur College was singing a hymn, a low murmur of piety easily pierced by the cymbals of Krishna and, for a moment or two, just as easily drowned by the steam hooter of the Serampur jute mill over the wall, which sounded to call the morning shift to work. Twenty minutes later the singing stopped and there was a knock on my door: my next-door neighbours the missionaries, having sung in the chapel, were summoning me to share their breakfast.

Mr and Mrs Knorr had said that this would be the best arrangement, otherwise I would have to share rice and dhal in the students' canteen. 'You should eat with us. It's no trouble. We've hired a cook.' The Knorrs were Baptists, energetic and practical Canadians with personalities so apparently unshaded by ambiguity or introspection or melancholy that they stood out in Serampur like a daub of primary colour on a sepia print. There was nothing false in them; to me, they were kind and direct. But Mr Das, their Bengali cook, seemed by contrast to represent a different race, separated not just by continent and colour but by an infinite wistfulness and obliqueness, as though he had stood in the wrong queue when the rations marked 'Energy' and 'Happiness' had been given out. Now he served the porridge with the silence and gravity, though not the precision, of an undertaker. Mrs Knorr arched her eyebrows. 'Poor Das,' she would say, 'he has simply no idea.' And then she bent her head as her husband said grace.

The Knorrs were not new to India—they had worked for decades in what they still spoke of as 'the mission fields' of the south—but they were new to Bengal and to this town thirteen miles upriver from Calcutta. They did not intend to stay long. Knorr said it was 'a kind of vacation'; he was here to consult the college archives for a book he was writing on early Baptist missions. They compared the district unfavourably with their old home in the uplands of southern India, a place of vigour and competence where the women wore flowers in their hair and the smell of fresh coffee drifted across station platforms to meet the morning train. The little they had seen of Bengal perplexed them. They saw lassitude and decay, a state government that was at least nominally Marxist and therefore perhaps nominally atheist, a lazy river in a flat landscape, small and squalid towns, tall mill chimneys made of brick, and a cook who made heavy weather of the porridge. On the journey from Calcutta they had passed station buildings and factory walls painted with hammers and sickles, portraits of Marx and Engels, and slogans urging the continuation of the class struggle. But Mrs Knorr discounted these as symptoms of energy. She said: 'I don't know why, but the people here have no go.'

We ate. Knorr said the college library was closed again that day, so we would have another day off: there would be no opportunities for research, either mine or his. Therefore the day guaranteed nothing but frequent meals. The Knorrs were hearty eaters. At breakfast, Das came out of his kitchen with bananas, tea and toast as well as porridge. At lunch there might be rice, vegetables, dhal, curried chicken, followed by fruit and a rich Bengali sweet of boiled sugar and milk. For afternoon tea, always promptly observed at half past four, the table was laid again with biscuits ('Britannia' brand), fruit, dishes of salty Indian mixtures made from lentil flour and dotted with bright green peas, and—perhaps the cook's greatest success—loops of sweet and sticky *jelabis* plucked crisp from the frying pan. Finally, for dinner, Das had been persuaded to switch to the old British mode which had reached him, perhaps more as a rumour than a recipe, via some previous employer. Soup would be followed by plates of chips, tomatoes and omelettes, rounded off with more fruit. Before each meal we bowed our heads as Knorr thanked Christ for what we were about to receive—almost, I began to think, more as a warning to the bowels than a blessing.

In the interval between eating that morning, I sluiced from the cold-water bucket again and walked along the riverbank. I was grateful to the Knorrs. For the past three weeks I had been travelling alone up-country in Bihar on a diet of hard-boiled eggs and oranges, and now the profound weight of so much food and religious certainty had a dulling, convalescent effect, burying the embers of my dream like spadefuls of sand on a fire.

Early morning is always the best time in an Indian summer. The sun is still friendly. On the road beside the river I passed old men in their dhotis and sandals taking their daily exercise, while in the river itself families bathed from the muddy shore; the men struck out boldly into the river and held their noses and bobbed under, while the women stayed close to the bank and soaped themselves discreetly under wet saris. Each splash sparkled in the sun. Crows cawed and the horns of cycle-rickshaws honked like flocks of geese down the bumpy road from the bazaar. The jute mill chimney put out more smoke and a low hum emerged from the weaving sheds. From this distance it was almost a noble sound—industry as Victorian idealists liked to think of it, something akin to the busyness of bees—but inside the sheds, I knew, the hum became a hellish clatter of shuttles and looms, so loud that communication was confined to a crude sign language between loom-hands and their foremen.

By midday it was too hot to walk and by afternoon the fierce light had bleached the landscape. Trees that in the morning looked green now looked grey, the brown and blue of the river had turned to a sheet of silver. The crows and rickshaws fell silent, the lizards stuck motionless on my bedroom walls. Even the Krishnaites sounded defeated, their chants ragged and tired. I lay under the fan and read, and slept and sluiced again. 'Hot enough anyway,' said Mrs Knorr over the teatime *jelabis*, though by that time the sun had slid down the sky and Serampur was coming back to life. When I went out again there were groups of students smoking cigarettes in the shadows of the road that ran along the river and the rickshaw pullers were beginning to light the oil lamps that were suspended from the axles of their tricycles.

I walked to the end of one of the little jetties that carried narrow-gauge railway lines from the jute warehouses, where barges were loaded with finished jute and towed downstream to Calcutta docks. Once it had been a considerable traffic, dotting the river with barges and steam tugs trailing banners of smoke upstream and downstream for dozens of miles. Now the river traffic was much less considerable—most jute swayed down the Grand Trunk Road in large, elaborately decorated lorries—but the shine on the rails and the grease on the crane indicated that sometimes a fleet of barges would still arrive and coolies would still push wagons to the end of the jetty and attach bales to an iron hook and watch the bales swing into the hold.

The river had changed from silver to dark glass. Downstream on either side chimneys pricked the evening sky from mills which bore

Scottish names: Dalhousie, Waverley, Angus, Kelvin, Caledonia. Nearer, a hundred yards or so upstream from the jetty on the same bank, stood a grand block of flats—impossibly grand for a place like Serampur; 'mansion flats' they would be called in London or Calcutta—with bay windows and balconies and crude classical pediments on the roof and the gateposts. That morning I had met an elderly Bengali out on his stroll and asked about this building: who had lived there? 'Scotch,' he said. The jute mill manager, perhaps? No, he said, the manager had a separate villa. Assistant managers, foremen, engineers, that kind of person had lived there. 'Scotchmen and their families, all of them. But they went away a long time back.' The flats were still occupied—I could see pale electric light shining through the shuttering on the third floor—but they did not look well kept. Damp from the monsoon had streaked the yellow lime-wash on the walls, the plaster of the facade was crumbling, the gardens had run riot.

The evening hooters began to sound, first from the Serampur mill and then from the other mills up, down and across the river. There was nothing alarming or rousing in the noise, nothing that suggested fires or air raids, or even that a day's work had been completed and a night's work was about to begin. It was a slow, reedy expulsion of steam and it resembled nothing more than a collective sigh, as though old men were turning in their sleep.

It completed a scene of the purest melancholy. I remembered my dream then, as I stood on the jetty and watched the flickering fire from the Krishna camp and the black silhouettes of the figures who walked and danced around it; the evening had renewed their vigour. That night I wrote in my diary of the dancers and the missionaries, Hindu and Christian: 'I suppose both are meant to supply a balm, if not an answer, to the universal human terror which seemed (was) so real to me last night. But in my family's case it failed and in my case it'll fail too. This morning I felt I'd grieve over this childhood memory of love and kinship until it died with me. And I suppose I shall—intermittently, of course, otherwise life would be both unbearable and insupportable. But I've too strong a sense of transience and what was, and almost none of what is to be.'

Did I really feel this commonplace so forcefully? I suppose I must have done; I wrote it down. The diaries of solitary travellers are often littered with banalities and depressions which seem unreal and over-heated after the writer has come home to the distractions of the social present. And then there is the old Scottish problem, of minds held in thrall to their childhoods and the sentimentalization of the past (think of Scott, Stevenson, Buchan, Barrie, all of them gifted with imaginations which in some sense were immunized from adult life; children's writers). Perhaps my dream owed something to each of these, the loneliness plus what might be called the cultural disposition. But Serampur, and more than Serampur—Calcutta, Bengal, Bihar, Bangladesh; all these places were reflected in it too. Sometimes as I travelled that winter and spring it seemed that these might be the last places on earth which preserved the old industrial civilization of Britain, people as well as scenes, manners as well as objects, frozen in the Victorian economy of the lower Ganges. Sometimes it even seemed, particularly in a place such as Serampur at dusk, that I had come home; or if not home, then to some tropical version of the time and country that my Scottish parents and grandparents knew, as if I might turn a corner of a Serampur lane and meet them dressed in dhotis and saris. That was absurd. But among the mill chimneys and the steamboats and the hissing locomotives this waking dream persisted, like a tribal memory.

India is different now and my mother is dead. As I say, the year was 1989. □

GRANTA

FOR YOU
The Libretto
Ian McEwan

This is not the final text. At the time of going to press, the composer, Michael Berkeley, is still at work on the second act. Casting has already begun, and rehearsals will begin in 2008 for the first performance in Brecon in May by the Music Theatre of Wales. Lines or parts of lines may change along the way. Square brackets denote matters of setting yet to be resolved. **I.M.**

Act 1

SCENE ONE

Lights down. The discordant sounds of the orchestra warming up. Violins on open strings, sudden runs on brass, woodwind etc. Slowly, this tangle begins to organize itself.

As it does so, **Charles Frieth** *comes upstage, baton in hand, towards the orchestra. He is an eminent composer in his mid-sixties, now rehearsing one of his own early works.*

From the shadows he is joined by his secretary, **Robin.**

Lingering in the background is **Maria,** *the Frieths' Polish housekeeper, a lame, ungainly woman.*

Charles Don't tell me.
I know that look of yours.
How long do I have them?

Robin Only twenty minutes more. No longer,
or we have to pay them overtime.
Maestro, you know the rules are very strict.

Charles Damn your rules man.

Robin They are not my rules.

Charles I said damn your rules.

He raises his baton.

This has been a long morning.
I'm tired and unhappy.
My temper is beginning to fray.
Let us try again, from D,
the tutti marked piano...

He mops his brow with a towel and lets it fall into Maria's hands. He conducts, the music finds its course.

Tenderly...
Sweetly...
Now attack!

Charles comes away, lost in thought, confiding while the music
continues.

It does not touch me,
this music of my younger self,
when my name was unknown
and I lived on nothing but sex
and cigarettes and fast food,
when I was in love again every other week.
I hear it clearly, each intricate part,
I understand it, even admire it,
but I cannot feel its passion,
the longing, the sharp hunger,
the lust for newness of that young man.
It does not touch me now.

The car is ready, Sir!
The usual table, Maestro?
The Minister of Culture is waiting.
A famous man with a rich wife—but
the dimmed perception, the expiring powers,
stamina, boldness, vigour wilting
under the weight of years.
The long descent to uselessness.
Every man's fate, how banal it is,
and still it makes me angry, the clock
that's beating me to extinction.
Stop! Enough! How can I make it stop?

He has returned to the orchestra.

And stop and stop and stop!
God fucking damn, I called a halt.
Am I standing here for nothing, waving my arms?

Through this, the orchestra comes to a slow, untidy halt. Silence.

I am not entirely deaf or stupid.
There was a note, a wrong note, a broken note,
an F sharp that should have been a G,
a hot needle in my ear.
It was the French horn. You, yes you, my dear.

Joan stands, holding her instrument. Anxiously, Robin comes forward.

[French horn obbligato?]

Robin Charles, she is a most promising player.

Charles You my dear. Yes, you.

Joan I did my best with what you wrote.

Robin Not this. Please God, not this again—

Charles Have you ever played that thing before?

Joan The note was high, almost beyond the instrument's range.

Robin Humiliation, then forgiveness, then seduction.

Charles Do you know which end to blow through?

Joan I'll try again. Please let me try again.

Trio

{**Robin**
{Charles, she is a most distinguished player.
{Not this. Please God, not this again—
{Humiliation, then forgiveness, then seduction.

{Charles
{You my dear. Yes, you.
{Have you ever played that thing before?
{Do you know which end to blow through?

{Joan
{I did my best with what you wrote.
{The note was high, almost beyond the instrument's range.
{I'll try again. Please let me try again.

Joan leaves, distraught. Charles leaves separately. Robin remains with the orchestra.

Joan *(offstage)* Please let me try again.

Charles *(offstage)* You, my dear. Yes, you.

SCENE TWO

The sitting room of the Frieths' London house. Charles's wife, Antonia, watches as Simon Browne, a surgeon, drink in hand, admires a wall of paintings.

Antonia It was kind of you to see me at home.

Simon I'm here as an old friend, not as your doctor.

Antonia I should be taking my turn in your waiting room.

Simon Another chance to see these beauties—
Ancher, Munther, O'Keeffe.
And you...

Antonia Yes, some say these women painters
were on the verge of greatness.
But Simon, look at me. I'm so full of fears.
Another operation. I cannot bear it.
Must it be so soon?

I need to ask you—is there no other way?

Simon A resection, and a biopsy to put our minds at rest.
A relatively simple procedure.
Trust me when I tell you, there is no other way,
and we must act now.

He pauses.

Is it your old fear that's haunting you?

Antonia Yes. It's ridiculous, I know.
My old fear,
the anaesthetic, the general anaesthetic.
The word 'general' sounds so sinister
to my ear.

Simon Perfectly safe these days. How many times
must we go through this?

Antonia I dread that moment of oblivion,
that rehearsal for death.
The cheerful porter with his trolley
coming to collect me from the ward.
I think of Charon, the boatman,
taking me across the River Styx.
Then corridors, fluorescent ceiling lights,
the elevator to a special little room,
the calming voices,
the cannula inserted, the chemical poison,
then coldness racing up my arm
with such violent speed,
and then, nothing, nothing.

Simon Exactly, nothing, and nothing to fear,
and when you wake...

Unnoticed, Maria comes in with a tray.

Antonia If I wake. What did the poet write of death?
The anaesthetic from which none comes round.

Simon Best not to think of Larkin at such times.

Antonia I know you think I'm a neurotic woman.

Simon I know you are an unhappy woman.

He pauses.

Where's Charles? Does he know?
I heard his concerto on the radio.
I don't pretend to like his music.
The notes seem plucked at random,
and what a din! A choir of tomcats!
But I'm a simple type who prefers Vivaldi.

Antonia He's working late.

Simon Again?

Antonia Working late again.
Working is the word we cling to,
Working is our household euphemism.
We live a privileged life of lies.

Simon *(softly)*
You must pack a case.
I'll come back for you tonight
if I can find a bed that's free.

He goes towards her, hesitates.

Too much to say.

Antonia Yes. Too much to say.

Ian McEwan

Simon Impossible to say it.

Antonia Impossible. And no need.

Simon Because you know.

Antonia We know.

Simon Only silence.

Antonia Silence will say it all.

Repeats, overlapping.
Simon takes his coat.

Simon I'm late. I must leave you. A doctor's duty.

Antonia The hospital? At this hour?

Simon A reception at the Garrick in honour
of a retiring surgeon. The glinting tray of canapés,
an indecent multitude of colleagues,
oily speeches of passionate insincerity.
I think we can all agree,
this is not an age of plain speaking.

Antonia, you must not worry,
it will work out well.

Antonia You must go.

As they turn, they notice Maria. Simon nods to her and leaves.

Antonia Maria. How long have you been standing there?

Maria I just came in this moment
with refreshments for your visitor.

Antonia I didn't hear you.

Maria The door was open, the doctor was just leaving.

She sets down the tray.

Will it be two for dinner tonight?

Antonia I shan't eat tonight. I'll be in my room,
and don't want to be disturbed.

Antonia leaves.

SCENE THREE

Maria Yes, I agree, a privileged life of lies,
But no one asks for my opinion—
Maria, who cooks his intimate
late-night suppers, who launders
the love-stains from his sheets,
removes the cup with its bloody
lipstick cicatrix, who sees it all,
the misery uncoiling because
in this house no one speaks.
Oh, the worthless, worthless women
he wastes his time on.

She complains, she whines about his
misdemeanours, the little crime she
longs to commit herself. But she prefers
virtuous hollow fidelity,
and sour long-suffering
so she can feel superior, and tragic,
while her illness is her only career.
She won't even kiss the good doctor
panting at her heels...

Ian McEwan

But she married the most exciting man
in the world. A lion among hyenas.
A genius, they say. I say, a god.
The room he enters fills with golden light.
It's the details that possess me—
the manly angle of his jaw,
the dark hairs curling on his wrist,
the pale hand that holds the baton,
the penetrating gaze of dark brown eyes,
a voice of warmth and power...
She married him, she has his name,
but she cannot keep him
from other women.

Ah, if only, if only...
I would give him what he wants—
I think I know.
Indeed I know his needs—
the little sensuous cruelty
he likes to inflict, and anal
and oral, and strange positions.
I'm more able than I look.
To drive all other women from his life!
Then all his music would be for me,
and I would make him joyous!
Delirious! Ecstatic!
Mine, and mine alone!

Robin enters.

Robin Oh, Maria, it's only you.
I wondered who was in here.
Be a sport and make some coffee.
I've had such an awful day with Charles.
What a piss-pot pompous fool he is,
a bully, a fraud, a mediocrity.
Oh God, I'm beginning
to sound like him myself.

A pot of coffee, and a cheese plate?

Furious silence

…with pickles?

Maria You know where the kitchen is.
I'm not paid to fetch and carry for you.
And don't leave a mess!

Robin Is everyone from Poland like you?

Maria In Poland we speak our minds.

Robin I always meant to visit,
but now you've put me off.

Maria relents and brings the tray to where he sits.

Maria

Song
Ah, Robin, you should go.
It's so beautiful and sad.
We have virgin forests
of the kind you lost in England
five hundred years ago,
where wolves and eagles hunt,
and clear rivers you can
put your lips to and drink.

Robin How romantic! I've heard the cities
are rather grim, and in between
are treeless potato fields.

Maria The conquering armies
from east and west forgot
to crush that lingering beauty,

though they almost crushed
our spirits. But now we are free
there's a newer sadness in our hearts.
The lovely town where I grew up,
is falling silent, becoming old.
We, the young, are fleeing west—
the plumbers, nurses, carpenters,
should be making a new Poland—
but money has lured us away.

Robin Don't blame money, blame yourselves.
If you really care about your hometown,
go back there, or stop complaining.

Charles *(offstage)* Robin! I need you.
Goddamnit man, where are you?

Robin Not again! Will I ever get a moment's peace!

Maria So resign, or stop complaining.

Enter Charles. Someone is with him, but we cannot quite see.

SCENE FOUR

Charles *(exultant, manuscript in his hand)* Ah! Robin,
the master of elusiveness!
Always hiding when I need you.
Tomorrow's rehearsal, the orchestral parts,
are they all done?

Robin I did them all last week.

Charles There's an insertion I need to make.
You'll have to work all night.
Thirty-two bars for solo horn...
floating, tumbling, sweetly falling,
gently sustained by muted strings...

Joan comes forward.

Robin *(aside)* A moment of pure beauty in bed—
an insertion he needed to make!

Joan So exciting!
We had our differences,
then we made it up in a flash.
Now we have a working relationship.

Charles And Maria, you dear, you wonderful woman,
without whom this house would fall apart,
we need champagne, and supper for two,
in the studio.

Maria Jugged hare or goulash?
Venison or bream?
Pommes purées or sautéed?
Beetroot in a crust of salt?
Figs in port with lavender ice cream?

Charles I don't care. Just bring it.
My Demonic Aubade, wild summation of all I know,
all I've ever felt, brought to new expression,
a new dawn in thirty-two bars.
Dear boy, history will count you privileged
to write out these parts.

Joan Not since Britten, not since Mozart,
did the horn have such a friend.

Robin To work till breakfast on my evening off—
I humbly thank you from the bottom
of my worthless heart.

Maria *(aside)* 'You dear, you wonderful woman,
without whom'… I'm in a dream,
I can hardly stand.

He's sending me a message over the head
of this ambitious tart.

Charles And Joan, a player of such sensitivity
and skill, such a gentle touch.
I feel she understands me.

Robin Who can doubt she does.

Joan For you, I'll always give of my best.

Charles Maria, a word in private if you please.

Maria Oh my heart...

She follows him out.

Robin Humiliation, forgiveness, seduction
in a single afternoon—oh,
the predatory vigour of the newly old,
spending the last of their small change.

SCENE FIVE

Charles's study.

Charles How was Antonia today? Did she see anyone?
Did she go out? Was she unhappy?

Maria No more than usual.
She moped in that restless way of hers,
tried to read, tried to eat, watched the TV
for half an hour, drifted round the house.
But her spirits lifted
when her good friend came, the doctor.

Charles He came again?
Simon with the soft-eyed bedside manner.

Did he stay long?

Maria I don't like to say this,
It's not my business...

Charles But it's mine, so tell me—

Maria I tried not to notice, I don't like to spy.
They were standing close,
he took her hand, she gazed at him,
he talked about a bed...

Charles A bed? He talked about a bed?
By what strange logic
am I feeling sick?

Maria He likes her...

Charles Likes?

Maria He's fond...

Charles Fond? You mean...

Maria I mean he loves...

Charles He loves her!
Ah, the knowing medical touch.
And she...

Maria Is still young. She's lonely,
she thinks she's beautiful,
she thinks she's ill,
she's full of sorrows.

Charles I'm sure you'll understand,
I need to be alone.

Ian McEwan

Maria leaves

Full of sorrows because
I neglect her for my work,
and for my...for my pursuits.
There's no justice in my anger,
but nor can I deny it.
Under my nose, in my house,
a man meddling with my wife
in the name of medicine!
I'll show him some double standards
with my fists! That smooth-faced bastard,
that cheat, that liar, that professional disgrace!

Am I going insane?
I know enough to know the blame is also mine.
'Still young', 'lonely', 'full of sorrow',
while the woman waiting next door
is my fifth this year, perhaps the sixth.
Reliable, loving Antonia,
this was always our arrangement.
But have I got the strength of will to stop?
I hate the doctor, and I hate myself.

Maria, I need you. Maria!
(Have I got the strength? I need someone
to shame me into keeping my word).

Maria enters

Maria, I've made an important decision.
Be my witness to this promise.
That girl you see will be my last.
I make this promise now,
in front of you.

Maria You are making this promise to me?

Charles Yes, to you. You know me well.
I'm making this promise to you.
She is the last, I swear to you.
I'm counting on you
to hold me to my word.

Charles leaves.

Maria I could tell myself it's a dream,
a psychotic interlude, pure desire
warping my senses,
wish fulfilment running wild—
but I know what I know.
Like all men, he barely understands himself.
Now at last he realizes
what I've always known.
He's made his [worthless] promise—to me,
And [but] he's almost, almost almost mine.

SCENE SIX

*Charles's studio. He and Joan are on a bed among a tangle of
sheets—becalmed.*

Joan They say an erection never lies.
But this is also eloquent,
when you shrink before my touch.

Charles I don't understand,
I just do not understand.

Joan You think I'm ugly, or too demanding.

Charles That's not it at all.
You're beautiful, and I love
your demands. Please don't get dressed.
This has never happened to me before.

Joan That's what men always say. [+ pause—perhaps
you're too old]

Charles [Don't say that] And don't get dressed.
Come and sit beside me here.
That's right. And kiss me, kiss me.
Now see. That's better.
I'll make it up to you, I promise.

They continue to embrace and kiss.

Joan Yes, that's better, Yes, I see.
I'm sorry for my angry words,
I love your kisses, and
I'm beginning to feel you now...

Charles My darling, everything will be fine.
My appetite is as strong as ever...

Maria bustles in, bearing a tray.

Maria For you...
Beetroot baked in salt,
venison to follow,
Just as you requested...

Charles This is kind of you, but...

Maria Figs in port, a hearty wine,
perfect for a working dinner,
for busy musicians who never know
when to stop.

*She fusses round them, determined to separate them, plumping
up pillows, arranging a table for Charles and Joan to eat in bed.
Before they can protest, they are lying side by side, in front of
their feast.*

Charles Maria, this is kind of you,
but you should have knocked.

Maria The tray was heavy and my hands
weren't free. Shall I open the wine?

She takes the bottle. A knock at the open door.

Charles Now who the hell is this?

Robin enters

Robin Ah, Maestro, you're busy. Never mind.
There's a problem with the score.
Four bars missing from the strings.

Charles Four bars missing? Don't talk rot!
For goodness sake, the violins repeat.
Are you blind? Can't you see the mark?

Robin There is no mark, and my eyes are good.

Antonia enters with suitcase, followed by Simon.

Charles My God! Now this. She's leaving me
for the doctor and his bed.

Antonia approaches.

Antonia We agreed you'd never bring your work home.
Is this the flute whose husband owns a bank,
or the harp with the autistic son,
or the cello with the house in Wales?

Joan None of these. I am the horn.

Antonia Of course. The horn of plenty.

Ian McEwan

Joan That's cheap.

Antonia No, my dear, it is you who are cheap.
Has he offered you yet your solo of thirty-two bars?
And promised a concerto?

Angrily, Joan gets out of bed.

Joan *(to Charles)* Is this how it goes?
Is this how it always goes?

Antonia You are but one variation on a theme.

Sextet
(Charles beseeching Antonia; Simon trying to draw her away; Robin addressing Simon; Joan furiously getting dressed; Maria aside.)

{**Charles**—I'm losing you, and I'm to blame.
{**Antonia**—Home and hospital—scenes of pain.
{**Robin**—Oh, the sorrow that follows the arrogance of fame.
{**Simon**—This is not an age for speaking plain.
{**Joan**—Offering thirty-two bars to a woman again!
{**Maria**—He's made his promise, I'm making my claim.

Tutti
Silence and deceit,
ambition and defeat,
love, music, self-delusion—
the elements of deadly confusion.

End of Act One

134

Act 2

SCENE ONE

Hospital. Around Antonia's bed are leads, tubes, life-support machines. The steady rhythm of the heart monitor sets the pulse of her thoughts as she begins to stir.

Antonia *(half asleep)* She said nothing at all,
and waited for him to come back.

She wakes

Song
On the border of memory and dreaming
I saw a couple on a London bridge
in an early evening snowstorm.
Hand in hand, wild in love,
with plans and hilarious cries
they strolled to the other side.
And oh what care they gave each other,
such intensive care in bed.
His work, her money, their freedom—
with no idea how grown-up life
could uninvent their love.

Then at last the idea came
with a roar of delighted applause
and with loud praise, and giddy fame,
profiles, parties, open doors.
And he grew to the shape of a lion,
his musical ambition swelled,
while she shrank to the size
of a household mouse.
Travel, concerts, hotels,
women in far-off places—
the world grew noisier and sad.

Ian McEwan

His work wouldn't tolerate children—
the house was silent and cold.

And I said nothing at all,
and waited for you to come back.

Fade up a low spot to reveal Charles in a chair, in his overcoat.

Charles I remember that snowstorm on the bridge
when we crossed the river to my first concert
at the Festival Hall, and as we walked
we were singing from The Magic Flute,
Mann und Weib und Weib und Mann—
my God, how happy we were.

He goes to her bedside.

Antonia Your oboe concerto, so graceful and free—
you told me it was a love letter in music.
And when the crowds could let you go
we drank champagne on a riverside rooftop—
the city below us was silent and white.

Charles That terrace belonged to a millionaire
whose name is lost to me.

Antonia And we danced on the snow...

Charles Drunk on music and love.

[Sudden shift]

Antonia *(aroused)* Then one month later, you fucked the oboist.
So began the endless succession—
what we kindly called your 'work'.

Charles Don't think of these things when you've
just come out of major surgery.

136

Antonia After such butchery, what better time?

Charles I can't ask you to forgive me for things I did
so wilfully. After all these years, one more apology
would be an insult.

Antonia *(subsiding)* For once you speak the truth.

Charles All I ask is your patience, give me
time to earn your trust, time to show you,
not in words but actions, that I have come back.
Let's cross another bridge together.

Antonia My limbs are heavy, I feel I'm sinking, but
by morphine's clear light I see it now.
I think you know there's a man who loves me.

Simon and a nurse enter, unobserved.

Your jealousy and pride have been provoked.
This is not sorrow, or a change of heart,
but blind possessiveness, the lifelong habit
you have of taking what you think is yours.

Charles *(rushes to her bedside)* Don't say that!
My darling, I want to show you how
I have changed. I've made my decision,
I've made a solemn promise...

*Accidentally, Charles knocks a monitoring machine to the floor.
Simon and the nurse rush forward to pull Charles away.*

Simon Come away from those lines! What are you
thinking of? Are you trying to kill her?

Nurse Her life depends upon these machines.
You must not come so close.

The nurse tends to Antonia, who is falling asleep.

Charles We were just talking of treachery, and I believe we were talking of you.

Simon *(moving Charles towards the door)* Leave her now. She needs her rest. You should go.

Charles I have to speak to her. We need to be alone.

Nurse Please...please, no violence here!

Simon You need to be alone; she needs to sleep. She's my patient, I know what's best for her.

Charles Yes, I've heard that's what you think.
Do you know there are ethical codes
for doctors and their patients?
And in my house,
there are rules of hospitality,
which you, my friend, have abused.

Simon And on my wards I have the final word.
I've asked you to leave. Shall I call security?

Charles *(furious, leaving)* A weak man hides behind authority—
It seems she's in your care. But listen doctor—
don't you dare exploit your position,
or I'll have you sacked. Whatever you say,
she's my wife and she belongs to me!

SCENE TWO

The Frieths' London house. Charles's studio. Maria is tidying up. Robin sits at a table surrounded by music manuscript in piles. On the floor, discarded balled-up sheets.

Robin Sixteen hours of writing out parts—

thirty-two bars for his latest squeeze,
then he wants to change the orchestration,
now he's unhappy with the strings—
I'm so tired these notes are swimming before
my eyes like drunken fish.
The rehearsal starts this afternoon.
My kingdom for a computer program—
but the old fool won't allow it.

Maria Count yourself lucky to be working for a genius.

Robin Aubade—a beautiful name for a poetic form—
the poet sweetly greeting the rising sun,
then parting sadly from his lover,
or tenderly begging her to stay.

But here comes 'Demonic Aubade'—
the great composer torments the dawn
with his fashionable racket. At his age
he should be thinking of the sunset.

Maria Pure jealousy. You want to be a composer—
I've seen the torn up pages in your filthy room.
But you know in your heart you have no talent.

Robin Does this mean that once again
you refuse to pour me a little cup of coffee?

Maria I've better things to do. This is
an important day, the important rehearsal
for his most important piece.
Destiny is calling him, history drives him forwards
and he needs my help. He's relying on me...

Robin To iron his shirts—you poor deluded slave.

Enter Charles, straight from the hospital, still in his overcoat, still angry.

Charles Not finished? Have you been asleep?
How much longer are you going to be?

Robin I need another half an hour.

Charles I want you to go to the rehearsal rooms now—
make sure the percussion has been delivered.
It's urgent—remember the disaster we had last time.

Robin *(keeps writing)* How can I ever forget?

Maria relieves Charles of his coat.

Charles Clash and suspended cymbals, tam-tam, roto-tom,
timpani, bass drum, temple blocks,
mark tree, side drum, vibraphone—
make sure they're all in place.

Robin But they're waiting for these parts...

Charles When I say now it's now I mean—
you can finish when you return.
Don't sit there man, get going!

*Robin leaves. Charles paces restlessly. Maria pours him coffee
from a flask and waits.*

Duet
Truly, Maria
I'm surrounded by fools on this crucial day
when my mind should be clear...

Maria *(aside)* Oh my love, I could comfort him now.

Charles ...clear of this anguish, this weight of sorrow.
If only I could live without a woman...

Maria *(aside)* He means without his wife.

Charles I should never have married her,
and tied myself up in lies.

Maria *(aside)* He dares not tell the truth about our love.

Charles How can I wipe away the past,
how can I persuade her that I'm in love?

Maria *(aside)* He's ashamed of his wretched marriage,
and now he must tell her that he loves me.

They come face to face. Maria offers the cup, he waves it away.

Was the operation a success?

Charles Oh yes, a success. Antonia will not die—
the good doctor has done his work,
but I could wring his neck, that loathsome snake.

Maria *(aside)* Angry with the doctor for saving her worthless life!

Charles If murder was among your household duties
I'd send you to the hospital now. Hah!

Maria *(aside)* To succeed where the doctor failed,
and end her misery!

Charles But I know that I'm a hypocrite and a fool...

*Calmer now, Charles is picking up some manuscript papers. Half
distracted, he glances at Robin's work as he starts to leave.*

Let me put to you a simple question—
Maria, have you ever thought of marriage?

Maria You're asking me! Oh no, I mean, but yes, but no,
but yes, I mean, my answer is of course,
it's yes of course, a simple yes.

Ian McEwan

Charles I didn't mean to embarrass you. Just think
carefully, is all I have to say. Most carefully.
Not only of the hurt that's done to you—
be careful of the pain that you might cause.
Remember my example.

He leaves.

Maria But my love, I'll never cause you pain,
and I know you'll never hurt me.

Charles *(off)* Send Robin to me when he's back.

Maria picks up Charles's coat and hugs it to her.

Maria

Song
When I hear your voice I feel
the pangs of greedy craving.
I know you suffer as much at least—
we share the hunger before the feast.

You set the matter out so well—
the command concealed behind a laugh,
and then you put your question to me—
do you think I didn't answer clearly?

My life was as dull as housework,
days forgotten in repeated chores,
lifting, wiping, cleaning—
now at last my tasks have meaning.

Let me lift your weight of sorrow
undo the lies, wipe clean the past.
My household duty is obedience—
my answer dear is a loving yes.

But I must bind you to me
before you change your mind,
[I've seen your ruthless ways]
[and] [I'll] make of love a gorgeous cage
where you, my sweet, can gently age.

SCENE THREE

*The hospital. Antonia in the ICU. The machines as before. The
nurse and a junior doctor are tending the patient as Simon enters.*

Junior Doctor All her signs are good. She's stable,
but she's weak, her pulse is thready.

Nurse It's too soon to send her to the ward.

Simon Then we'll keep her here another day...
before you go I want to tell you this:
her husband is certain to come back,
and when he does you must let me know
at once. His state of mind is dangerous—

Nurse This morning when he went towards her bed
I thought that he would kill her.

Junior Doctor The whole hospital is talking of it.
Hard to believe of such a famous man.

Simon Jealous fantasies, greed about her wealth,
the pressures of the creative life,
even a psychiatric disorder—
who knows—these may all be stupid stories,
but we'll take no chances—do not leave him
alone in here.

The nurse and junior doctor leave.

Ian McEwan

I cannot leave him alone with her—
but who will ever forgive this abuse
of professional power, or cure
my feverish sickness of deceit?

When I performed the tricky operation
I knew I was saving her for myself,
I've told no one of our connection,
that I've loved her and waited seven years.
Love has made me a specialist in fraud,
senior consultant in deception.
Now he wants to take her back, stake a
forceful claim to what he fears he'll lose.
He'll wheedle, threaten, repent, atone—
I dare not leave him alone with her.

Antonia *(stirring)* And waited for you to come back...

Simon Antonia...

Antonia He'll never change my mind.
I've told him. He knows...

Simon Yes, he knows, and he wants you back.

Antonia He cannot touch me now that I'm with you.

Simon With me—that's what I've longed to hear.
But Antonia, are you fully awake?
Do you know what you're saying?
Do you know where you are?

Antonia I'm drifting high above an endless plain
that's green to the curved horizon.
I'm moving towards you,
from misery to warmth,
from coldness to truth,
from silence to joy.

Simon No need for silence.

Antonia So much to say.

Simon Yes. So much to say.

Antonia And at last we can say it.

Simon The misery is over.

Antonia Because we know.

Simon We know.

Antonia Only joy.

Simon Joy will say it all.

Repeats, overlapping. They kiss. Unseen by them, a dark figure in a black coat moves downstage in low light.

I'm needed in theatre.
I'll come back soon.

They kiss again.

Antonia I'll sleep now, my darling.
But come when you can.

Simon leaves.

Antonia *(falling asleep)* On the borders...
On the borders of dreaming and waking
I saw a couple...
I saw a couple falling in love...

Maria moves quietly upstage.

Ian McEwan

Maria What agony, to stand in the shadows
listening to this conniving pair—
her hateful pride dressed up as virtue
and he a compulsive liar
by his own confession.
How dare they call it love,
this cringing, timid, dishonest affair.
How can it measure against my own?

She goes towards the bed.

Only the rich sleep so deeply,
so sweetly unconcerned.

The final impediment to bliss.
My instructions were clear,
and I'm not strong enough
to resist the power of their logic

My household duty
is to uproot the weeds—

*She wrenches out leads from the life-support machines. Slowly,
deliberately, she lets Charles's coat slip from her shoulders to the floor.*

No one saw me arrive,
no one will see me leave.

Maria melts back into the shadows.

Antonia *(softly)* I'm cold, so cold,
The house grows silent and cold.
And I can say nothing at all
while I wait for you to come back,
while I wait for you, while I wait...

*Her fading voice is steadily overwhelmed by the rising din of an
orchestra tuning up.*

SCENE FOUR

The rehearsal room. The tuning-up continues. The A is sounded
and taken up. Charles comes upstage towards the orchestra, baton
in hand. Robin is with him. Maria is to one side with a fresh towel
for her master.

Charles Is all the percussion here?

Robin Every last item safely delivered.

Charles You've got rid of that horn player?—
I've forgotten her name.

Robin Yes, her replacement is that bearded fellow.

Charles takes up his position.

Charles Ladies, gentlemen,
I'm deeply honoured that your famous orchestra
will give the world premier of Demonic Aubade.

The orchestra applauds. Charles raises his baton, the piece begins
while he describes it.

A dust-reddened sun lifts itself
over the cold desert rim.
Soon we feel the harshness of the rays,
the searing white heat of creation
like the imagination
striving in its birth pangs.
Straining to give life.
This music too is a rising sun,
ever more fiery as it proceeds
until we must avert our gaze...

Robin *(aside)* Or stop our ears...

Ian McEwan

Charles And find shelter. The sun becomes
the face of God at which we may not stare.

Charles comes away from the orchestra.

The light of artistic creation is also blinding.
The artist can't see the suffering he causes
to those around him. And they'll never
understand the purity of his goal, how the heat
of his invention won't melt
the ice in his heart.
He must be ruthless!
No religion, no purpose except this:
make something perfect before you die.
Life is short, art is for all time—
History will forgive my ways because
I wrote this beautiful piece.

*Enter unobserved a plainclothes police woman, Detective Inspector
Black; a uniformed woman police constable, WPC White; and Simon,
distraught. WPC White holds over her arm Charles's coat.*

Charles returns to the orchestra as the Aubade reaches its climax.

Charles It lifts! It soars!

DI Black Is he the one?

Simon This is the man. This is her husband.

White, Black If you don't mind, sir.

Charles Nothing can withstand its power!

White, Black We'd like a word.

Charles It's fury and its heat!

148

White, Black This won't take long.

The orchestra comes to a ragged halt.

Charles How dare you intrude like this!

DI Black They told us we would find you here.

WPC White Is this yours?

Charles You've found my coat. How awfully kind.
Give it to my man, then, ladies, kindly leave.

White, Black We have some questions for you.

The exchange becomes fast and stormy.

Charles Questions? Questions? Questions?
Do you realize where you are, and who I am?

WPC White Did you leave it at the bedside
of your dying wife?

White, Black, Simon This coat you say is yours!

Charles Dying? Did you say dying?

DI Black You left in a hurry. Were you disturbed?

Black, White, Simon You ran for your life!

Charles Dying? I don't understand.

Simon Did you kill her because it was me she loved?

White, Black, Simon Your jealous frenzy!

WPC White Was it her money you wanted?

White, Black, Simon Your vicious greed!

DI Black A nurse and doctor saw you make
a failed attempt upon her life.

White, Black, Simon You can't deny it!

Robin Surely there's been a misunderstanding.
Why don't you sit down.

Maria *(aside)* Every minute brings him closer to me.

Charles Am I going mad?
What is this talk of killing and dying?
How can I answer your questions
when my wife is not dead?

Simon What odious pretence of ignorance!

DI Black *(as WPC White applies handcuffs)*
Not dead! A good defence.
You can put it to the judge.

WPC White Not dead—a matter of opinion, perhaps!
Hah hah! This way, my friend.

She begins to lead him away.

Charles *(softly beseeching)* Please tell me Antonia is not dead.

DI Black You'll find no one who can tell you
she was not murdered in her hospital bed.

Charles Murdered...
Who could murder sweet Antonia?

He has come face to face with Maria.

No…no…

Maria remains silent.

But why?

WPC White This way now sir. Our car is waiting for you.

Maria For you, my sweet. For you.

White and Black begin to lead Charles away.

Charles Maria! You must tell them the truth!

Maria The truth is this. I know you better
than you know yourself. I know your
prison years will teach you how to love. [at last]
I'll make your cage a happy one.
In the desert of empty time, my visits
will be your sweet oases.

Charles Are you completely mad?
Tell them the truth!

Maria Like heroes in a prison movie, we'll
press our hands together against
the thickened glass.

Charles This is the killer. Arrest her!

White, Black This way now.

Maria And when at last they set you free,
and you are old and frail
I'll take you home with me
and care for you, and care for you.

Ian McEwan

Charles I am not the killer. Please listen to me!

White, Black, Simon, Robin, Maria
The lonely years in your happy cage,
the sweet oasis of her (my) visit.

Maria This is the gift I brought—

White, Black, Simon, Robin, Maria For you!

Charles I am...

Maria I am the only lover.

White, Black, Simon, Robin, Maria For you!

Charles I am already...

Maria And I will wait—

White, Black, Simon, Robin, Maria For you!

Charles I am already in hell.

White, Black, Simon, Robin, Maria She (I) will wait for you.

Charles is led away.

Maria remains.

Ends   □

GRANTA

THE UNKNOWN KNOWN

Martin Amis

Martin Amis

Even as we enter the age of cosmic and perhaps eternal war, it remains remarkable: the nuanced symbiosis between East and West. Here at Strategic Planning, or 'the "Prism"', there are three sectors, and these three sectors used to be called, not very imaginatively, Sector Three, Sector Two, and Sector One. Sector Three dealt with daily logistics, Sector Two with long-term missions, and Sector One with conceptual breakthroughs. But now, following certain remarks by the American Secretary of Defence, the three sectors have been renamed as follows: Known Knowns, Known Unknowns, and Unknown Unknowns—a clear improvement. There is of course (this goes without saying) no sector called Unknown Knowns. That would be preposterous and, moreover, a complete waste of time. Only a madman would give the idea any serious thought. There are no such things as Unknown Knowns—though I have to say that I can imagine such a category, such a framework, when I contemplate my physical extinction (which, I admit, I am increasingly inclined to do). I work in Sector One: Unknown Unknowns.

Our camp lies on the Northern Border. Picking up on certain remarks in the Western press, other groups in the region—affiliates, rivals, enemies—have seen fit to call 'the "Prism"' a 'jungle gym' operation, a mere 'rope ladder' or 'monkey puzzle' bivouac which the Americans, should they ever find out about it, wouldn't take the trouble to destroy. According to them, we're not worth so much as a cruise missile—or even, if you please, a Hellfire warhead from a Predator drone. They call us 'daydreamers'; they call us 'sleepwalkers'. Well, all that is about to change. Soon the whole world will whisper it—in the East with tears of pride, in the West with bitterness and horror: 'the "Prism"...'. I refer of course to my own initiative, my 'baby' if you will. Its codename is UU: CRs/G,C.

To the right of the drill-yard, the first longhouse: Known Knowns. This is where we all started out. When you think about human society in a certain way—i.e., with the sole objective of hurting it—the entire planet resembles a pulsing bullseye. The continents themselves hang there like great soft underbellies, almost pleading to be strafed and scorched and slashed. True, our activities here in Known Knowns are hands-on and bread-and-butter: shells, landmines, grenades, petrol bombs. But one's induction will include action in the field: oh yes. And it goes on being dangerous work, what with the frequent gas leaks and accidental fires and the almost daily explosions.

Later, when, with some pomp, you cross the yard and enter the second longhouse, Known Unknowns, you begin to understand that civilization isn't *entirely* defenceless. It is no walk in the park, trolling around North Korea in search of the fabled twenty-five kilograms of uranium; it is no picnic, going from factory to factory in Uzbekistan in search of weapons-grade anthrax or aerosolized asphyxiants. True, doing that is better than actually being in Known Unknowns. In *Bio*, for example, the conditions are far from sanitary. In one stall a comrade tests a sarin compound on a donkey; in the next stall along, another channels a 'mosaic' toxin of smallpox and VX into a garden sprinkler. The regular and lethal epidemics are not always easy to contain. Accordingly the breath of a Sector Two comrade always has a tell-tale tang, that of potent cough-drops, moving about as he does among vats of acids and tubs full of raw pesticides.

Unknown Unknowns is not to be found in a third longhouse. In fact, there isn't a third longhouse. No. For Unknown Unknowns you go behind the wash-huts and over the sheepdip and then you see it, a deceptively modest wooden cabin, called, sinisterly, 'Hut A'. An outsider, putting his head round the door, might find the atmosphere somewhat casual and unfastidious—even somewhat torpid and scurf-blown. But these are the necessary motes and postures of intense concentration. The thinking, here, is pointed-end, cutting-edge. Synergy, maximalization—these are the kind of concepts that are tossed from cushion to floor mat in Unknown Unknowns. Now a comrade argues for the dynamiting of the San Andreas Fault; now another envisages the large-scale introduction of rabies (admixed with smallpox, angel dust, and steroids) to the fauna of Central Park. A pensive silence follows. Sometimes these silences can last for days on end. We sit there and think. All you can hear is the occasional swatting palm-slap, or the crackle of a beetle being ground underfoot.

Every evening, after prayers, I flex my impeccable English, reading aloud our write-ups in *The New York Times* and elsewhere on a faulty and outmoded computer borrowed from *Cyber* in Known Unknowns.

Martin Amis

Paradigm-shift is what we're in the business of. But paradigm-shift represents a window, and windows will close. The much-ballyhooed operation of September 2001, to take the obvious example, is now unrepeatable. Indeed, the tactic was obsolete by ten o'clock the same morning. Its efficacy lasted for exactly seventy-one minutes: from 8.46, when American 11 hit the North Tower, until 9.57, and the rebellion on United 93. The passengers on the fourth plane grasped the new reality, and acted. They didn't linger for long in the vanished praxis of the 1970s (and how antique and diffident that now seems!): the four-day siege on the tropical tarmac, the shortages of food and water, the festering toilets, the airing of 'conditions' and 'demands', the phased release of the children and the women—then the surrender, or the clambering commandos. No. They rose up. And United 93 came down on its back at 580 miles per hour, twenty minutes from the Capitol.

For different reasons, UU: CRs/G,C launched but not yet completed, is also unrepeatable. From the outset it relied on something we may never have again: the full resources of a nation state. That's gone, thanks to the biblical, the mountain-flattening rage of the Americans. Indeed, given the heavy price we have had to pay for it, many of us, here in Unknown Unknowns, regard September as almost criminally lax. We would have deployed scores of planes nationwide, and our targeting would have been much more adventurous. Not just the landmarks: we would have sent a message about all the other things we hate—nightclubs, music halls, women's institutes, sports arenas. Think of it. A 767, in the evening glitter, descending like an incensed seraph on Yankee Stadium...

UU: CRs/G,C was launched in July 2001. If everything had gone according to schedule there would have been a second 'September surprise' for the Americans. Now, four years later, my actors are at last on US soil and poised to strike: my CRs are at last homing in on G,C. The difficulties along the way have been unexpectedly numerous. I don't know—twice a day I have attacks of fluttering uncertainty; I mistake the dawn for a sunset, the sunset for a dawn, and a part of my mind involuntarily anticipates failure, if not fiasco. Thereafter it is hardly the work of a moment to refresh my belief that God will smile on UU: CRs/G,C.

On top of all this I am not getting on very well with my wives.

Last night I had a visitor: a colleague from Unknown Unknowns. Now might be a good time to explain about our aliases. We in 'Hut A' have, over the years, become theorists and visionaries, but we all started out in Known Knowns, seeing action in various theatres (Chechnya, Thailand, Kashmir), and our aliases are reminders of the way we made our bones on the front line. Again the 'nuanced symbiosis': for these names are taken from our coverage in the Anglophone media, and then lightly transliterated. I cannot exaggerate the ineffable reverence, the tender solemnity, with which we murmur our *noms de guerre*. My visitor, my colleague—*his* name is of the very best: bold, virile, and self-explanatory. Unlike mine. I didn't say anything when they gave it to me, but I have grown increasingly unhappy with it. My name's 'Ayed', and it derives from Improvised Explosive Device. But Ayed's *already* a name. The little Tajik who limps into the village once a month, to grind the knives, *his* name's Ayed...

'I had a message today, "Ayed",' said my guest, 'from the One Eyed One.'

The tea I was drinking abruptly changed direction and came sneezing out of my nose. 'Continue, "Truqbom",' I said when I was able. As was now my habit, I'd been hoping that the One Eyed One was dead.

'He asks after UU: CRs/G,C. He asks: "When will the great day come? When will it be, this day?" '

'... *July 29!*' I always imagined that, when I said those words for the first time, they would echo with geo-historical resonance (this, after all, this was a date that would for ever burn in the soul of the West); but it came out as something of a whinny. It was now July 25, and my CRs were still in a pit near a swamp in East Texas.

'July 29 of this year?'

'Definitely. I virtually guarantee it.'

'He understands, "Ayed"—*we* understand—that there have been setbacks.'

I laughed with unexpected shrillness, and found myself saying, 'It is so, is it not, comrade, that you've never been introduced to my wives?'

And before he could answer I summoned them from the kitchen with a mighty clap of my hands. In they filed. I had spent my lunch hour, that day, sadly gazing into the small pond, or large puddle, under the plane trees behind the wash-huts. And it now seemed to me that my wives resembled four gigantic tadpoles. What would they eventually mutate into?

'Oh, we're very advanced here you know,' I cried. 'Oh yes. My wives quite often "meet". Have some purified water, comrade, cooled in my refrigerator.'

He left at once, naturally, stalking off on that noisy tin leg of his. This afforded me some temporary relief, and then of course I gave the wives the rough edge of my tongue.

All night I sat there on the lumpy hassock with my face in my hands. What extraordinary behaviour: my wives most certainly do *not* 'meet'! And now I have offended the notoriously sensitive and traditionalist 'Truqbom', with his ugly muscles—my patron and my peer.

It was he, you see, who sponsored my initial audience with the One Eyed One (aka the One with One Eye, the Mullah, the Emir, the Commander of the Faithful) that June: the June that preceded September. There has been much speculation in the press about this—about whether the Mullah actually approved the attack on America. The truth is that he voiced his doubts and, at first, withheld his blessing. And his doubts were not the obvious ones—that he would a) forfeit his country, and b) spend the rest of his life in hiding.

No. What worried *him* were considerations best described as 'ideological' (I quote from *The 9/11 Commission Report*, which, with rather exaggerated nonchalance, we are all passing around). The One Eyed One wanted the autumn initiative 'to attack Jews' (ibid.). Already aware of this settled emphasis of the Mullah's, I mildly exaggerated the anti-Semitic component (at that point non-existent) of UU: CRs/G,C when I came to make my presentation. The prospect of September 11, by the way, did not deter the Mullah from going ahead with, or getting started on, his autumn campaign against the Northern Alliance, solemnly inaugurated on September 10.

Having made the six-day journey to our second city, I joined the queue in the back yard of the One Eyed One's modest villa. Many of my fellow supplicants were representatives of organizations similar to but much grander than 'the "Prism"', and I heard the usual sly remarks about swings and hammocks and treetop dens. My clothes were creased from successive nights on packed buses, and I would have dearly liked a minute alone with a cloth and a faucet. Overall, my confidence was far from high. I had, as it were, auditioned CRs/G,C (it did not yet bear the 'UU' imprimatur) before the thinkers of 'Hut A', and it was greeted without the slightest sign of enthusiasm, to put it mildly; it was greeted, in fact, with chilled dismay and then outright mockery. I also had an unpleasant suspicion that 'Truqbom' had intervened on my behalf in a facetious spirit, to bring upon me not only much trouble and expense but also humiliation and perhaps even punishment. Despite all this, I cherished the hope that the One Eyed One would somehow grasp the wayward, the vaulting genius of CRs/G,C.

Once I got inside it was possible to watch the petitioners as they took their leave of the fabled chamber. You could see them backing away, and then turning towards the open front doors. Some came out looking almost farcically gratified; some (I counted nine) seemed utterly crushed—and two of *them* were promptly marched off by the guards. The overwhelming majority, admittedly, were neither happy nor sad: they were merely caricatures of bafflement. But by this time I had a near-irresistible desire to bolt: I could feel my body trying to do it, trying to burst away from itself and be gone. My turn came and I stumbled in.

The warrior poet lay half-submerged by the heaped cushions, an imposing figure in his dishdash and his flip-flops. I found it difficult to return his one-eyed gaze, and during my presentation I looked elsewhere, at the rugs, the tea tray, the large tin box brimming with US dollars. When I eventually fell silent and straightened my neck, Mullah Omar said slowly,

'Answer me this. What should we do with the buggerers? Some scholars say they should be thrown from a high roof. Others maintain that these sinners should be buried in a hole and a wall should be toppled on them. Which?'

I said with hesitation, 'The hole and the wall sounds more unnatural, and thus more pious, my Leader.'

And I saw that he was smiling at me. A strange smile, combining serenity and severity. Perhaps this is the way God smiles.

I returned to the north-east in a two-door Datsun pickup. Brashly I sounded the horn, and watched the unloading of my recent

Martin Amis

purchases (the water purifier, the battery-operated refrigerator), suitably impressing my wives.

UU: CRs/G,C? It's simple. We're going to scour all the prisons and madhouses for every compulsive rapist in the country, and then unleash them on Greeley, Colorado.

Ah, my wives. As I keep saying to all my temporary wives, 'My wives don't understand me.'

And they don't. For instance, I am of that breed of men which holds that a husband should have sex with his wives every night. Or, to put it slightly more realistically, every twenty-four hours—without fail, except for the usual calendric exemptions. My wives have of course never denied me, but they sometimes show a certain resistance (more by demeanour than by word or deed) to my forthright amatory style. It is fairly clear by now, I think, that what they object to is my invariable use of the 'RodeoMaMa'.

The 'RodeoMaMa' is a Western frippery I picked up, by mail order, during my sojourn in the United States and didn't have the heart to leave behind. It consists of a 'weight belt' and the prow of a leather saddle. You attach it to your wives' waists, so that the saddle hovers over the lower back. If the 'RodeoMaMa' has a fault, it is its unwieldiness, or its bulk. My wives always know when I am off to see one of my temporary wives, because I take my 'RodeoMaMa' with me in its ragged old sack.

I was fourteen when my father, a gifted poppy-grower, took me to America. One day I was a contented young student, never happier than when about my tasks of recitation and memorization; the next, I was hurled into the hellhouse of Greeley, Colorado. I arrived in midwinter, which muffled the shock—in several applications of that verb. A mother blimplike in her padded parka, an infant daughter, as rigid as a capital aitch, in hers; and the snow, seen at first from above, like a flood made of milk, then on the ground like a sugar coating that also imparted silence. The shock was muffled, but it came. Scarcely crediting my senses, I began to notice that there were women motorists, women police officers, women *soldiers*; I felt all this as a multiple, a compound ignominy. Yet nothing prepared me for the spring and the summer.

A thousand times a day I would whisper it ('But her *father*...her *brothers...*'), every time I saw a luminously bronzed *poitrine*, the outline of underwear on a tightly packaged rump, a thin skirt rendered transparent by a low sun, a pair of nipples starkly staring through a pullover, a white bra strap contending with a murky armpit, a stocking top arresting the architecture of an upper thigh, or the very crux of a woman sliced in two by a wedge of denim or dungaree. They strolled in swirly print dresses across the Walkway, indifferent to the fact that anyone standing below, in the thicket of nettles and poison ivy, could see the full scissoring of their legs and their shamelessly brief underpants. And when, in all weathers, I took a late walk along the back gardens, the casual use of a buttress or a drainpipe would soon confront me with the sight of a woman quite openly undressing for bed.

Worst was Drake Square in early July: the students, in the week before summer recess. A slum of bubblegum, sweet drinks, cigarettes, and naked flesh; the girls on towels and blankets, with limbs and midriffs raw to the sun, waiting to be *checked out* (such is the brutal patois) by any man with eyes to see. Sitting on a bench, trying to apply myself to a book, I would despairingly conclude that in the universal war between the flesh and the spirit, the spirit was tasting ruin, its armies crushed and broken-winged. And yet the birds sang, and the grey squirrels bobbed across the green. On the way to Drake Square from the bus stop I would pass, each morning, an inanimate reminder of what a woman ought to look like, cherished, sequestered, exalted: I mean the curve-cornered matt-black postbox (check *that* out) in front of Thurgood Assurance on City Boulevard, which I would often glance at as I sprinted by.

It was at this time, too, that I received a cruel blow to my self-esteem. Back home, every little boy, at the age of five or six, experiences that lovely warm glow of pride when he realizes that his sisters are, in one important respect, just like his mother: *they* can't read or write either. Well, that pride was painfully retracted in Greeley, Colorado; and there were other familial developments that caused enormous suffering for me and for my brothers—and for my poor father. What can you do when your daughters start consorting with *kaffirs*, with *koofs*? You can't live with them, and you can't kill them (not in America); so the women stayed, and the men came home.

Martin Amis

I wonder. Will there one day be a book called *The 7/29 Commission Report*, running to 567 pages, including 118 pages of notes? I still believe there will. And what a tortuous tale it will tell.

The One Eyed One, the One with One Eye, referred me to another one with one eye, his Justice Minister, who referred me to his Justice Minister (another one with one eye). The initial scouring of all the country's prisons and madhouses yielded 423 CRs. It was a hazardous journey they faced (there would be attrition), so I authorized a second sweep with a different kind of inmate in mind: compulsive paedophiles. This realized an additional 62. The 485 compulsives were corralled in a barracks near the capital and prepared for departure with heroin and straitjackets. As a further refinement, those who didn't have it already were infected with syphilis D.

When I went to America, I went there by plane. But I hardly needed telling that the unscheduled arrival of a jumbo jet crammed with scrofulous sociopaths would have raised some eyebrows at US Immigration. The first leg of the compulsives' journey, then, was a 900-mile drive in the trunks of old taxis. When we performed a 'test run', using a dozen assorted criminals and lunatics, the fatality rate turned out to be one hundred per cent, so we were careful, next time, to poke a few more holes in the back panelling, and we reluctantly reduced each load from four to two. This meant that the drivers had to come back for a second batch while the first took its ease in holding kennels at the port. Although I was inflexibly resolved to lead UU: CRs/G,C myself, a sudden indisposition forced me to stand down; so all authority in the field devolved upon the ferocious figure of Colonel Gul, commander of the First Mechanised Battalion. On August 3, 2001, chained to the hold of a disused container ship, my compulsives boldly set sail for Somalia.

NOTE: At which point (for reasons I will later mention) I abandoned this skeletal typescript of 'The Unknown Known'. The much fuller manuscript version followed the compulsives on their sanguinary journey to Greeley, Colorado (Greeley, after all, is the cradle of Islamism: it was there that Sayyid Qutb's Milestones, *known as the Islamists'* Mein Kampf, *was decisively shaped). The disused container ship is hijacked by Filipino pirates; the surviving compulsives spend*

162

two years in a punishment block in Mogadishu; they are then death-marched across Ethiopia into Sudan, where they encounter a host of some 30,000 janjaweed, *who kill all the compulsives under thirty 'as a warning'; the remainder (now consisting entirely of paedophiles, plus the implacable Colonel Gul) continue west by bus and on foot; they are severely mauled by a child militia in Congo, armed with pangas... And so on. Finally, one CR makes it to Greeley, Colorado, where, half-dead with syphilis D, he is found weeping in a cinema car park. Meanwhile, Ayed's marriages decline to the point where he retools his RodeoMaMa in the outhouse called Known Knowns, and resolves on a paradigm shift, an Unknown Unknown, which is sure to succeed: a suicide operation in his own home. The unknown known of the title is of course God.*

I abandoned the story for many reasons, all of them strictly extraneous. As I have said, Islamism is a total system, and like all such it is eerily amenable to satire. But in the end I felt that the piece was premature, and therefore a hostage to fortune; certain future events might make it impossible to defend. If I live to be very old, I may one day pull it out of my desk—at the other end of the Long War. □

GRANTA

TURN OF THE CENTURY
Photographs by
Bruce Frankel

Mid-1970s. New York was centre stage. It seemed as if everybody had a camera. For the neophyte photographer, originality was the goal. While the reference for serious photography remained black and white, I was drawn to colour. (I didn't know what colour was, didn't have a black-and-white darkroom, found a lack of compelling polychromatic work.) Through the luxurious qualities of Kodachrome I learned about light and the properties of film. Eventually, understanding colour would lead me back to black and white in the early 1990s. There were two extremes that I experimented with: one, orthochromatic film with its inherent high contrast, low speed and no grain; two, high-speed film, pushed to the maximum, to exploit the grain fields.

New York was a rich source for these explorations, and no subject had such a unique visual impact as the World Trade Center. The twin towers held great possibilities: volume, shape, spatial arrangement. Tragically it would be the symbolism of these two tall buildings, and their fate, that would mark the changing of centuries for New York, the self-proclaimed capital of everything. □

42nd Street, September 1973

Fifth Avenue, February 2000

Duffy Square, February 2000

Central Park, February 2000

Central Park, February 1996

West 52nd Street, May 1999

Williamsburg, looking west, February 2001

World Trade Center, May 1999

World Trade Center, October 2001

New York Bay, October 2001

"This collection of photographs and commentary presents a relentlessly tragic vision of the ongoing conflict in Iraq. . . . Not yet 30, Gilbertson has clearly studied James Nachtwey, Robert Capa, and David Douglas Duncan; this impressive book shows he has absorbed their lessons."

—*Publishers Weekly*

"A stunning new book. . . . This is the kind of reporting we so desperately need: free of false bravura, free of agenda, free of inflated urgency. . . . For this reason, the book belongs less with other histories of the war than on the same shelf with Hemingway's *A Farewell to Arms* and Vonnegut's *Slaughterhouse-Five*."

—TED GENOWAYS, *Mother Jones*

260 p., 230 color plates
Cloth £19.00

Trade enquiries to: UPM, 0117 9020275
Distributed by John Wiley, 01243 779777

THE UNIVERSITY OF CHICAGO PRESS
www.press.uchicago.edu

WHISKEY TANGO FOXTROT

A PHOTOGRAPHER'S CHRONICLE OF THE IRAQ WAR

ASHLEY GILBERTSON

the new 8
photography magazine
reserve your limited edition copy now
www.foto8.com
+44(0) 207 253 8801

GRANTA

HUMAN SAFARI

Lucy Eyre

Hamar villagers and a European tour group, Omo valley, 2006

Human diversity is the new wildlife, apparently. Every second honeymooner has glimpsed a lion or stalked a buffalo, but people—ebony-skinned, half-naked, scarred, painted people—are the new wildebeest. Going to photograph and stare at people untouched by the modern world (ignorant of the life and work of David Beckham) is state-of-the-art adventure tourism. Unfortunately for the participant in the human safari—the white one, that is—one's arrival tends to mean that these subjects are no longer untouched. No doubt this is unfortunate for the spotted as well as the spotter, but their opinion—as opposed to their photo—is rarely sought.

The Omo valley, in south-west Ethiopia, is home to more than twenty distinct tribes. Some of them understand each other's languages and intermarry; others raid cattle and kill each other. The Omo valley is part of the clumsily named 'Southern Nations, Nationalities and Peoples' Region' (SNNPR) of Ethiopia. Southern Omo epitomizes several stereotypes—or prejudices—about 'native' Africa: bare-breasted women with lip plates and heavy iron ankle rings; near-naked men with spears or feather headdresses; children smeared with coloured body paint; murderous inter-tribal conflict over cattle. That this should be in Ethiopia—boastful of its long Christian heritage, hierarchical, bureaucratic, isolationist and conservative, where the word for black African (in Amharic) means 'slave'—is almost as extraordinary as the fact that it still exists more or less as it always has. Apart from the tourists, that is.

Tourism is rather undeveloped in Ethiopia, though the country offers ancient rock-hewn churches, breathtaking mountainous landscape and the ability to see the outside of a shabby stone cottage in which sits, we are assured, the original Ark of the Covenant. In 2005 my partner accepted a posting with the British government's Department for International Development, and we moved to Adis Abeba, Ethiopia's capital. Last year some friends came to stay with us. 'Omo valley looks interesting,' they said. I was working on a book set partly in that region, and needed to go back there as I'd been only once before on a brief, overwhelming trip with someone who was taking photographs for an NGO. Our friends visited in August, a month when the highlands of Ethiopia are battered by the rainy season and the walls of Lalibela's famous rock-hewn churches sprout green moss. Since the cultural attractions were damp, Omo seemed a more appealing proposition.

Lucy Eyre

So six of us set off, with some reservations, for the inaccessible Omo valley, that lowland, 'pagan' and generally un-Ethiopian part of the country. We drove for more than two days from Adis Abeba, though it can also be reached by a six-hour drive from a grass airstrip usually occupied by sheep and goats. The tourist facilities in the Omo region are beyond basic. As the *Bradt* guidebook notes of one of the larger 'towns' in the region; 'Whether the marginally cheaper and even more sordid National Hotel represents better value for money is the sort of burning question that will help see you through the night should counting cockroaches fail to cure any insomnia brought on by the heat and the dirt.' Generally, people camp.

Most visitors go with a tour group. These are run by Adis Abebans who feel no affinity with the tribes, despite being their countrymen. On my first visit, the driver from Adis Abeba shouted at people as we sped past, our large car kicking up dust. I couldn't understand the words, but the tone was clear enough: 'Oi, get a load of those feathers! Put some clothes on.' On my second trip, I saw mainly southern Europeans (who hunt in packs in August) going from campsite to campsite: families from Spain in matching khaki; Italian backpackers with loud tie-dye T-shirts and louder voices. They were transported in a convoy of white Toyota Land Cruisers, with a piece of A4 paper taped inside the back window of each, numbered 1, 2, 3 and 4. We were travelling independently in our private cars—white four-wheel drives with diplomatic plates—so we felt superior, though I expect the distinction was lost on the locals.

One of the larger tribal groups in the Omo is the Hamar. At first glance—which is all that is generally taken—Hamar men come across as fey, preening, vain birds. The women, by contrast, are tough, sturdy and no nonsense. The men wear short—sometimes very short—striped wraps and little else. Sometimes shoes, sometimes not. Their main, show-off feature is their hairstyle. Young men will spend days working on each other's hair. They have headdresses—clay caps with feathers sticking out the top. The feathers are supposed to indicate that the wearer has killed a dangerous animal or human enemy in the last year. I'm not sure if this is really so—or whether 'dangerous' is liberally interpreted. A Hamar man's most prized possession (after his cows and, if he can afford one, his gun) is his stool, which he will have carved himself. It is about six inches high and long, and has two functions, both of which are integral to a Hamar male's sense of well-being: sitting down to contemplate life, and careful sleeping to preserve his elaborate hairstyle. A Hamar man will lie on his side, prop his neck on the stool at an uncomfortable angle and, somehow, fall asleep.

The women wear small short plaits—not braids but stringy twists—cut in a bowl-like fashion, coated with butter mixed with red ochre. Their heads resemble animated orange mops. Their bodies—or at least their chests and shoulders—are often also shiny and red with the same butter. Married women wear heavy iron neck-rings (usually three)—those with a protruding piece on the top ring are first wives; the others are second wives. They wear goatskin skirts and, often, a goatskin piece over their shoulders, trimmed with rows of cowrie shells. Their breasts are usually exposed. They have tight brass spirals wound round their upper arms. Married women are all ochres and browns: skin, butter, goat-hide skirt. The unmarried girls are colourful: red, yellow and blue beads round their necks and decorating their leather skirts. They also go bare-chested, and are most sought after by the prowling tourists with cameras.

The Mursi men—neighbours and mortal enemies—appear much more impressive than their Hamar counterparts: manly and beautiful, posing as great warriors with spears. The ones we saw were almost naked, with blankets hanging loosely down from their necks or shoulders. It's easy to stray in to colonial porn here: the flashing smiles, firm thighs and blue-black buttocks of the native. Hamar women draw your eyes, but Mursi females defy your gaze. They wear enormous, disfiguring lip plates; those who aren't wearing them have long, saggy lower lips, hanging up to ten inches down in a droopy echo of the missing clay plate—a parody of a surly teenager.

These living covers of the *National Geographic* know their value. There's not much to see in southern Omo. Indeed, almost nothing beyond the inhabitants. The palette of the landscape is muted: browns, dusty yellows, bleached greens; the blue sky rinsed out by the unforgiving sun. It's a harsh landscape in the dry season (when the tourists come): most of the limited growth consists of shrubs that only the hungriest goat would consider eating. The thirsty eye is quickly drawn to the occasional tree with shocking pink flowers, a blaze against the drabness. You don't come for the views: the highlights are village visiting, gawping at local markets and, perhaps, seeing a traditional ceremony.

We were lucky enough to see the spectacle of a Hamar ritual— a privilege, as it turned out, offered every day to tourists during the season. One worry about tourism is that it undermines traditional cultures; but does it, paradoxically, conserve them as a show for the tourists? This ceremony involves whipping the women, a practice which inevitably makes a modern Western liberal nervous. We worried that, as spectators, we were implicated in such brutality. This initiation festival would have happened without us, but the family sometimes needs to wait until sufficient money is saved up to brew beer and kill goats for the participants. There must have been at least forty *ferengis* (white people) watching the ritual; if everyone paid the same price as us, then the tribe or the family would have received well over £200. (The standard wage for a construction worker in Adis Abeba is just fifty pence a day.) The ceremony is a genuine tradition, and the Hamar, naturally enough, make the most of its appeal to the tourists, whom they never courted. But should we help to preserve it? Ought we to refuse to watch? And who is exploiting whom, after all, when one is clearly paying a (relative) fortune for a ring-side seat? How would we feel if our luxury wedding could pay for itself by letting a few strangers from a very different culture wander through the proceedings, pointing and taking photographs? Would we all sell our wedding party to *OK* magazine if they asked us?

The rite we saw was the Hamar initiation ceremony where a young man leaps across a line of cattle and is, subsequently, permitted to get married and carry a phallus-shaped piece of wood tucked into the waist of his skirt. It goes like this. The Hamar women (and the *ferengis*) gather in a dry riverbed. The women sing and dance, clacking their heavy ankle rings together. Some of them have bells tied below their knees, which jingle as they jump. After more than two hours of the women blowing atonal horns and singing loudly in the midday sun, a few men approach. The women wail in response. The men carry fistfuls of long, narrow, stripped-birch branches. A woman approaches a man and 'provokes' him by blowing her horn loudly in his face and jumping. She will raise her right arm ready to be whipped. Other women may push her out of the way, wanting to go first. The man, seemingly reluctant, will whip a birch branch round the woman's left side, the tip flicking on to her upper arm and her back. He drops the stick in the sand and reaches for another. Each woman will be whipped several times.

Oddly enough, or perhaps not, it was the men (both European and Hamar) who were most uncomfortable with the whipping. It seemed that the women asked for it. The Western men were confused by this, as were (apparently) the Hamar men. As a tourist it's difficult to know how much of the refusal to whip, and the insistence on being whipped, are show, when so much of what goes on with the Hamar remains completely incomprehensible. An anthropologist who has lived with the Hamar writes, in her wryly named article 'Beating About the Bush', that the women are whipped to prove their loyalty to their kinsman who is being initiated. In return they will get gifts and he will take care of them in future. The scarring on a woman's back functions as an IOU. Yes, our European men agreed, women initiate it—but do they have a choice? Isn't this unreasonable pain required by the—male-dominated—society in order to succeed, or even belong? A bit like a full Brazilian, observed a female member of our party. It's faked, one *ferengi* man said, hopefully: look, it only catches them lightly on the arm. I pointed out the fresh, bleeding stripes on a young woman's back. He wandered away, thoughtfully, and sat down. How is a modern European man supposed to react to this spectacle—the whipping, the noise, the heat—except by filming it on his camcorder? The *ferengis* appeared to think of themselves as disembodied, invisible. Some of them had no qualms about crowding the participants to obtain their photos—literally shoving cameras through Hamar legs to get a better view.

The Hamar men's part in the ceremony appeared to consist of much sitting around, some beer drinking, and a little face- and leg-painting. Older men painted their legs white and pale green, which made it look disconcertingly as if they were wearing 1980s-style cropped leggings. One of the drivers from Adis Abeba was filming the men with his mobile phone. A Spanish woman had her face painted. This is men's business, really, but—despite her quest for the authentic—she was not, it seemed, prepared to be involved in whipping. The men did have one crucial task. Once the other business was done—the dancing, the trumpets, the whipping, the painting—the men arranged the cows in a line, side by side. The twenty-year-old initiate, naked and with electrified afro-style hair, jumped up on to the first cow, ran across the line (of about ten animals) and hopped down. He then jumped up from the other side and ran back. This happened four times (twice each way) and then it was over. Stand on a few cows—big deal. At least you don't have to get whipped. Or have eight children, fetch the water every day, clean the house, cook the food, grow the crops or grind the grain by hand with heavy stones. But none of this makes a good spectacle.

You pay a fee to watch the ritual and then you have full access and permission to take unlimited photos. Visiting a village or market is somewhat different. You pay to enter the village (though not for the market), then you must negotiate separately for each photograph. There's not really much to see in a Hamar village: four round huts, perhaps, a large goat-pen built out of thorny shrubs and, amazingly, almost no Western artefacts beyond some plastic jerrycans and cigarette lighters or digital watch straps worn on necklaces. And us, of course, looking ridiculous with our designed-and-tested walking boots, insect repellent, suncream and cars full of essential equipment—camping stoves, tents, sleeping bags, extra clothes, toothbrushes, tins, tin-openers. (Actually, we forgot the tin-opener.) When we got changed in the campsite, local children would ask for our T-shirts. The assumption, naturally enough, was that you clearly didn't need it if you had taken it off and swapped it for another one. We look at the Hamar; the Hamar look at us. 'But you're here!' both groups are thinking, with somewhat different emphasis. It's a two-way zoo.

Having paid over a hundred pounds per day for a car and guide, cushioned camping and cooks, not to mention flights to Ethiopia (none of it to the Hamar or the Mursi), tourists are reluctant to pay the people themselves—their *raison d'etre là*—the going rate: six pence per person per photo. Tourists *bargain*—twelve subjects for the price of ten—and they turn off the sound on their digital cameras to pretend that they have only clicked the shutter once, when they have taken several shots. It's as if the very handing-over of money for the privilege of photography is sordid; that the actual exchange makes it so, not the presence of aliens with their cameras pretending to have discovered an exotic tribe. Most tourists don't want to interact with the people—find out their names, ask about their lives—they want to see them, and get photographic proof that they've seen them. In any case, their guides from Adis Abeba probably don't speak the local languages. If you do ask the Hamar what they think, they are bemused: 'Why would someone follow me to take my photograph just to show it to his people in his country? They don't even know me.'

The Hamar, Mursi and others possess a scarce resource that is in demand. It's a tenet of capitalist economics that monopoly sellers should exploit their position. The Hamar's hard-nosed demands for money reveal that this tourist is not the first; other visitors have taught the Hamar their worth as photographic subjects. But the ghostly, and actual, presence of the other tourists spoils things. One cannot pretend to be pioneering while surrounded by fellow pioneers. Tourists may try to ignore each other, as lines of Land Cruisers pass on the rutted road, but the reactions of the local children (chasing cars, shouting 'caramelo') make the context clear enough. There's a parallel with hunting, and some of the vocabulary even carries over— 'I bagged that shot'—but if the 'prey' acknowledges your presence and negotiates terms, then it's closer to engineered grouse shooting than big game hunting. Often, in the markets, people will approach a *ferengi* and demand that a picture be taken—the hunter hunted. That is most unsatisfactory. The visitor wants to capture a photo of an exotic creature to take home like a leopard skin (and then, most likely, ignore), and the chase is soured if the subject talks back and demands money. Eventually one emerges from the village, emotionally soiled, and with hands and clothes covered in ochre-coloured butter that has rubbed off from the Hamar.

The southern Omo region may be geographically and psychologically remote from our world, but it's not all cockroach-counting or camping: there is the extraordinary mirage of Murle Lodge. We drove for three hours and saw almost no sign of life. The only evidence of human habitation was, in fact, a few humans—very few—who materialized and waved at the car. There were no visible human markings on the landscape: no buildings, no rubbish, no artificial colours; just bare nature. Suddenly, we spotted an airstrip and, after hours of nothing, a tidy gateway to a lodge which charges seventy pounds per night for a double room.

Lucy Eyre

Murle Lodge was beautifully situated next to the famous Omo River. We stayed in the attached campsite, which was four times as expensive as the other campsites in the area, but a bargain compared to the lodge. It was run by a mild young man from the north of Ethiopia. He had been imported for six months. 'I can't control these people,' he said of his local employees. We asked about the facilities at the lodge. Could we, for example, take a boat trip? 'It's for professional hunters. Very expensive,' was all he would say. Is that where the guests eat breakfast? 'That is where the professional hunters eat breakfast.' It was a happy fantasy that 'professional hunters' would land in private planes and track crocodiles on the wide Omo River. Every tourist is an amateur hunter, taking potshots with a digital camera, but I doubt that the spirit of Hemingway is to be found in the back of Land Cruiser 3.

What is the appeal of the human safari? It's not a particularly modern brand of sightseeing. Travellers have always aimed for remote places, the inaccessibility of which is confirmed by the 'noble savagery' of the inhabitants. In the age of globalization (or perceived globalization, where 'everyone and everywhere is the same'), utterly exotic people are an increasingly endangered species. Perhaps visiting them is intended as a defiance of the miseries of this homogenizing trend, though without the fanatical step of altering one's own comfortable life for more than two weeks. It's hard not to see a sense of superiority in this. The traveller may feel superior to those who have stayed at home. This is why the photographs are required: to display as proof of adventurousness. But also, in at least some cases, superiority to the Hamar, the Mursi and their neighbours. These people don't read; their lives haven't changed for generations; we can visit them but they can't visit us; they walk for miles, we drive past in powerful cars. We'd hate to be them, though we love to see them. It is, for the Hamar, astonishing that *ferengis* will travel so far simply to watch them doing what they always do. But if the visitors insist on gawping (and they—we—do), then the Hamar know their price.

□

GRANTA

HIGHLIGHTS

Alan Hollinghurst

Alan Hollinghurst

1.

They were at Gatwick, Colin and Archie, waiting to check in, and Colin refusing to think about whether it was a good idea. Already Archie was talking to the young Italian ahead of them in the queue, who had the new kind of iPod he wanted. Colin knelt down by his suitcase to get out his copy of *I promessi sposi*, which he was still working his way through in Italian. He wasn't wholly pleased to find Archie could speak Italian too, albeit only in the present tense; he didn't want him running off speaking Italian all over Rome. Now Archie was sending the young man his mobile number, and asking him something about a *discoteca*. Oh, God, thought Colin. Surely we're not going to Rome for discos. Though with a tiny part of himself he thought it might be rather thrilling to come back having gone to one.

Colin Cardew was fifty-two, and worked for Latimer, publishers of the well-known cultural guides. He lived alone, drank a bit too much, and was thought to be duller and older than he was by people who met him at book parties. He had been to Rome twenty years before, with a friend who had later died, and a sense of awkwardness and regret had kept him away from the place ever since. Archie was told nothing of this, and in a way his ignorance was the beauty of the plan. He had asked to be taken there, asked to be shown something new. Colin glanced discreetly at his small, neat form, the fashionable inches of underwear white above low-waisted jeans. There hadn't been sex, or anything close, since the previous May. Archie would wriggle away or say, 'Goodness, I'm hungry!' and they would go to the local trattoria. He had made himself, touchingly but frustratingly, into a friend: Colin still paid, but for dinner rather than fifty minutes in bed. Well, he knew you could never spell these things out, but he felt fairly sure that by accepting a free weekend in Rome his young companion had agreed to something more.

On the plane Archie insisted on the aisle seat, claiming a tendency to claustrophobia. As soon as everyone was belted in and the doors were closed the first officer announced a delay of eighty minutes. Archie showed great forbearance for the first one and a half of these minutes, but after that he said, 'I knew we should have flown BA.'

Colin went over one paragraph in *I promessi sposi* several times, stung by the criticism of his arrangements, and unable to see why BA should be any less subject to delays on the tarmac than Alitalia. Well, it was a useful reminder: that Archie, though he liked to be paid for, didn't care to be planned for. He could fret if he wasn't in charge of arrangements, and treats and surprises didn't always go down well with him. Sometimes, if he got wind of a plan, he took it over himself and changed it, so that it turned into a surprise for Colin instead.

Colin said, 'Well, at least you can start getting in the Italian mood,' and passed him the *Latimer Cultural Guide to Rome.*

Archie said, 'Right…' with a worried frown; and then laughed and rested his head on Colin's shoulder in a gesture of trust and affection, child-like as much as lover-like. 'I just want to get to Italy,' he said.

'I know,' said Colin, suddenly encouraged. 'So do I.'

'I'm very lucky to have you to show it to me.'

'Yes, you are,' said Colin; and then, thinking it was probably time for their first lesson, 'So, who are the two great architects of baroque Rome?'

Archie detached himself and leaned out to gaze down the aisle at a retreating steward.

'You haven't answered the question,' said Colin.

'Um…' Archie smiled dimly and sent his eyes from side to side in a mime of thought. 'Yes…now…who are they?' he said.

'Well, they're very easy to remember. There's Bernini and there's Borromini: the two Bs.'

'Oh!…right. So it's Bernini—and…what was it again?'

'Borromini.'

'*Bernini,*' said Archie. 'And *Borromini.*'

'And there's also a third one, called Pietro da Cortona, but I'm not going to bother you with him till we get there and can actually visit a church by him.'

It wasn't clear that Archie had imagined their actually visiting churches. 'Okay…' he said; and then, 'No, the two Bs are probably quite enough for my little brain.'

'I thought,' said Colin.

'Look at this guy's biceps,' said Archie, as the steward, colossal in his short-sleeved shirt, sauntered back down the aisle. Archie grinned at him, and got a sly raised eyebrow in return.

'You'll see much finer examples of that in Rome,' said Colin gamely, reopening *I promessi sposi* and reading the faintly familiar paragraph for the fourth time.

2.

The lift at the hotel was very small, but then it was a small hotel, family-run, in a historic building, and close to the Forum... Colin hoped these advantages were evident to Archie as he edged into the space between him and the porter and their two cases. Despite the awkward comedy of the lift, he had a sense of ritual, in being taken upstairs, with a handsome young man, to the bedroom he knew already from the website, with its view of the Forum, its cable TV, and its 'matrimonial bed'. That matrimonial bed was a bold decision, but the smiling porter seemed to solemnize it. He wasn't really a porter, he was Silvio, the son of the owner. As the lift door closed they all started speaking in Italian at the same time, so that Colin missed what Silvio was saying, quickly and humorously, to Archie— it was something to do with the telephone. Archie frowned and shook his head as if to close the subject, and shifted to give Colin a wide close-up smile. It was a smile that seemed full of shared expectancy. Colin blushed and looked down, abashed by the presence of Silvio, who was laughing contentedly.

At the end of a narrow landing Silvio unlocked a door and went ahead of them into a room of which all Colin saw at first was a wardrobe and a shuttered window and the high coving of the ceiling. Archie strolled in after him, with a quick scanning glance, and Colin, his smile in the mirror looking almost sarcastic with tension, came last. 'Ah...' he said, as Silvio brandished the TV control and then crossed to open the bathroom door. 'Um...!'—for a minute Colin's Italian failed him; while Archie was saying, '*Perfetto!*' and pressing an absurdly large tip into Silvio's hand. 'Um...yes,' said Colin, scrambling to repossess himself and looking round, as the door closed and they were left alone, at the wardrobe, and the bowl of fruit, and the two high bolstered single beds.

3.

They had breakfast next morning on the rooftop terrace, which did, strictly speaking, have a view of the Forum. A distant wedge of ruined wall could be glimpsed between the neighbouring house and the awnings on the roof terrace of the much grander hotel in front of them. Their own roof terrace had a bar with a coffee machine, half a dozen tables with paper cloths clipped against the breeze, and pots of geraniums wired to its wrought-iron railings. Colin said, 'You can just see the top of the dome of S. Luca and S. Martina; which is indeed two churches, S. Luca on top and S. Martina beneath. It's rather fascinating.'

It seemed unlikely, from Archie's look, as he spread some red jam on a white roll, that anything had ever fascinated him less. He leaned back to signal to the waitress for more coffee. 'It's by Pietro da Cortona,' Colin went on.

'Right...' said Archie.

'Well, you'll see,' said Colin. 'I hope it will be open. Last time I was here it was closed for restoration.'

Archie brightened a little at this. 'You are going to take me shopping, aren't you?' he said.

'Well, what do you want?'

'I don't know yet, I want to see what there is. And we've got to get you sorted out, too: get you some nice jeans, something a bit more casual, Colin. That's my task for this weekend.'

Colin drank his little glass of concentrated orange juice. 'We'll want to do some sightseeing first,' he said. 'You haven't forgotten about the two Bs?'

To his relief this seemed to be a game Archie was prepared to play. His smile was happy, and confusingly like smiles he'd given Colin in the past. 'Ah yes, now...who are they?' he said.

'You can't have forgotten,' said Colin, still excited by the remembered smiles.

'They're B...B...'

'Bernini,' Colin murmured.

'Bernini! Yes, they're Bernini and...B...'

'Borromini,' said Colin.

'Exactly!' said Archie.

It wasn't clear who'd won the game, once they'd played it. Archie sipped his hot coffee and sank back into a vaguely critical silence. Though the silence itself, the untuned and rhythmless hum and squeal and nearby clatter of the city, had for a minute or two past been eaten into by the strident electronic bleeps of a reversing vehicle. Only their recurrence, after nine or ten seconds of peace, made Colin start to picture the van, some narrow negotiation in the street below.

'God, I can't stand that noise,' he said.

'Forget about it. It'll stop in a minute,' said Archie, who tended to meet impatience with patience, and vice versa.

Colin got up and leaned over the railing, but he couldn't see where the noise was coming from. 'I wonder if a single injury has ever been prevented by those bloody things,' he said.

'Well, we'll never know, will we?' said Archie. 'I mean, you can't count things that don't happen.'

Colin sat down again, frowning madly, wondering if Archie would let him make a joke about the things that hadn't happened the night before. 'How very true,' he said.

Archie was cool and practical. 'We need to get going,' he said. 'We haven't got much time here, you know.' But just then there was a different bleep: Archie had a text message, in fact two text messages. He sat there thumbing and chuckling to himself for the next ten minutes.

4.

As soon as they were in the street they saw where the noise was coming from. Behind the hotel a large building had been demolished, and they looked down into the excavation where two mechanical diggers were shifting and levelling the rubble. Forward they rushed, from different sides, clanking and jolting, to scoop up dirt and twisted metal and broken Roman bricks; they seemed to bow to each other with their scoops. Then almost together came the bleeps, and the trundling erratic reverse. No one else was on the site, but the warning was sounded. It was piercing and implacable, with an echo that came back dead off the buildings like a knock. Colin laughed thinly at his continuing bad luck.

He marched Archie up the hill, to the high open-sided piazza on the Quirinal, where they had their first view across the whole city, with the dome of St Peter's in the distance and the wide brown jumble of roofs below. Archie seemed to like that, and the twenty-foot-high naked statues of Castor and Pollux. Size was in general a mark of authenticity, for Archie. They pondered the colossal fig leaves of the two young gods, colossal absolutely, but proportionally on the small side, and Colin made a joke about 'Pollux's bollocks', which Archie seemed to enjoy more than anything since they'd left London. Colin wished it was the sort of remark that came to him more easily.

Harnessing the mood of childish hilarity, he hurried them along to the pair of neighbouring churches, where Archie would have his first taste of the two Bs.

His own first feeling, as the door of S. Andrea thumped softly shut behind them, muting the roar of the traffic, was, It's still here. The mild light on grey marble, the cherubs and the gilding, the candle trays and parish notices, the one woman praying: it was all as it had been twenty years ago. The notices referred to a new famine and a new pope, but the mood was the same, the mid-morning vacancy of a church in Italy, with the rumble of lorries and whine of Vespas in the long hot street outside. He walked slowly around, tipped his head back to look up at the elliptical dome, with a dull protest from his neck. He smiled to encourage Archie, and also, in a way, himself. It wasn't quite working for him, great though it was. He felt that if Archie would say something, smile, make even a tiny gesture of surrender, it probably would work: his own long-ago sense of discovery would revive.

He went over to Archie, who was still standing near the door, with his hands on his hips. Colin kept smiling purposefully, but Archie's half-smile was that of someone not easily taken in.

'Isn't it wonderful?' said Colin.

Archie glanced around. 'It's quite small, isn't it?' he said.

'I know,' said Colin, and nodded enthusiastically.

A twinkle came into Archie's eye. 'I was just looking at you there, Mr Cardew. You're getting quite a pot on you. We're going to have to get you down to the gym when we get back; do some work on those abs before it's too late.'

'Oh, it already is too late, for that,' said Colin.

'Never too late,' said Archie, with charm, and the way he had of seeming to allude to Colin's fantasies, and play on them. He reached out and squeezed his shoulder. 'Let's get on,' he said, as if Colin had been dawdling intolerably. 'We haven't got long here, you know.'

Out in the street, Colin said, 'We'll just have a quick look in S. Carlo alle Quattro Fontane, shall we?'

'S. Carlo alle Quattro Fontane,' said Archie, with a certain stoniness under his mimicry. They bustled along the narrow pavement, Colin fiddling with his top shirt button, as he did when he was nervous and responsible. It was hard to talk because of the roar of buses and taxis. 'God, this city's polluted,' said Archie.

'I suppose it is,' said Colin.

'I can hardly breathe,' said Archie.

As they drew close to the church, on its busy crossroads, Colin said, 'We ought to cross over to see the facade properly. It is rather amazing.' But Archie had already dropped behind, and when Colin turned round he was standing with his mouth pulled down and his fist rubbing at his left eye. 'Are you all right?' said Colin.

Archie was somewhat abstruse. He said it was his allergies, and also that he had a bit of grit in his eye.

'Let me look at it,' said Colin, and after a minute of blinking and squeezing, Archie let him look, with the child-like submission and bravery that anyone will show when they have something in their eye. 'I can't see anything,' said Colin, keeping Archie's head steady with one hand while he held his eye open with the thumb and forefinger of the other. It didn't escape him that this was their most intimate moment in over a year.

After Colin let him go Archie carried on frowning and rolling his eyes. He was breathing noisily, as he did in his sleep. 'I've got to have a drink of water,' he said. 'I'm so dry.'

'Well, all right,' said Colin, with a smirk that showed he wasn't easily taken in either. They set off in search of a cafe, leaving the church unvisited.

'Rome is so beautiful,' said Archie airily, taking Colin's arm for a moment. 'What's that over there?'

'It's the back of the post office,' said Colin.

5.

In the afternoon, Colin tried a different tack, and took Archie to the Baths of Caracalla. 'I think you'll like this,' he said, as they got into a taxi. 'It's both old and large.'

'Great,' said Archie, sleepy but mischievous after two martinis and a bottle of Corvo. 'You know, it's all new to me,' he said, with a yawn.

'It's where Shelley wrote *Prometheus Unbound*,' said Colin, as if that might focus it for him.

At the entrance to the site there was a little kiosk, where they bought plastic bottles of water. Colin took his jacket off, and led Archie through the deserted grassy precincts towards the great broken vaults of the baths. It was splendid, but perhaps a little dull. It required some patient reimagining, which on a hot April afternoon seemed somehow beyond them both.

'They are quite large,' Archie conceded.

'I think Shelley somehow got right on the top,' said Colin, looking in the *Latimer Cultural Guide*. 'He talks about the "mountainous ruins" and "immense platforms".'

'Mountainous,' said Archie. 'Immense.' He hopped up a low mound, and sat down against a ruined wall, facing the sun. Colin scrambled up beside him with some difficulty in his leather-soled shoes. 'I've been thinking,' said Archie.

'Oh yes,' said Colin.

'We need to get your hair sorted out, get you a new look, something a bit younger. Have you ever thought of having some tints?'

'What, a blue rinse you mean, I suppose.'

Archie laughed happily at this. 'No, not yet,' he said. 'No, just some highlights, a few little blond streaks. You know, just as if you'd been in the sun. It would take years off you.'

'I doubt it,' said Colin. 'Anyway, I'm happy the way I am.'

'Are you?' said Archie, with a devilish grin.

His own hair colour had changed several times since Colin had known him. When he'd first had him round it had been straw blond; now it was a reddish brown, which was probably nearer the natural tint.

'You forget that I'm twenty years older than you, or is it twenty-four years older? You must let me know when you stop being twenty-eight.'

'Colin,' said Archie reproachfully, undoing three buttons and then pulling his shirt over his head. 'Well, I'm going to get some sun.'

'Hmm...good idea,' said Colin, though he waited till Archie was napping before he took off his own shirt and then his shoes. He lay uncomfortably on the stony grass, looking at Archie's pale body.

6.

Colin's mood of anxiety, going up to Nino's salon, was heightened by the large framed photos of women that lined the staircase, and by a stifling smell that he associated with his mother, and her formidable perms. Staunchly unfeminized, Colin had the feeling, as he was greeted and gowned, of seeing something he wasn't meant to, like a glimpse into the ladies' lavatory at a theatre. Sunday, too. In his Rome you couldn't have done this, but new European Rome seemed perpetually open for business. Archie had looked into it: now he was talking confidentially with Nino, and responding to the dapper old man's remarks with Italianate gestures of his own.

'It's *my hair*,' said Colin firmly into the mirror, 'and I'm just having it trimmed a bit. I'm *not* having any highlights—' and here his voice jumped, so that he wondered if he was about to make a scene.

In a minute Archie went away, like a prudent parent, leaving Colin to brave it out. What was Archie going to do, unsupervised, Colin wondered—he seemed to disappear with a sense of purpose. Nino approached, smiling remotely, and fingered Colin's bushy grey hair, which was, in truth, a bit longer than usual because he'd thought Archie might find it more romantic; though what he meant by romantic was as vague as it was ineradicable. Nino, like any professional, wanted to flatter him but also to suggest there was serious work to be done and paid for. He pursed his lips and pushed Colin's hair around, then nodded competently before sending him off to be washed.

Half an hour later, Colin was sitting with a large art book in his lap and numerous twists of silver foil in his hair. Nino, it turned out, was a member of a special Borromini society devoted to restoring the master's works, each one of which was the subject of a beautiful scholarly book. He brought out several of these from his office to keep Colin distracted as the colouring took hold; Colin said how much he liked the buildings, and found himself wanting to impress Nino, who, he saw now, was a rather distinguished old man. He spoke to him as though what was happening on top of his head was not a pathetic surrender, to Archie's will and to some tiny speculative vanity of his own; as if it was normal and indeed benign. After all, who would say no and mean it when offered the chance of growing ten years younger, which was Nino's casual prediction? They would just be highlights, very subtle, very natural, as if the signore had been in the sun. Then the signore was left alone with a cup of coffee, hardly daring to look at the freak in the mirror. Behind him, in the white salon, women were reading under driers or chatting candidly with the stylists. He wondered, with sudden horror, what the people at work would say. From time to time Nino drifted back, peeped cautiously inside a silver tress, then wrapped it up tight for a further baking.

When Colin was back in the street, it was nearly lunchtime. He went hurriedly towards the hotel, knowing everyone was looking at him. The whole treatment had cost 190 euros, to which, in complex embarrassment, he had added a handsome tip. He couldn't quite look at what had been done to him, but now, as he glanced in a dark shop window, he saw the effect, architectural as much as painterly, that Nino had produced with his scissors and heaters and silver foil. Still, he managed a tense grin for Archie, who was hurrying the other way, perhaps to meet him, and who walked straight past without recognizing him.

7.

In the restaurant, after a quickly dispatched martini, Colin said, 'Please don't keep looking at it.'

'Looking at what?' said Archie.

Colin signalled to the waiter for another drink. He could tell that Nino had gone a bit further than Archie had expected. Archie had wanted him to make Colin less embarrassing, but it seemed he had ended up making him more so. This was an irony in which Colin himself could take only a limited satisfaction. The whole thing was a botch, and it would need a visit to another Nino to redress it.

'Your hair, you mean,' said Archie. 'It looks great...amazing!'

'You think I look a fool,' said Colin.

'Really, Colin, no one will notice,' said Archie.

'Well, make your mind up,' said Colin.

Archie gave him the wounded look of the well-meaning meddler. 'Well, I think—' he said, but then his phone bleeped, and he had a text message to deal with. The second martinis came, and Colin sipped at his, feeling the alcohol sharpen his resentment of Archie's mobile, and of these friends whose mere illiterate texts were apparently so amusing. Well, you could hardly call them texts. He watched Archie press Send, and put the phone down beside his glass, ready perhaps for a reply. 'That was Aldo,' he said.

'And who might Aldo be?' said Colin. 'Someone you met this morning?'

'Aldo—we met him when we were checking in. With the little goatee? We're going to a club with him tonight.'

'Are we?' said Colin, and found his martini had gone already.

'Well, you may have to wear a hat,' said Archie. 'Joke! Joke!'

They drank a bottle of wine with their main course, and when Archie said, 'Shall we have another?' Colin said, 'Why not?' He saw the day could sensibly be disposed of this way; and when they were drunk together the blur of a chance of fun seemed to shine through the misery, the expensive folly. Colin could take his drink, but he was wandering a bit as he went to the lavatory. He heard his name, looked round stupidly for three seconds, and there at a corner table were the Gortons.

'We didn't like to interrupt,' said George suavely.

'He looks rather super,' said Emma. 'Good for you!'

'Oh...yes,' said Colin, with a little gasp.

They eyed each other, jovially but warily. 'You're looking well,' said Emma. 'You've done something to your hair.'

'Oh...gosh,' said Colin, who had actually forgotten this fact as he approached their table. Now, he ran his hand through it. It felt silky but stiff.

'Very dashing,' said George.

'Very bold,' said Emma. And since Colin just stood there: 'Well, lovely to see you. Don't let us keep you from your friend. We haven't exactly been spying on you, but we can see you're having a marvellous time!'

8.

Really very drunk, in the street, barging each other as they went along. Colin put his arm round Archie's shoulders. It seemed absurd, but then again perhaps only prudent, to have another drink. 'I suppose we should go to St Peter's,' he said.

'Umm...' said Archie, distracted by the window, the interestingly priced Armani suits. 'Shall we go in here?'

Colin was saying, '...of course we could just go back to the hotel and have some fun.'

Archie, abstracted for a moment, staring across the crowded square... 'Yes!' he said.

'Great!' said Colin, of course it was all going to be all right.

'Yes! I know what we must do,' said Archie. 'We must go for a ride in a carriage. I cannot go back to London without first having had a ride in a carriage.' Pulling at Colin's arm.

'Don't be ridiculous,' Colin said.

'Oh, please,' said Archie. 'Please, please, please.'

'I'm not going for a ride in a carriage, and that's that,' said Colin.

'It'll be something to remember,' said Archie. Stumbling him towards the rank, with three or four carriages waiting. Crocheted cushions, plastic flowers.

'It's a total tourist trap,' said Colin, smelling the horse dung. 'They're a total rip-off.'

'I'll pay!' said Archie.

'You haven't got any money,' said Colin.

'I can make some! I'll pay you back.'

They were almost scuffling, Colin heaving him away; Archie had started talking to the driver, he was being handed up the listing step of the vehicle, agreeing to the mad first price that was mentioned. Colin said, 'No, no, no, that's fifty quid as near as dammit,' reaching up, tugging hard on Archie's arm—anyway, they went in the carriage, Archie on the mobile to Aldo and making Colin speak to him too. Colin slid down on the plastic cushions, dreading being seen by the Gortons.

9.

He woke at 6.25, and lay for a while measuring the violence of his headache and the sundered intimacy of their two beds. The digital clock cast a faint green light across the table between them and drew Archie's face very dimly out of the blackness. He was sleeping steadily, open-mouthed, eyebrows raised, as if phrasing a question.

Colin felt the horrible tightening under his ribs and pure instinct hurried him out of bed, patting and stumbling in the near-darkness—the blaze of the bathroom lights was like the spasm of his own body, swallowing wildly to gain the two seconds he needed to reach the bowl and double up.

In the shivering frailty afterwards, tears blurring his eyes, the tiny unaccountable prickle of pride... He rinsed his mouth out and cautiously drank a glass of water, leaning against the edge of the basin. In the mirror he saw the bony moppet, ghastly with age, grey-jawed, its grey-and-gold hairdo squashed tall by sweat and sleep. The vein in his temple twitched with its pain, and behind it, slipping in one against the other, the disordered images of the night, the shared taxis, the insane new friends, the cash machines, the immense walk home, and somewhere, in the second club, an image seen only from the corner of the eye, Archie signalling to Aldo that Colin was blind drunk and that this was their moment. A moment that had seemed a long weekend to Colin, gripped by his own simple but absurd idea.

He got his nail scissors out of his sponge bag and, tilting his head forward in the mirror, started hacking at his gold highlights, which came away in small jagged tufts, mixed up with the adjacent grey. He kept moving his scissors in the wrong direction, snipping at the air, poking at his scalp. This showed he was still very drunk. He piled the rough clippings on the glass shelf beside his toothpaste and the cologne he had bought for Archie at Gatwick. A whorish cologne, he'd felt at the time, though that was the one thing he could never say to his young friend, companion, whatever the hell he was.

'What are you doing?' said Archie, sounding bored, barely awake.

'I've just been violently sick,' said Colin.

'Hmm,' said Archie.

'I hate this hair,' said Colin.

Archie looked at him in the mirror, and what might have been guilt, or maybe some harder impersonal sense of comedy, twitched for a moment under his sleepy frown. Colin put down the scissors.

'What's the matter?' said Archie amicably, but as if he had limited time for the answer.

Colin looked at the little offering of his own hair. 'What's the matter?' he said. 'Um…yes, what…is…the matter…'

His heart was pounding at the scale of the opportunity; he held the edge of the basin and looked into it with a pant of panic. He saw that if he started to answer, if he opened that padded and studded door a chink, he would be answering all day, all the way to the airport, and on the flight, and in the long anti climax of the train to Victoria.

He managed to sleep again, with his fist against his forehead, to equalize the pain. Archie was sleeping too. At eight the piercing bleeps of the diggers began. It was Monday morning, it was that time already, they had started and they weren't going to stop. Archie pulled the covers over his head, and Colin lay across from him, looking at the shrouded hump he had become. There were the brief intermittences, distant rumbling and clanking; and then the bleep again, the bleep of a thousand busy reversals. ☐

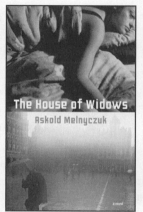

Isabel Allende

'Isabel Allende, what is your passion?'

'I would say my passion is life itself, everything that happens in life. This is why I am a writer, because I want to tell of all people's lives. I want to fix it all in writing so that it won't be forgotten.'

Jewelweed
Ashley Capps

Red haw   hog apple   much-branched

shrubs and small trees   we

discovered a row of old theatre seats   red velvet

and smoked   and followed all day   through binoculars   birds

that shone like earrings.

         Such

was the cinematic   effect

we loaded those seats up   cursing

and dragging delivered them slantwise

         onto the porch.

*

She might

in her sleeve-

less white

night

gown

wake up

with it

stuck

to her arm

What

That egg

My sister

said

she grew

afraid

to sleep

by me

I bled

too much

She pictured

an egg

the size

of a pearl

but

she loved

me I

was still

enduring

my night-

mares

Move

over

on your

towel

*

I grew lilies from scales   knew whip and tongue graft   grew
my mother's   touch-me-not   from seed that flew   at Old
Man's Creek   when capsules brushed   sit here she'd say   and
watch the leaves   we watched her comb   she   was a woman
nothing   my father said   the entire history of beauty   could
have prepared him for   sit here   it   was supposed to be
the Leonid Meteors the night   a neighbor dog   ate our spike-
tailed kittens   that had just got their sea legs   and it snowed
in October

The stars did not depart   for which we'd lugged that   relic
home   the ferns turned blue   in a shell of ice   the last wild
roses held one note   I found that dog where he'd tried to claw
out   after he'd been buried   after he'd been shot   a thickness
of grit   on his wildering eyes   where he tried to claw out
where snowbells grew   and the worst untruth   that had
ever been told   was the one about goodness   directing the
earth

But   we spoke of the killing frost   and a silver thaw took the
tops off the fir trees.

GRANTA

CHICKENS AND EGGS

Doris Lessing

A Sitting Hen

'What a scatterbrain, what a feckless girl'—so my mother would say of me to a guest, a visiting policeman, a neighbour coming over about some farm problem. 'What a harum-scarum!' Did she believe in the evil eye? No. And the Chinese, who, we are told, may say of their own, 'This is my worthless wife', 'This my useless son'. Are they averting the evil eye? 'She's such a flibbertigibbet,' usually said with a fond little laugh. What could she have meant? But the real question came much later, for if you are thirteen, fourteen, what she says has to be taken as true. This knot of wants, needs, angers, attitudes, a confusion of emotions, amounts to being a scatterbrain, the feckless child? Later you had to ask, how could she have used those words on this over-serious, critical bookworm of a girl? A mystery.

Was it in order to cure my flightiness that she said I must look after the sitting hen 'from start to finish'? Was she curing me of irresponsibility? But I was already bound to the hen, kneeling in front of her cage, an hour, two, most passionately identifying with this incarcerated one, who was as united with those eggs as if tied to them, peering out from the bars as the long hours, and days, went by on our farm in the old Southern Rhodesia.

Before my mother had made the hen my charge, I was gathering up her eggs. A hen, doing what her nature suggests, lays eggs under a bush, returning to add another, and another, but it is unlikely that an unguarded egg could survive more than a day or so. Wild cats, porcupines, hawks, rats, the watchful little mammals of the bush, would see the egg, and eat it on the spot, leaving a telltale smear of yolk, or roll it away to their own nests. If you wanted a hen to sit on a reasonable number of eggs you had to hunt about in the bush, find where she had hidden them, keep them safe, and then, when there were enough, show them to the hen. She might or might not be broody. A sly trick, that, to feed a spoonful of sweet sherry to the hen, who then nearly always went broody, her cluck changing to the deep maternal clucks and calls appropriate to a matron wondering what had happened to those eggs she had left, she thought, in a good place. And here they were, all together, brown and white and fawn-coloured, some at least hers. This hen was a Rhode Island, the big heavy hen that can brood sixteen, seventeen eggs, really big eggs, not the 'large' eggs of the supermarket, which are only half their size. A slender white Leghorn, the other kind of hen pecking about over the hill, could sit on only twelve eggs.

These eggs were bound to hatch. A device a long way from the expertise of laboratory, was a sheet of cardboard, and in it were various sizes of cut-out egg shapes. The deep dish of eggs in their nest of straw stood waiting, and, too, the cardboard, and a candle. Each egg was fitted into the relevant size of hole and the contraption held up to the candle. And there could be seen the tiny knot in the fluid emptiness of the egg that meant fertility; from that little blot of blood there would be a chick. The hen approved our makeshift device, for at first she did not refuse any egg, but clucked, trod into the nest, and settled, her wings curving in and close.

But she was not in the bush under a shrub or a fallen tree trunk, where she would last five minutes. She was behind a front of wire netting, confined, caged, for her own good and for the good of the eggs.

Once a day I lifted off the wire frontage and she carefully trod out over the eggs, drank from a newly filled tin, ate a little, not much, stood tall and flapped her wings, and then—and I waited for this— she took a run, flapping her poor probably stiff and aching wings, and ran a few yards as if about to take off into the air, but no, she was a hen and earthbound. She pecked about a little, drank some more and then, after perhaps half an hour, trod carefully back into her nest. Was she thinking, Oh, please don't put back that wire? But I did, and in the evening, before the light went, I opened the wire again, but often she did not want to go out. She had sat there unmoving all day, through the heat or the cold, dozing a little, but always on the lookout.

The packing case was set deliberately where people passed all day, going from house to storeroom. Probably she would have preferred some dark hidden place, but there she would be too much of a temptation. We saw rats lurking, saw a hawk's shadow flicker on the earth, and the bird peering down to see the hen. She would be a match for a rat, but the danger was the snakes. They could slither through the mesh of the wire and there was nothing she could do. In the corner of the packing case was a tin of water. The hen could not be expected to sit thirsty all day and all night, but there was a danger that a snake would come up for the water. When we thought of putting out a lure for the snakes, a dish of water some yards away, we were warned by the servants that this water would bring snakes up from the bush. Better rely on the dogs, which roamed free at night. Lying in our beds we would hear barking, and think, Is that a snake? I might go out to peer through dark or moonlight and fancy I saw a snake sneaking away.

Every day when the hen was out for her half-hour's exercise, I flicked tepid water on to the eggs 'to soften the shells and help them hatch'. All the farmers' wives did this. I remember wondering, If the hen had managed to keep her eggs safe under the bush, would those eggs hatch less easily than ours, which were in blood-hot water every day? The hen did not seem to mind the eggs being a bit wet. But at some point in the sitting she deliberately rolled an egg, and then another, from the mass of eggs under her. I put them back, anguished that they would not have a chance to hatch, but she rolled the same eggs away from her warmth. And now it was my job to lift away those condemned eggs and throw them into the bush. They were addled and the hen knew it. They plopped on to a rock, the earth, a tree trunk, with a hollow sound I did not hear again until a long while later when I stood in the Tottenham Court Road and saw a young man come sailing over the handlebars of his great motorcycle, and his head crashed down on to the pavement yards away. The sound as his helmet hit the pavement was the same implosion as that of the addled eggs, in the bush.

Twenty-one days it takes to hatch eggs, twenty-one nights, and there sits the great fierce hen who had accepted me as protector and jailer for that time. Sometimes she pecked me a little as I slid my hand under to feel if the eggs were there, and marvel at the scorch of that brooding warmth. My wrists and hands had her beak marks, but she seemed to know that I meant her well.

Time must pass so slowly for a sitting hen. Does it run a little faster as the three weeks near their end?

Three or four days before the end, holding an egg that was so heavy and portentous to my ear, I imagined I heard the peck-peck of achievement. The egg seemed to pulse, to announce itself. The hen watched me listen to her eggs and pecked me as I slid them back under her. Only three days now, only two... The hen seemed to know her eggs were due to hatch. With her beak she moved them around her great feet that never trod down on egg or chick. Eggs must be moved about or otherwise the chicks might be born lop-sided. So we thought, but did she?

One more day. And I hardly moved from my position crouched before her nest. And at last, when I held an egg to my ear, I heard the faint peck-peck of the chick inside. On the smooth surface of the egg appeared a minute dusting of shell. That is where would appear first a hole and then the beak of the chick that would have on it the tough integument that enabled the beak to tackle the thick shell, peck-peck. The hen didn't like me lifting out an egg now. She watched me, her eyes full of warnings.

Everyone seemed to be aware and waiting, watching. The dogs sat at a small distance. The servants made excuses to pass close. Then, I lifted the hen slightly, and from under her came the many sounds of the pecking, hatching chicks. At last, when I lifted her, there were eggs that were still whole, and a mass of broken shells, and the first chick, the little dinosaur, so ugly with its great feet, slimy from the birth. Soon, all around the hen were the tiny heads of the chicks, fluffy and yellow, fit to be on postcards and calendars.

The hen sat on until the last egg hatched, then I lifted off the wire, and she stood up, giving the throaty croodling call of the hen with chicks. She stepped out, the chicks with her. One egg remained. It had not hatched. For some reason that chick had died under her. But now, scratching and drinking and showing the chicks what they had to learn, she trod about among them, drinking from the water tins, trying a little grain and scratching it towards them. We watched, the dogs watched that proud hen and her chicks, and we knew how the predators bided their time in the bush.

The hawks were up there too, watching.

The hen wandered over the hill with her chicks, who every day were fewer. At night the hen retreated to her packing case and seemed not to mind being shut in.

Soon those minute chicks became gawky and leggy and they could run fast as a hawk's shadow dipped towards them over the earth. And then they were cockerels and pullets, and another hen sat in the packing case behind the barrier of wire.

Some people had incubators, but a really good one was an expensive item.

The Incubator

And so here I was, alone in the house on the kopje, alone on the farm, and Mr Watkin's Studebaker had just taken my father and mother off down the hill to Salisbury and the big hospital. My father was ill again with a crisis in his diabetes. Doctors were not then as skilled as they are today with diabetes, and the crises that kept occurring would not happen now. All that year I was at home my mother would appear, white and trembling: 'Your father is very ill again.' I used to drive them the seventy miles in, an hour or less in the fast, good cars of our neighbours, but in our rattling Overland, and on those roads, it might take four or five hours, with my father half dying on the back seat and my mother's, 'Drive more slowly,' 'Stop a minute. He must rest.' Those were nightmare journeys, and how relieved I was not to have to do it.

The reason was an incubator full of eggs three or four days off hatching, and my mother's, 'You'll have to stay. We can't afford to lose all those eggs.' That dreadful 'We can't afford it' of the impoverished middle classes, with behind it an indictment of the bitter unfairness of the world, had always fallen on my ears like an accusation. I did not know how it could be my fault unless it was my very existence, but I dreaded the refrain. As I did the next: 'We can't expect Isaac to do it. They aren't responsible enough.'

Isaac was the cookboy (they were all 'boys', even when they were old), and even if he wasn't 'up to it', then who could blame him? I was afraid I wasn't 'up to it' myself. The incubator had probably been knocked together by a local carpenter. It was a large box that had some random holes drilled in the sides. In it were tiers of eggs, eight dozen, on egg racks borrowed from the store at the station. Each egg had been laid by our hens,and each had been tested, held against a light so you could see if it was fertile. The contraption was warmed by a small lamp, and it had a tiny shade and above that, at a height of a few inches, a metal cap that directed hot air through a funnel into the box of eggs. The flame was minute. 'We don't want roasted eggs,' jested my mother, nervously enough since my father, always afraid of fire under that shambling thatched roof, said the thing was a fire hazard. The flame had to be no more than a glimmer, or the metal cap would be too hot. The incubator was constantly monitored, and at night my mother would creep from her bedroom through mine, and check the flame, which must never go out.

When this do-it-yourself box would eventually give up its ninety-six chickens, they would be mostly dispatched in boxes across the veld to neighbours who had already booked half a dozen or a dozen day-old chicks.

I would be alone for at least two nights, perhaps three.

It would be easy for me now to make a real drama out of the situation, particularly as the Liberation War and its brutalities, and Mugabe and his excesses, have intervened. 'A white girl of seventeen all alone and the neighbours miles away, surrounded by blacks...' First, when I say 'alone' this is to ignore the labourers who would be in the compound half a mile away, and who would certainly come rushing over if the thatch did decide to go up in flames. About the lunacies of what was then called the colour bar I feel inadequate to comment, particularly as a kind of moral exhaustion sets in even to think about it. Whole books could be written about the ironies, the contradictions. Recently I read that in the southern states of America, when they were trying to integrate the schools, because the whites did not mind standing up with the blacks, only sitting down with them, the desks were taken out of the classrooms and the children, black and white, had to stand up to study. This tale could be paralleled with a hundred about the colour bar of southern Africa.

In the short hundred years' history of Southern Rhodesia, from occupation to liberation, there was one rape case, black on white. During the two world wars women stayed alone on the farms while their men went off to fight, perhaps with a farm manager (black) to help them, and there is no record of anything untoward. It did not cross my mind to be afraid 'alone' in that house. I used to wander around and through the bush by myself and had for years. My mother began by moaning that I was inviting rape, but that was no more than routine rhetoric, of the kind the colour bar invited. 'Then, don't go far from the house,' she ordered. Once, miles from home with my gun, I was spotted on a bush track when the old car appeared. My mother, seeing me, waved and said, 'Oh, there you are. Oh, good, you shot us a guinea fowl, I see. Let's hope it's not too tough to cook for supper.'

The servant, the cookboy, had been instructed 'to look after the little missus'. More rhetoric. He would make meals for me, feed the dogs and cats as usual, and, though told to bring up his blankets to our kitchen and sleep there, I knew from his averted eyes and the stubborn set of his shoulders that he would do no such thing. Besides, the scornful logical mind of the adolescent was silently commenting, 'If in fact I was assaulted, it surely would be Isaac who would be accused?' He knew I would not expect him to sleep in the kitchen, and I was determined not to ask him as otherwise he would lie, and then that would be my fault.

The real difficulty of the business, watching the tiny flame which was the safeguard of the future of the chicks, was the cold and the wind.

On the high veld it was cold at night. Six thousand feet. It doesn't sound much, but the rule was, hot and even burning days, with a clear blue sky, and then mild or cold at night under brilliant stars. This was winter. It was cold and the wind was sharp. The house, built to last four years, was now thirteen years old (and would last a good few years yet until a veld fire did in the end destroy it). It was built of pole and dagga, mud slapped on poles, which had dried, and cracked and shrunk off the door and window frames. The thatch was thin in places, particularly where birds had flown off with some of it in their beaks for nests. Wind poured through that house, shook it, tugged at the thatch and rattled the frames. In hot weather it was a house of cool breezes, but at this time of year it could be unbearable. Only in bed under a heap of blankets was I warm. It was freezing— but really. A little film of ice stood on the dogs' water bowls. I have never been as cold as I was that winter, and particularly during those days I was in that old house waiting for my parents to return.

I could have lit the charcoal stove in the sitting room, but the thing scared me. My father said, 'A dog could knock it over and the whole house could go up.' True. The dogs were cold. They went into the kitchen and lay as close to the stove as they could. The cats were there too.

The day my parents left was not too bad. Wrapped in sweaters and blankets, I lay face down on my bed, reading, and occasionally going to check the glimmering flame. There, if you quickly lifted the lid, stood the tremendous battery of eggs, white through fawn to dark brown.

In due course the dazzling white eggs would give forth the White Leghorns, and the big brown ones the Rhode Island Reds and the Australorps, and the creamy and fawn ones, some speckled breed whose name I can't recall.

When I read remarks to the effect that you cannot hoodwink the populace, 'truth will out' and so forth, I remember that some authority in Britain simply abolished white eggs. A survey said that people preferred brown eggs to white, and behold, soon there were no more white eggs, unless you wanted to go to some gourmet shop. That old treat, the stark white egg, coupled with the dark brown egg, side by side on the plate—gone. If you ask some youngster they will say, 'No, of course eggs are never white. There never were white eggs.' So easy is it to brush out of memory a fact that someone in power has decided is uneconomic.

As the day went on it was colder, and when I had had my supper and Isaac had gone I did not ask where, I longed to go to bed to get warm. The wind was hissing and buffeting and occasionally even shrieking. My mother rang from Salisbury to ask if I was all right, and say she would bring my father back tomorrow if certain tests had been done. 'What would she do if I said, No, I am not all right?' commented that cold observer.

The incubator stood on a table in the end room of the house close to the door to my bedroom and my bed, which was right against the door. Leaning up on my elbow I could peer in at the incubator and the tiny flame. The oil, a small spoonful, lasted twenty hours before it had to be refilled. I woke in the dark and switched on the torch; there was nothing wrong. I listened to the wind and knew that any random gust could blow that flame out. And so we all got through the night. Breakfast. The dogs and cats would not leave the warm kitchen. I could not go off into the bush, with or without a gun. I could not leave those eggs. Very well then, I went on reading.

Oh, it was cold, so cold.

Isaac brought me morning tea as usual. I saw him through the kitchen door, sitting as close to the stove as he could, a tumble of dogs and cats all around his feet. He had his blankets around him. When I called him to replace the paraffin, he came with a blanket around his shoulders. I let my hand move gently among the top tier of eggs, and then I sprinkled them with tepid water, and wished the incubator were the old hen, with her warm feathers.

If I were a hen I would be turning the eggs with my big feet, so that each would have equal access to my warmth. But here the air was supposed to move gently around and about the eggs. I leaned to stare and stare, thinking of what was in those eggs. Three or four days off, the hatching. Nothing very pretty, the coiled-up chick with its great feet and its blind eyes, just there, just inside the shell. If there were any dud eggs in that mass, we would not know until the end.

My mother rang to say no, they would not be back that day, but probably tomorrow. 'He's very ill,' she insisted. I didn't doubt it. I wandered through the freezing house, and looked at the equipment for my father's illness, the syringes, the test strips, the burner for the test tubes which though small was much larger than the one that fed warm air into the eggs. This was the apparatus that enabled my father to stay alive. Three or four times a day he stood holding the yellow urine in its test tube over the flame, to check for blood sugar, and another test tube with urine that had added to it a different chemical, checking for something called acetone. The urine bubbled up sea-blue, a very pretty colour, or turned gungy yellow, oh bad, very bad indeed—how familiar I was with these things; so was my mother, who at night as in the day monitored it all.

How I did wish she was there on that second night, in her nightgown with a candle in her hand, creeping past my bed to check on that glimmer of flame.

It is strange that one may be much colder in countries known for their heat than ever in a really cold country, which knows how to make fires and central heating.

What use was a hot-water bottle that was cold and clammy by midnight?

Perhaps a nice friendly cat would come and lie on my bed and keep me warm, but no, they weren't going to leave the kitchen.

I knew Isaac was in his hut in the compound, lying near one of the big logs that always burned in there. If he stayed in our kitchen the stove would go out by midnight and the whole kitchen would chill. Perhaps then those ungrateful cats would come and...

A howl of wind woke me and I leaped into the next room to see that the light was out. I fumbled for matches, could not get one to light, because of the draughts, but finally relit the flame. How long had I been unconscious there while the eggs cooled? I felt them; they were not cold but were definitely chilling. What was I to do? I lifted off the top of the box and folded over the eggs an old eiderdown, to keep whatever warmth there was in it. I spent the rest of that night wrapped in another eiderdown, sitting near the box, with my eyes on the flame. If they closed, I did not know it, but the flame was there in the morning. I took the eiderdown off the eggs and waited for a call from my mother. It was too much for me, this task. I had let the flame go out. Probably the whole mass of eggs was already dead, dead chicks inside their shells. It was all my fault. And I could hardly keep awake, it was so cold.

I did not tell Isaac what I had done. *He* was unreliable, was he? What a joke. I had probably ruined the ninety-six eggs and *we could not afford it.*

The selling of day-old chicks was not a big enterprise, but one of the many my mother tried so as to earn a little cash. A lot of care had gone into gathering those eggs. Meanwhile, out in the pens a hen that showed signs of going broody had been dosed, just a little, with the warmed sherry, and while she clucked and brooded the dummy eggs meant to keep her in the mood, perhaps the eggs that we planned to be her progeny were already dead.

Isaac made me tea, told me I should eat. He fed the dogs and cats and went off to the compound. I saw him go. I would have liked him to stay. I wanted my parents back, even if I was going to have to confess that my mother was right, that yes, I was irresponsible, feckless and unreliable.

How would she tell the neighbours the dramatic news that she had left a seventeen-year-old girl for several nights? She wouldn't. I was known among the neighbours as the clever Tayler girl who was a bit odd, wandering about through the bush with a gun, like a boy.

My mother would simply forget to mention my being left alone. She rang to say they would come back the next day. She had run into Mr MacFadyen in the hotel and he would bring them back.

I don't think I slept the third night. I certainly wasn't in bed. I sat on the floor, wrapped in everything warm I could find, my eyes on the flame. The wind rushed through the house but this time did not extinguish the flame. And next afternoon my parents turned up. I had decided not to tell my mother about letting the flame go out, but in the event I could not help myself. 'You should never tell lies.'

But she did not seem to take it in. 'He nearly died,' she said. 'He seems all right now, though.' And off she went to her main charge, my father.

And in three or so days the eggs cracked open everywhere in the tower of eggs, and little chicks flopped about looking hideous, but instantly drying into exquisite chickness. They drank water eagerly before they were sent, in warmly wrapped boxes, across the veld to the neighbours. The broody hen accepted her twenty-four foundlings and behaved as if she had hatched them herself.

Through all this hustle and bustle I waited for my mother to say something about my letting the flame go out. She did not. The line between her eyes was drawn deep and sorrowful, and she kept saying that life was so difficult. She had forgotten my delinquency? I could not. The moment that I had seen the tiny black crater of the lamp, lightless, kept coming back to me.

Then Mr Watkins came around and we were back with, 'My flighty daughter', 'What a pity she's so scatty', 'I sometimes think I've given birth to a real frivol.' But this did not seem to refer to my letting the flame go out.

My father listened to all this and chose his time.

'Your mother says you were all alone here. How long? I don't think I was taking in much, wasn't feeling too good.'

'Three days and three nights.'

I wasn't going to get Isaac into trouble. 'You see, it was so cold. Of course he wanted to be in a nice warm hut, with a fire, instead of our kitchen. That stove is cold long before morning.'

This was an argument I could not conceivably put to my mother, but my father said at once, 'Makes sense, yes. Yes. Your mother had better not know. And I don't really see what Isaac could have done to help.'

'No.'

'You did pretty well, I think. Well done.'

And now a bit of a pause.

'You know, your mother does rely on you. She does let things get on top of her, I know that.'

'Yes.'

And then, 'Did I ever tell you about when I was in Norwich that winter and it was so cold? The weather was coming straight down the North Sea. Then it began to snow and...'

Back to normal, then.

Soon I went off to start my life as an adult person, leaving the farm for ever behind. But how often in that year I was on the farm did I sit, head in my hands, staring into the dark that so adequately reflected my incomprehension, my bafflement—that pose surely most characteristic of the adolescent. 'What on earth does she mean? Why? But they are all mad, barmy, loco, gone. It's all mad, isn't it? What else can you call it?'

What a pity that into that dark hadn't come a thought from the future, years ahead, when all of a sudden I understood it all.

My mother, whose mother died when she was three, leaving her with a cold authoritarian father, didn't get many cuddles and compliments when she was growing up. She worked hard to please her ambitious father, and came first in everything. Then, defying him, she became a nurse, which he said was not for middle-class girls, and he said, 'Then you are no longer my daughter,' and she went through the four years of training with no help from him. The pay for nurses was minuscule, and she was often hungry, she said, could not afford to buy a pocket handkerchief, or good soap. She did brilliantly in the exams, and he longed to forgive, but she could not forgive him. She nursed the wounded of the First World War.

Only late in my life, listening to tones in her voice I had not really 'heard' before, I realized how much the war years had cost her. Then she married my wounded father and found herself, delightfully, in Persia (now Iran), living a life she was born for. She was social and gregarious, all picnics and musical evenings and parties, part of 'the legation set', enjoying every minute, while my misanthropic father told her she was frivolous. And then, that was over and she was on a farm in the middle of Africa, with a husband with one leg, who had suffered a bad breakdown, 'shell-shock', and who soon got diabetes. Hard work all the way, every day, particularly when my father became ill, and more ill, and then very ill. 'Lucky we don't know when we are young what's going to happen to us.' She often reminisced about 'the best time of my life'—Persia—and told how, at a fancy-dress party, she was dressed as a cockney flower girl, and a young subaltern said to her, 'Why, Mrs Tayler, I didn't recognize you. You look so pretty.' This was told again and again, and the tears came rolling down her cheeks. As for me, the cold, heartless, scornful teenager, I heard this for the twentieth time and inwardly mocked. 'She actually cares that some snotty little soldier said she was pretty.' And late, very late in my life, I understood who the flighty and feckless imaginary girl was. It was herself, projected on to me, in an extension of her fantasies. She had never in her hard life been allowed to be flighty and feckless, was never anything but responsible and sober. (Except for those five years in Persia.) She had certainly not been pretty. Her coldly religious stepmother would not have tolerated that. □

Gary Shteyngart

'Gary, what are you going to do in ten or twenty years when people stop reading literature or novels completely?'

'I think I'd like to do something with my hands. I'm not sure what it would be. But I love foods. And maybe I'll go to some part of the world where I love a certain dish like Tom Yum Kung soup in Thailand. And I will apprentice myself to some master Tom Yum Kung maker or a master paella maker or, in Argentina, a master empanada maker. And I will devote five, ten years to making that food. And maybe I will come back to New York and open up a little shack, not a restaurant, but just a place with a couple of tables. Because the less people read for some reason, the more they seem to eat. So I think there is some direct correlation there. That's what I would do.'

End of the Pier Show

Michael Hofmann

It was—what?—the triumph of hope
over experience. But what triumph
(and what hope)? The continued display
of a kind of unreasonable fortitude,

the man—Beowulf—stooping
to pick his severed head off the sawdust,
and doing it again and again. And she,
the woman, sold, to her mind, on love

as a kind of motor syrup—a green linctus –
that was slowly replacing her blood.
Perhaps lycanthropy. A pessimistic sublime.
They had made their bed and they

were jolly well going to lie in it.
The woman's persistent complaint
that it wasn't a life, the man shrugging,
going away, battening down,

daring her to do worse, if not her worst.
Siege conditions. And she bringing out
in him strange abysms of new behaviour.
Everything went so peculiarly,

spectacularly skewed. They were fascinated
by what they seemed to have contained.
Unspoolings of truths. Such dire sayings
of hers. Such vehemence out of his mouth.

Just as well really his doggish gloom
met her prickliness halfway.
Attritional chafe, chafe, bridle and chafe,
and, periodically a grin and tears.

Her good will expressed itself
in a strange persistence of affection
that he not unreasonably supposed
would last forever.

(It wasn't to do with him, was it?)
When it stopped, he didn't believe it.
He didn't know what to do.
He went hunting around for the trip switch

that had made this darkness, this withdrawal.
(Alas, he was never much of an electrician.)
What happened to their lovely
puppet theatre, their grand knockabout?

GRANTA

GREENLAND
Isabel Hilton

The Ilulissat Ice Fjord in September 2007

There was a moment, towards the end of a long flight to Greenland, when the banality of dense cloud cover suddenly gave way to a luminous whitescape that announced another world: an endless plateau of ice, the slanting sun casting deep shadows on successive frozen waves that seemed to stretch to the horizon.

The Greenland ice cap covers an area of 1.5 million cubic miles. It is the storehouse of ten per cent of the world's fresh water, more than a mile thick and so cold at its surface that it creates its own freak climate: minus 20 degrees centigrade at its surface, warmer at two kilometres above. It is so heavy that the land beneath it has been pushed down below sea level. For nearly ten million years it has defined Greenland and influenced the climate of the northern hemisphere. Now it is melting.

The plane banked and the ice cap gave way to deep red and brown tundra dotted with azure lakes. We landed at Kangerlussuaq, the civilian relic of a former US air base on Greenland's west coast. Other travellers have spotted musk ox at the end of the Kangerlussuaq runway. All I saw were metal fences and a scattered collection of functional but unlovely buildings set in a bleak landscape of shale mountains; a long prefabricated building housing the terminal at one end and announcing a conference centre at the other; a tourist signpost that marked the spot as equidistant between London and the North Pole. Across the street, a small, prefabricated building advertised pizza, a children's playground of swings and roundabouts in orange and purple and a few apartment buildings painted in vivid red and blue seemed to have spilled out of a sack of objects bound for elsewhere. Not for the last time I wondered how Greenlanders stayed sane.

But Greenlanders have always lived in the margins of the habitable world, surviving on their skills and their capacity to adapt to the harshest conditions on the planet. The world has come to them in many guises: Viking settlers, looking for fresh lands to colonize; European explorers, ill equipped and unskilled, looking for the fame that heroic undertakings would earn them; whalers and traders, missionaries and hunters.

Many explorers died; most depended on the locals to feed and guide them. The Inuit, on the whole, were generous in their help and sometimes poorly rewarded for it by visitors who treated them at best as curiosities and at worst as exotic trophies. In 1576 the English explorer, Martin Frobisher, in his repeated search for the North-West Passage, kidnapped an Inuit man, woman and child from Nunavut in the Canadian Arctic and took them back to Bristol, where they excited some interest in the month they survived.

Others were to follow Frobisher's example, and the kidnapping of Eskimo people as trophies continued into more recent times. In 1897, the American explorer Robert Peary brought a young boy, Minik, his father Qisuk and four other adult Inuit from northern Greenland to New York. He promised them, falsely, they would all be returned to Greenland after a short visit, and failed to tell them that they were to be exhibits—and objects of study—in the American Museum of Natural History. The adults died of tuberculosis in short order, and the profoundly distressed Minik pleaded for his father's body to be given into his care for burial and to be returned to Greenland. His pleas were ignored. Qisuk's skeleton was put on show in the museum, where it remained for nearly one hundred years, and it took Minik many years to escape. The remains of the dead adults were finally returned to Greenland in 1993, after a writer, Kenn Harper, took up their cause.

Some visitors came to stay: in the eighteenth century Danish missionaries arrived and ordered the Inuit to abandon communal living and live in nuclear families on the Danish model. Later, whalers came, some to marry and settle. The Greenlanders have kept their language, but few families have no trace of incomer ancestry.

Our own group was neither exploring nor trading, though there was, perhaps, a hint of preaching. I had come to join a shipboard symposium on religion, science and the environment, led by the Ecumenical Patriarch Bartholomew, the archbishop of Constantinople, a prominent dignitary of the Orthodox Church who, every two years for ten years, has brought together scientists, religious figures, writers and journalists in different parts of the world to discuss and draw attention to the world's multiple environmental crises. We had come to Greenland, drawn by the melting ice cap, victim of the carbon follies of industrialized countries thousands of miles to the south. If it melts entirely, the ice cap will drown the coasts of those countries that have so recklessly pushed the climate of the frozen world over the edge.

A short connecting flight took us to Ilulissat, a town of just over 4,500 inhabitants, 120 miles inside the Arctic Circle at 69.13 degrees North. Like most Greenland settlements, Ilulissat is not a strong contender for any architectural prizes, but it sits in an astonishing land- and seascape: it perches on the edge of the Ilulissat ice fjord, at the seaward end of the gigantic Sermeq Kujalleq glacier, which pushes twenty million tons of ice into the North Atlantic every day. The fjord is the most likely source of the iceberg that sank the *Titanic*. It is littered with icebergs in various stages of transformation, some as stately as castles, others eroded into fantastic shapes, ethereally luminescent. They float out, children of the glacier, turning and melting as they drift on the currents.

Greenland towns are messy tributes to human resilience and ambition. The harbour at Ilulissat is crammed with small fishing boats that sail no more than a mile or two away from shore, bobbing about under the nose of the glacier, catching their fish in the icy, nutrient-rich waters.

The houses are wooden imports from Denmark, painted in turquoise and mustard, blood red and aquamarine and set at haphazard angles, both to each other and to the rocky slope. Arctic detritus is scattered over the spaces between: surface pipes for sewage and water, fishing nets, huts, sledges, fish-drying racks festooned with haddock—and dogs. On the outskirts of town, dozens of huskies lie around, the adults tethered on long ropes, the puppies roaming free, bored with a summer of restraint and idleness. From time to time they erupt in a howling parliament that echoes to every corner of the town and reverberates off the mountain slopes. The dogs have an honoured place in Greenlandic life, but they are expected to live rough, a treatment that suits them for the hardship of the ice pack.

The landscape of Greenland is almost impossible to see. The sheer scale of the place is only visible from the air. It is a geologist's paradise of rocks and glaciers, the land barely inhabited. The mountains are too forbidding, the roads all but non-existent. Greenland's 57,000 people live on its fringes, looking to the sea. It was the frozen sea that was the human highway, the route by which the polar peoples migrated tens of thousands of miles, on which they lived and hunted with ingenious self-sufficiency.

Isabel Hilton

The ice gave them their winter freedom, their food and the ability to roam. It was the intimacy and the beauty of the ice, the dog sleds, the fishing, the animals that lived on and under it, that lay at the heart of Inuit culture. It was the ice that defined the place and its people and gave the long winter, dark for months on end, its power and attraction. 'Summer is boring,' a Greenlander told the American writer Gretel Ehrlich, who travelled there in the 1990s. 'It's in the winter that we are happy.' Ilulissat's dogs have been chained up all summer, waiting for the winter, for the freedom of the ice and a rich diet of walrus and seal. But last year, the ice didn't come to Ilulissat. Nor did it come the year before.

The Arctic has lost about a third of its ice since satellite measurements began thirty years ago, and the rate of loss has accelerated sharply since 2002. In August 2007, the North-West Passage between the Atlantic and the Pacific oceans was reported to be free of sea ice for the first time in recorded history, and at the present rate of melting, the summertime Arctic could be entirely ice-free by 2030. In the polar north of Greenland, the last of the Inuit hunters struggle to live as they always have, eating walrus, seals and polar bears, hunting across the increasingly dangerous ice on dog sleds.

On the southern tip of the island is sub-arctic Greenland, where Eric the Red landed in 987. He gave the place the name by which we know it and established a Viking colony that lasted nearly five hundred years. Eric had no way of foreseeing that the period during which he landed on the green shores of the fjord would later be called the medieval warming, or that four hundred years later it would end. When the climate began to cool, the sheep farming failed as the growing season for grass shrank away. Sometime around 1450, the last survivor died, the cold settling inexorably on the settlement and no more relief ships arriving. Did he—or she—still scan the fjord, hoping for the sight of a sail or a long ship? Did he sit by the tiny churchyard and worry that there was no one left to bury him?

As the Norsemen sickened, far to the north a fresh wave of Eskimo migrants was thriving. They had arrived at much the same time as Eric, but with their specialized technologies—their kayaks and harpoons, their dog sleds constructed from the bones and skins of the animals they hunted, their clothes that allowed them to survive Arctic temperatures, their ice houses and highly adapted diets—they were to flourish for the best part of the next thousand years. Eric's colony could have survived too had they moved north and learned how to live as the Inuit. Now the climate is changing again and the Inuit polar hunters are in trouble. Animal migration patterns have changed. The sea ice comes late, and in some places not at all. It is thin and unreliable and dangerous. Men, dogs and sleds fall through. Two years ago, for the first time ever, the government had to fly dog food to the north of Greenland: five hundred hunters had managed to feed themselves, but their dogs were starving. In Eric's old colony the sheep are back and farmers are thinking of trying cattle.

Written in the rock and ice of Greenland, if we know how to read it, is the story of the planet's past and dark hints as to its future. Minik Rosing knows how to read part of it. Half Danish, half Greenlander, Rosing calls himself an apprentice Eskimo. He was born in a small settlement near the Greenland capital, Nuuk. Many such settlements were closed down by the Danish government, which has ruled Greenland since 1721. The scattered populations were moved into coastal towns, where boredom and alcoholism set in. Rosing's birthplace, though, just ceased to exist when the family left. 'We closed it down ourselves,' he said. When he and his brothers needed to go to school, his parents had moved to Denmark. 'That was pretty much it,' he said.

Rosing's brothers chose professions that they could bring back to Greenland: one became an architect, the other a doctor; they both live in Nuuk. Minik became a geologist. Now a professor in Copenhagen, he returns to Greenland to probe the story written in its rocks. In 1999, he stumbled across a rock that was to backdate the beginnings of life on earth by one billion years.

The rock lies in Isua, a boulder-strewn valley high in the mountains above the Nuuk fjord. It was a valley that excited geologists because it was known to be the home of some of the oldest rocks on the planet. We reached it by helicopter, flying up the long fjord and into the forbidding mountain landscape, dusted that summer afternoon with a light covering of snow.

'Greenland has a memory of four billion years of the history of the earth,' Rosing said. 'I didn't go there expecting to find life, but I was very interested in what Earth was like then. These rocks are

3,800 million years old and they were formed on the surface of the earth so they contain a picture of what conditions were like. They are a snapshot of the very beginnings.'

But a lot has happened in that valley since then: rocks of different ages are jumbled together, creating static in the record. Rosing was trying to develop a theory of observation: how to read the rocks in their environment, how to distinguish which characteristics belonged to their moment of origin and which came later.

'For a geologist that valley was like being lost in Tokyo and not knowing the language, not being able to read any signs. Then I saw this outcrop—and it was as though I had met a cousin who could explain everything,' he said. 'It was a window back in time.' The earth was young when this rock was formed, just 700 million years old. The sun was seventy-five per cent weaker and lunar meteor showers set off violent explosions. The continents had not yet emerged. It was not much more promising than anywhere else in the universe as a place where life might begin. The rock was sedimented in clearly identifiable layers. Rosing took samples back to his lab in Copenhagen.

A snowstorm started as he spoke. Flakes of snow swirled around us, cold descended. 'The first thing you do with a rock like that is take a sliver twenty-five microns thick and put it under a microscope. At first I was disappointed. I thought it was dirty and it was hard to resolve. Then I realized that the dirt was part of the rock. It was unambiguously carbon. The only way carbon gets into a rock is through organic material separating it out. So then I had a rock that was full of carbon—and it was from the sea floor, which meant that it was not a freak occurrence.'

It took ten years from the first discovery to analyze the rock and publish the results. When he did, it proved that life had formed from the very beginnings of the earth one billion years earlier than had previously been thought. The carbon was the result of photosynthesis: irrefutable evidence of life.

The scientists in the group talked about life as though it had a personality. Life, one of them said, invented photosynthesis to store the energy from the sun. From this beginning all else follows—the regulated health of the planet that made it possible for humans to evolve in a brief moment of geological time, between the last ice age and the present.

Greenland tells the story of life on Earth in other ways. The ice cap is a detailed record of the Earth's atmosphere that goes back 100,000 years. The Ilulissat ice fjord is one of the pulses that scientists are taking to diagnose the fever that is gripping Greenland. What they are finding is full of omens. High up on the ice cap they probe the moulins—the deep holes that have appeared in the glaciers, internal cataracts that accelerate the melting of the ice, eating it out from inside. Greenland's ice cap is roaring with internal torrents, dripping and running, melting and dissolving. Since the summer of 1992, when teams of scientists extracted two complete ice-core samples from its summit, they have been able to study the climate record for the last 100,000 years, through the Holocene and the last glaciation to the previous interglacial, reading the mix of gases in the ice bubbles that track the cooling and warming of the planet. What they have found has revolutionized their understanding of climate: instead of a pattern of gradual change, they have learned that the story of the Earth's climate has been punctuated by sudden shifts from warm to cold, abrupt and unexplained reversals, some happening in the course of a few years. It does not matter to life on the planet, but it matters a great deal to human beings, who have built their complex societies within dangerously narrow boundaries of tolerance.

The oceanographers, the Arctic scientists, the ice specialists, the biologists and botanists voice their growing alarm at the catalogue of unusual events—the unprecedented Arctic winter temperature shifts that leave reindeer herds pawing at sheet ice unable to reach the lichens on which they feed, the plagues of insects that can strip a boreal forest in a season, the alterations in animal migration patterns and, above all, the gathering pace of the thaw. Bob Corell, an American scientist who studies the ice cap, has watched the Sermeq Kujalleq glacier double its speed in the last ten years. 'Seven per cent of the ice that leaves Greenland comes from here,' he said. 'Ten years ago the glacier was moving at three to four kilometres a year. By 2003 it was measured at eight kilometres a year. The ice is more permeable than we thought, and the glacier is melting from within. It's sitting on water now and it is speeding up.' The pace of melting is causing the scientific literature to be rewritten. 'We didn't used to believe that ice could permeate all the way down a glacier,' he said. 'Glacial earthquakes are increasing, and now we think that this might destabilize the lower slopes. It could collapse very suddenly.'

Every day, this glacier is delivering into the ocean the equivalent of a year's supply of fresh water for a city the size of Beijing. It is altering the chemical balance of the oceans, changing the shape of the seas, disturbing the life of the coastal waters. Eventually, when it all melts, sea levels will have risen by seven metres, drowning coastal cities across the world. Just by melting it will accelerate the earth's warming: polar ice is like a giant planetary cooling system, reflecting eighty per cent of the sun's energy back into space. Without this albedo effect, that energy will be absorbed, melting the tundra that stores millions of tons of methane, a far more dangerous greenhouse gas than carbon dioxide.

The scientists continue their catalogue of runaway change: the oceans have been absorbing increasing amounts of carbon, contributing to an acidification that is making it hard for any form of ocean life that needs to calcify, including not only corals and molluscs but also the microscopic phytoplankton that are at the bottom of the ocean food chain. Jane Lubchenco, an eminent American oceanographer, talks about the effects of the rush of fresh water into the seas and the fear that the ocean circulation might weaken or reverse, as it did in the Younger Dryas, or the 'Big Freeze', 11,000 years ago. Then, it took 2,000 years to return. 'We don't know,' she said, 'what triggered it or how close we might be to the tipping point.'

Her more immediate concern, though, is the dead zones that have begun to appear on certain coasts, the result, she thinks, of changes in the coastal winds that drive the currents. Instead of alternating to produce cycles of up-welling and down-welling warm and cold waters that renew the nutrients in the rich waters, the cycles have stalled, generating suffocating layers that kill all forms of life unable to swim or scuttle fast enough to the edges.

The crystalline seas around Greenland are now highly polluted by the toxins of the industrialized world: technetium from Sellafield, DDT and heavy metals from Russia, POPs (persistent organic pollutants) from flame retardants, mercury from Chinese coal burning, toxins that accumulate in the body fat of seals, the walruses, the polar bears and finally in the bodies of the people who eat them. The sense of apocalypse begins to grow.

For Greenlanders who have already lived through an advanced dose of climate change, talk of mitigation, of limiting emissions, of constructing global agreements to curb what Minik Rosing called 'mankind's passion for burning things' is already too late. The warming of Greenland is already so advanced that it is transforming all other climates, from the economic to the strategic and the political.

Greenland's cold has largely protected it from exploitation. Now the receding ice is uncovering its mineral treasures and oilmen and miners are beginning to sniff the air. With the prospect of mineral wealth and a prosperity that might allow the country to dispense with Danish government subsidy, Greenland has begun to negotiate with Denmark for its independence. The world of treaties and boundaries, resource competition and exploitation scarcely mattered in an ice-bound Arctic. As the ice melts, strategic rivalries have sharpened.

For the United States, Greenland is a link in a strategic chain. It maintains a secretive base at Thule, far to the north, established first as a monitoring station watching for Russian rockets and retained now as part of the grandiose illusion of missile defence. Fifteen Inuit families were moved to make way for the base in September 1953. It was 40 degrees below zero and the promised houses did not arrive for months. Aleqa Hammond, Greenland's finance and foreign minister, told me that half of them died in the move. The survivors are still battling fruitlessly in the Danish courts for their right to return.

On August 2, 2007, Russia claimed that, for the first time, a submarine had reached the ocean floor 4,000 metres under the North Pole and planted a Russian flag. The event was illustrated on Russian television with footage that an alert teenager recognized as a clip from the beginning of the film *Titanic*, but this comic incident had a strategic purpose: it demonstrated, according to Moscow at least, that the Lomonosov Ridge, extending from the New Siberian Islands in the east of the Laptev Sea towards the Canadian Arctic archipelago, is a submerged geological extension of the Siberian platform and part, therefore, of the Russian continental shelf. The North Pole, and any continental riches it may contain—the Russians are saying with their flag—is theirs. 'It's nonsense,' said Aleqa Hammond. 'Everybody knows that the North Pole is ours. That's where Santa lives.'

Until now, Santa has had the Pole pretty much to himself, but if Aleqa Hammond's vision of the future of Greenland comes to pass, he will have to defend his claim against some determined competition. He may lose his workforce to more lucrative employment: the giant multinational company Alcoa is planning the world's second largest aluminium smelter in Greenland, to be driven by the hydropower generated by the melting ice cap. Two others are under consideration. Stranded hunters and elves will have the option of retraining as foundry and factory workers. Greenland will enter an industrial age, a perverse and unintended consequence of the rest of the world's industrialization.

One evening, in the cultural centre in Nuuk, along with the town's intellectuals, professionals and politicians, we were served reindeer fillet and musk ox, smoked salmon and halibut tartare. Two choirs sang Greenlandic songs in a Moravian a capella style imported by Danish missionaries. A middle-aged actress told a story of how happiness came to the people of Greenland, a thin man played the guitar. The entertainment had a quality of self-conscious innocence that was belied by the conversations around the buffet, where rumours of Danish intransigence over future mineral rights in the independence negotiations were traded, contradicting the public declarations of goodwill from Copenhagen towards Greenland's ambitions.

In the bars of Nuuk, Greenlanders who had not been invited to the reception fell to drinking in less elegant fashion. They are on the front line of the gathering emergency, their physical world shifting around them, their melting landscape a magnifying mirror of the planet's changing state. For them, a new cycle of adaptation has begun. In the quiet of the Arctic night sky, aurora borealis traced a ghostly luminescence, whispering of cosmic energy. Human settlement never seemed so fragile. □

GRANTA

TO THE CITY
Tash Aw

 O ne day, not long after he turned thirteen, Adam ran away from home. He woke up that morning and decided he would look for his mother.

For some weeks before this he had been feeling strange, not at all himself. He would be annoyed by the smallest thing: the mewing of the fat white cat outside his window, or the squeaking of his bed-frame every time he turned over on the too-thin mattress, or his cupboard door that never closed properly—things he would not normally have noticed. He was irritated by Karl, too—by his uneven club-footed gait, by the pinky-whiteness of his skin, which seemed obtrusive against the dull green landscape, and, above all, by the way Karl mumbled to himself: indistinct words in an indistinct language, spoken under his breath without even realizing he was doing it. Outbreaks of this muttering could occur at any time—whether at breakfast or during those peaceful moments late in the evening, when they had finished dinner and settled down to some reading—but it always seemed more intense whenever there was music playing. At first Adam tried to ignore this, carrying on with his own reading or homework, but before long he found that he was unable to stand much more than several seconds of Karl's mumbling. As soon as that dreadful inarticulate half-whisper started, Adam felt a curious sensation in his head, a little pinprick that welled up quickly into a hot, almost burning feeling that filled his skull, pressing especially insistently behind his eye sockets. He would no longer be able to read or concentrate on what he was doing, and would be so overcome by this pressure in his head that he would have to leave and retreat to his bedroom. There, on his bed with his pillow over his face, he would still be able to hear Karl's dull drone. Every other noise would be shut out except that wretched mumbling.

As if guilty by association, the music soon began to annoy Adam too. It made no difference what it was: the moment Karl began to walk towards the record player, Adam's back would stiffen. Violins that previously thrilled him now seemed harsh and screeching; operatic voices, amusing before, were suddenly ridiculous. Adam took to leaving the house altogether. Heading for the sea, he would clamber over the rocks and make his way as far up the shoreline as possible until even the faintest strains of Karl's dying heroines were drowned out by the hush of the waves. One or two little outrigger

249

canoes would be floating on the steel-blue sea, their tiny sails trembling gently in the breeze; small nets would be flung from the boats, the fishermen hauling in meagre catches of mackerel and skipjack and anchovies. Adam would sit watching until his head felt clear and calm once more, the anger draining from his body.

That was what it was, this thing that filled his head: anger.

'What's wrong with you? Why are you so angry?' Karl called out after him the first time he got up and left the room, mid-aria, and ran down to the sea. Since beginning his New Life with Karl, Adam had never truly known what it was to feel angry. He wondered what this was a sign of, whether this anger meant that he was somehow changing, and if so, how. He would lie awake in bed thinking, Why am I angry? and, finding no answer, would become angrier still.

At school he suddenly became conscious of what he was: an orphan. He had never been aware of this state of being, for many of his classmates seemed to be orphans too. Every so often someone would drop out of school to work in the rice fields or help with the nets, and Adam would learn that their father had drowned at sea or their mother had died in childbirth; now they were an orphan. On this island it seemed entirely normal not to have at least one parent. But one day they had a new teacher, a young Sasak who had studied at the Universiteit van Indonesie. He taught them the difference between orphans who had lost one parent and those who had lost both. There was a word that distinguished the two: *piatu*. It was important to be precise with our Indonesian language, the teacher said; we had to use it carefully and with pride. This revelation troubled Adam greatly. Had he been orphaned once or twice? Was he a *true* orphan, more pitiful than the others? He went home and consulted Karl's dictionary, kept on the highest, dustiest shelf like some forgotten, forbidden relic. Perhaps he would be less of an orphan in Dutch. This was what he hoped. He would discover that in every language other than his own he was an ordinary, unremarkable orphan. He remembered the Dutch for 'orphan' but he could not understand the definition. He copied it down on a piece of paper and, in the privacy of his room, tried to make sense of it using what little Dutch he knew. No luck. It left him more frustrated than ever.

O ne evening, just before dinner, Karl put on some music. They sat down to their meal: overcooked mutton curry and rice.

'Not hungry, Son?'

Adam did not answer; he did not even bother to shake his head. With his spoon he built little mounds of rice on his plate, and then mashed them into the shallow pool of curry before rebuilding and remashing them. The edge of his plate was decorated with faded purple flowers whose stems disappeared into the brown swamp that he had created; one of them was missing a petal, replaced by a tear-shaped chip.

'Adam,' Karl said, 'please don't play with your food. A lot of people on this island are surviving on one meal every three days, and I mean one meal of rice mixed with tapioca.'

Adam dabbed at the curry. He found a morsel of meat and tried to cut it using the side of his spoon, but the mutton was tough, full of tendons.

'Use a knife, Adam. You're making a mess.'

Adam went to the kitchen and returned with a blunt butter knife. He began to saw at the piece of mutton listlessly, as if he had already given up.

'Please,' Karl said, 'don't hold your knife like that. Put it between your thumb and forefinger—you're not holding a pencil.'

Adam looked straight ahead, avoiding Karl's gaze and glaring instead at the piano. Then he smacked the knife down on the table, catching the side of his plate and upsetting a thick glob of curry on to the lino tablecloth. He felt his eyes well up with hot tears, his head prickling with that burning sensation that he now knew to be anger; and this time the anger seeped downwards too, filling his chest and belly.

'Don't you leave the table, Adam,' Karl said, his voice still calm. 'You're going to stay here and finish the meal that you are lucky to have. If there is something you are not happy about, say it—but don't you dare leave food on your plate.'

Adam had already risen, his chair pushed back, his hands clutching the side of the table. He remained in this state of limbo for some time, making no attempt to wipe away the thick streams of tears flowing down his cheeks.

'I want to know,' he said at last, 'I want to know about my family.'

Karl sighed. He placed his fork gently on the edge of his plate and then leaned forward, resting his elbows on the table. He held up his hands and looked at his palms intently, as if trying to decipher the secrets of his own life. He lowered his face into his hands and sighed again. 'I found you at the orphanage, that's all. You know the whole story. There's nothing more to tell.'

Adam's breaths were stifled by sobs as he remained clutching at the table, still looking away from Karl. 'Everyone has a history, you told me that yourself. I want to know about my life—my *real* life.'

'But this,' Karl said, gesturing weakly with both hands at the space around him, '*this* is your life. Isn't this enough?'

There was no breeze that evening. The lace curtains over the always-open windows did not stir; Adam stared at the pattern of chrysanthemums and palm leaves on the thin, rose-coloured fabric. The room suddenly felt airless and utterly still.

'Your mother was not local.' Karl spoke in a measured monotone, as if he had rehearsed saying these words a thousand times before. 'Some people say they had seen a fair-skinned woman in the village the day before you were found. She had the complexion of a Sumatran or a Malay, and she spoke differently, with a big-city accent—Jakarta, some people thought, but no one was sure; it was difficult to understand what she was saying. Someone asked her where she had come from and she said, "from a place far away from here". She asked directions to the orphanage. She had a baby. It was so silent and still that some people thought it was dead. There was an infant too, a little boy with glassy eyes that never blinked. The villagers saw the woman walking along the paths leading out to the hills, along the rice fields that were very green that year. The next day she was gone and there were two children at the orphanage. This is all I know.'

Adam remained motionless. He noticed that he had, quite suddenly, become curiously clear-headed and calm. His breathing had slowed down to a bare whisper, and he did not move at all. He wondered why he could not react more powerfully to what he had just heard—it did not seem like a revelation but a mere affirmation of something he already knew; it annoyed him that he should feel soothed, not agitated, by this news.

'So she went back to Jakarta,' he said eventually.

'I haven't a clue. She could just as well have been from Surabaya or Medan or even Singapore. This is what they told me when I came to the orphanage. They mentioned nothing else—no father, nothing.' Karl reached across and laid his hand on Adam's arm; Adam felt it on his skin, cold and clammy and heavy. 'Son, please believe me, that is all I know.'

'What about,' Adam said, hesitating, 'what about my brother?'

'They say he was taken to somewhere far away—Kuala Lumpur, they thought. The people who adopted him did not want to say where they were taking him.'

Adam looked at Karl's furrowed brow and watery red eyes. He moved from the table, and felt Karl's grip on his arm loosen and fall away limply. Karl remained at the table, staring blankly at the remnants of their dinner that lay on the chipped china plates, illuminated by the stark light of the single bulb hanging low over the table. It was as if they both knew that by the next morning Adam would be gone, and there was nothing Karl could do to stop him.

The idea of Jakarta or any other big city held no terror for Adam. For several weeks now he had been constructing his own metropolis, building it in his mind's eye as he went about his daily chores. While sweeping the yard he summoned a vast flat plain circled by distant hills; while feeding the chickens he painted an aquamarine sky, troubled by rich rain clouds. After dinner he would hurry to bed, longing for that intense, magical hour during which he could return to the focal point of his Jerusalem: a small, neat bungalow, a modern one with whitewashed brick walls and a roof of red clay tiles and a compound filled with plants in pots. This was the house in which his mother lived. There were a few cats—sleek, blue-grey ones— which his mother would pick up now and then and caress. There was a child too—his brother—but it was more difficult for Adam to picture this boy, who resisted his attempts to bring him to life and so remained consigned, for now, to the shadows. Adam concentrated instead on building the streets around his mother's house. They were clean and modest, busy with scooters and *becaks* and bicycles, lined with houses like his mother's, simple and unadorned, lived in by decent people; but beyond this unsullied heart the city grew darker, murky with unseen danger. There were wide avenues that stretched into the distance, running into nothingness; there were great silvery buildings full of people doing things that Adam could not comprehend;

there were areas of brilliant coloured light and slums where there was no light at all. Sometimes the streets were full of urchins and millionaires, sometimes there would be no one.

He imagined this city into existence, and now it seemed more tangible than the barren place in which he lived. He knew he had to leave. He knew he had to find this faraway city.

The ferry was not as big as he had expected, and there were many people. The bus journey from the other side of the island had not been so bad, and he had a pocketful of dollars that he could feel pressing on his thigh; he had endless possibilities. Setting off from home that morning, he had been so light-headed with excitement that he almost felt sick. It had been one of those rare cool mornings when the sun kept low behind a thin veil of cloud, and there was no dust in the air, just a hint of rain. But now, standing alone at the docks, the sun was high and he was hot and tired. The boat that lay just beyond the jetty seemed too small and flimsy to withstand the crossing to Java. It must once have been painted gaily in greens and yellows, but now there were only a few curled flakes of paint on the dark, slimy timbers. Its single deck was already full of people, but the crowd nonetheless insisted its way forward, bottlenecking at the gangway: there was no more space on the ferry. There was no shouting, no agitation, just an eerie hum of voices as people tried to force their way on to the boat. Adam could not understand. There was no discernible space on board, and yet the mass of bodies on the jetty continued to shuffle forward. There were men reaching across from the edge of the boat to take small children whose mothers held them out pleadingly, and occasionally a bag would be tossed from the crowd on to the boat, from invisible owner to unidentifiable recipient.

Adam noticed a boy standing next to him. He was older than Adam and wore a clean T-shirt with a bright orange globe on it; he did not look like the other boys hanging around the docks. 'You'll want to hurry or you'll miss your chance to go across,' he said.

Adam squinted, shielding his eyes in the sun.

'Everyone's leaving because of the drought. They think it's better over there, over in the big cities where there are foreigners, but it isn't. I've come from there, I should know.' He laughed as if he had told a joke, and Adam could not tell if he was serious. '*Woi!* It's one big turd, this whole country!' He shouted in the general direction of the ferry and giggled. 'There's no escape!'

Adam began to move away.

'Hey, do you want to get on board?'

'No thanks,' Adam said. 'I'll come back tomorrow.' He did not know how he would achieve this; he had no idea where he would sleep or eat or hide from the crowds.

'It will be the same story tomorrow, my friend,' the boy said, catching up with Adam, 'and the day after and the day after and the day after. But listen, I can get you on board.'

Adam stopped and looked at this boy. He looked normal, just like Adam. 'How?'

'I know people here. People who can get you on board.'

'Really?'

'Sure. All it takes is a bit of money. You have money, don't you? We don't need much—enough for a pack of cigarettes, plus something for me. Hey, fair's fair, isn't it? I'm only asking for some coffee money, no more.'

Adam hesitated but found himself nodding.

'Don't worry, I like you. You're my newest friend! Don't give me anything now. When you get on the boat, a friend of mine will come and find you. I'll tell him you're my buddy—just give him enough cash to buy some *kretek*. How about that? My God, you're so helpless, look at you. Okay, don't worry, don't give him anything. We'll do it for free. This is your lucky day—we'll do you a favour. Just remember, if you ever get to Jakarta and make it big, remember me: Sunny.' He pointed at the logo on his T-shirt. 'That's me, unmissable, unforgettable, just like the sun.'

'Thank you,' Adam said. 'But how do I get on the boat?'

'Okay,' Sunny said, putting his hand round Adam's shoulders, guiding him back towards the overcrowded jetty. His voice dropped and he sounded very serious. 'This is the hard part. Stand with me in the crowd, pretend we're just going to go forward. That's good, just like that. Slow down, just ease up a little. I'm going to leave in a few seconds but don't panic, I'll be back—that's it, just there, steady now, not too fast. Wait until I come back for you. Don't shout or draw attention to yourself, just wait here for me. Good luck.'

Adam felt the hot crush of bodies around him, the sour smell of perspiration making him feel ill. The crowd did not seem to be moving forward, and Sunny had vanished. Adam waited patiently, hoping no one would see him. Ahead of him there was a little girl holding a painted cage with a songbird in it. She stared at Adam with clear watery eyes.

'They've closed the gangway,' someone said.

'*Cis!* It's the third day I've missed that boat.'

'Can you afford to bribe someone? I can't.'

'Come on, let's go. No chance today.'

When the crowd had dispersed Adam remained at the docks with the nursing mothers and listless infants, and the old men and women who did not dare to venture too far from the jetty. Tomorrow there would be another boat, they said, as they watched the boat draw away, carving a smooth V in the steel-blue water behind it. It seemed to move so slowly that Adam felt he could have swum after it. He waited for Sunny for a very long time before giving up.

His throat began to feel numb from thirst, and he could not swallow. He walked back towards the village, beyond the coconut groves where some families had begun to build makeshift shelters from lengths of tarpaulin and driftwood they had found on the shore. He would buy some food in the village, he thought, and he would find somewhere to sleep. Someone would give him a bed. They would not refuse him, for he had money, American dollars.

He stopped at a shop that sold drinks. There were men playing cards and drinking coffee, and Adam suddenly felt very hungry. He wanted a bun, one of those sticky sweet rolls that Karl bought him whenever they went into town. Across the shop there was a small brown box sitting on a counter, stained with grease that seeped through the cardboard in billowing patches: countries on a map of some strange, invisible world.

'Leave those cakes alone, you little thief,' someone called out.

Adam turned to face his accuser, a plump woman with a mole at the edge of her mouth that made her look as if she was smiling cheekily. 'But I have money.' As he heard his own words Adam thought, That sounds as if I'm lying. At the same time he realized that it had been a while since he had been aware of that comforting wad of notes pressing against his thigh. He put his hand in his pocket: nothing. The other pocket: nothing.

'You kids are getting worse every day,' the woman with the mole said, smiling her lopsided smile that was not really a smile. 'You're like mangy scrounging dogs, you lot. Get lost.'

Adam went back to the docks. It was turning dark now and a baby was crying. It was thirsty, Adam thought, so thirsty it could not even cry properly. Its thin dry cough drifted over the sound of the water licking at the quay and the distant chugging of a tugboat. He sat against a low wall, next to an old blind woman, and pulled his knees up to his chin.

Later, in his half sleep, his imaginary city came to him once more, even though he did not want it to. He regretted having created it and wished it would go away; he wanted it to leave him tonight and every night for the rest of his life. But still those images filled his head, at once glittering and hazy; there was nothing he could do to stop them. Yesterday they had made his sleep rich with excitement; today they made him feel hollow and sad. He knew he would never find his mother. He was no longer sure he wanted to.

It was very late when Karl found him asleep at the base of the wall, his head resting sideways on the small bony pillow of his hands. He looked as if he was listening for a heartbeat deep in the ground.

'Let's go home, Son,' Karl said softly.

The car had never felt so comfortable. It smelled of beeswax and Karl's clean clothes, and its engine rattled in a patient monotone. Karl gave him a flask of water and some biscuits wrapped in newspaper. They drove along darkened roads, the broad sweep of their headlights illuminating thin clouds of insects. Karl put his hand on the back of Adam's neck; it felt broad and very cool. The fresh evening air eddied through the open windows and Adam realized he was weeping. □

Marie NDiaye

'Marie, why do you write?'

'I've been writing for a long time to try and establish a little bit of order in what seems to me like one big confusion: the world, language, thoughts. I want to get all of this clear, focus it as you do in photography: at the beginning all is blurred. But then you start to focus and the object appears in all its clarity. For me it is the same with the act of writing. Writing is the focusing of what surrounds us.'

The Swing

Don Paterson

The swing was picked up for the boys,
for the here-and-here-to-stay
and only she knew why it was
I dug so solemnly

I spread the feet two yards apart
and hammered down the pegs
filled up the holes and stamped the dirt
around its skinny legs

I hung the rope up in the air
and fixed the yellow seat
then stood back that I might admire
my handiwork complete

and saw within its frail trapeze
the child that would not come
of what we knew had two more days
before we sent it home

I know that there is nothing here
no venue and no host
but the honest fulcrum of the hour
that engineers our ghost

the bright sweep of its radar-arc
is all the human dream
handing us from dark to dark
like a rope over a stream

But for all the coldness of my creed
and for all those I denied
for all the others she had freed
like arrows from her side

for all the child was barely here
and for all that we were over
I could not square the ghosts we are
with those that we deliver

I gave the empty seat a push
and nothing made a sound
and swung between two skies to brush
her feet upon the ground

GRANTA

HERACLITUS

Salman Rushdie

Salman Rushdie

When the cartoonist Charles M. Schulz announced that he was going to stop drawing the *Peanuts* comic strip, he allegedly received a flood of reader requests, all asking for the same thing: *please, just once before you stop, let Charlie Brown kick the football.* But Schulz set his face against his readers' wishes, and followed the logic of his characters instead. If Lucy van Pelt allowed Charlie Brown to kick the football, if she didn't whip it away at the last moment from his eternally trusting, eternally betrayed feet, then she would cease to be Lucy. If Charlie Brown kicked the football, he would no longer be Charlie Brown.

For Charlie Brown and Lucy, their *ethos*, as Heraclitus said two and a half thousand years ago, their way of being in the world, is their *daimon*, the guiding principle that shapes their lives. And their author, having created them, is no longer omnipotent, but bound by his creation. Pinocchio is no longer a marionette; he once had strings, but now he's free. He's a real, live boy.

Heraclitus himself was lost and never found, and all that remains are quotations from him in the works of other writers, some in the original Greek, some paraphrased or translated into Latin, just a few broken potsherds numbered from 1 to 130 like fragments in a drawer in a museum. In these remains he comes across as something of a mixed bag, part wise man, part fortune cookie:

51
An ass prefers a bed of litter
to a golden throne.

69
The way up is the way back.

70
The beginning is the end.

84
Goat cheese melted
in warm wine congeals
if not well stirred.

99
The ape apes find
most beautiful
looks apish
to non-apes.

It's hard to take some of this stuff seriously, although there are many wise people who take it very seriously indeed, and to these wise people one is tempted to say:

109
Stupidity is better
kept a secret
than displayed.

And yet Heraclitus was a remarkable fellow by all accounts, a genuine seeker after truth. Like the Buddha, he was born a prince, in his case in and of Ephesus, and like the Buddha, he renounced power in order to seek what he would have called wisdom (*sophos*), which the Buddha called enlightenment. And some of the fragments have plenty to say to me. For example:

4
People dull their wits with gibberish,
and cannot use their ears and eyes.

Or:

13
The eye, the ear,
the mind in action,
these I value.

Although obviously I'm disappointed to hear him say:

14
Now that we can travel anywhere,
we need no longer take the poets

and myth-makers for sure witnesses
about disputed facts.

Then there's fragment 121, which has attained the status of one of
the grand self-evident truths about life and tells us, as it told Charlie
Brown, that a man's *ethos* is his *daimon*, or, as Saul Bellow puts it in
the opening paragraph of *The Adventures of Augie March*: 'A man's
character is his fate.' Character is destiny. The key to the art of the
novel in seven syllables, or so people have long believed. Captain
Ahab's character, driven, obsessive, fixated on the whale to the point
of selling his soul for the right to kill it—'from hell's heart I stab at
thee'—makes his death inevitable. There he is at last, lashed to his prey
by harpoon-ropes and drowned, the two of them bound together, man
and whale, inseparable in life and death. The survivor of the wreck of
the *Pequod*, the one who lives to tell the tale, is the disengaged figure
of Ishmael, or at least we think that's his name. 'Call me Ishmael,' he
tells us, not 'I am Ishmael' or 'Ishmael is my name.' Ishmael may be
an alias, like the name 'Alias' adopted by the character played by Bob
Dylan in Sam Peckinpah's great western *Pat Garrett and Billy the Kid*.
'Call me Alias,' Dylan says, playing Ishmael to Pat Garrett's Ahab (Billy
the Kid being, I suppose, the hunted whale), and when Garrett asks if
that's his name, he replies, with an opaque little Bob Dylan smile, 'You
can call me that.' So, call-me-Ishmael—the outsider, the one who
doesn't buy into the passion and fervour, the grand obsession, of the
quest for Moby-Dick—Ishmael survives, because survival is the game
he's in, it's his character, so it's his fate. Ahab, because it's his fate,
because it's what he wants, goes knocking on heaven's door.

Then there's character as refusal, the refusal, for example, of
Bartleby the scrivener, who prefers not to, without ever giving a
reason or even a hint of an explanation. But can Bartleby be called
a character, or is he simply that refusal, enigmatic, infuriating,
important for its effect on others and not for itself? I think he can,
because the refusals are not random, they cohere. Bartleby has
needs—he is homeless and close to penniless and is living secretly in
the scriveners' office, and when he is surprised there *en déshabillé*,
he prefers not to let his employer enter until he has tidied himself.
He has, too, a strong sense of himself as a worker, working
assiduously at his copying, but preferring not to go over his work

with anyone else. His professional pride may be misplaced, but it reveals that this is a man who sets boundaries in his life. He will do this, he will not do that, and he will politely adhere to his private rules, whatever the consequences for himself. Is he, then, some sort of passive-aggressive zealot? I don't think so, because he has no ideas to impose on anyone else. In the face of poverty and even death he has chosen the path of dignity, preferring not to deviate from it, and accepts his fate. So if character is destiny, then the characteristic of acceptance is as potent as that of refusal. Bartleby both refuses and accepts. He prefers not to, but he also, silently, prefers.

I'm thinking, too, about another refusal, the refusal of Michael Kohlhaas the horse-trader, in the great story by Heinrich von Kleist that bears his name, to accept that justice will not be done. He insists on only what the law has decreed, that the two beautiful, glossy, well-nourished horses unjustly seized from him by Junker Wenzel von Tronka and allowed to decline into 'a pair of scrawny, worn-out nags' should be returned to him in the same condition they were in when they were taken, along with his other lost possessions, a neckcloth, some imperial florins and a bundle of washing; and when his small grievance is not addressed he embarks on a course so violent that it half destroys his world, and himself as well. His character becomes his entire community's destiny as well as his own. But when, at the story's end, and after deeds of terrible violence have been done, he gains full restitution for his losses, he accepts that justice must also be done upon him, for his own deeds. Having received satisfaction, Kohlhaas is prepared to give satisfaction to the state, and submits without argument to the executioner's axe. Once again, refusal goes hand in hand with acceptance.

A century and a half after it was written, *Michael Kohlhaas* inspired the American novelist E. L. Doctorow, who based the character of Coalhouse Walker in *Ragtime* on Kohlhaas. Coalhouse Walker, the dandyish African-American with the fancy car that gets wrecked by racists, insists, like Michael Kohlhaas, on restitution, insists peacefully and civilly for as long as he can, beyond the limits of most men's patience, and only turns to extreme measures when modest ones have failed. A sense of injustice will drive a man to extremes—many of the world's present discontents can be attributed to such a sense—but what makes these men special, Kohlhaas, Coalhouse, Bartleby, is their belief in civility, their refusal to step towards incivility or violence until all other avenues have been exhausted, their preference for non-violence, even though, in two of these three examples, there is violence aplenty lurking below the surface.

The almost karmic willingness to accept what life sends is also at the heart of the nature of Mr Leopold Bloom, Odysseus recast as modern picaro, as the wandering, but also Irish, also Quixotic Jew. Mr Leopold Bloom, who eats with relish the inner organs of beasts and fowls, who loves his wife in spite of her wandering eye for Blazes Boylan and who, after his sojourn in Nighttown, brings Stephen home in the 'Ithaca' chapter of *Ulysses*, the lost son Bloom never had who's in search of a lost mother, *O, it's only Dedalus whose mother is beastly dead*, and afterwards, in bed with Molly, speaks to her of him, presents him to her for her pleasure, allowing her to intuit what he doesn't know himself, *hes an author and going to be a university professor of Italian*, Molly ruminates about Stephen, *and Im to take lessons what is he driving at now showing him my photo*, meaning Bloom, what is Bloom driving at, *I wonder he didnt make him a present of it altogether and me too... I suppose hes 20 or more Im not too old for him if hes 23 or 24.*

How poignant it is, at the end of Bloom's long day's journey into long night, near the end of the chapter's long catechism, and just before Molly's overwhelming voice is unleashed upon us, to discover that there's a refusal in Bloom, too, a refusal beneath his acceptance: he accepts her infidelity because he refuses to lose her, he enters the marital bed and finds there 'the imprint of a human form, male, not his,' and lying beside his sleeping wife lists to himself the names of his wife's lovers, that list of which he is not even the last term, and experiences, sequentially, 'envy, jealousy, abnegation, equanimity', and yet is aroused by her and loves her in spite of what he knows. Then, in that beautiful gesture in which the cuckold's humility joins with the husband's lust, he kisses 'the plump mellow yellow smellow melons of her rump, on each plump melonous hemisphere, in their mellow yellow furrow, with obscure prolonged provocative melonsmellonous osculation'. And as for Molly Bloom, Molly the Yes, she's nothing but character-as-destiny, is soliloquizing Molly, nothing but Fate, lying on her bed, sleeping, waking, doing and remembering. No character was ever Destiny more than she, everyone's destiny as well as her guiltless, sensual own.

So: game, set and match to Heraclitus, you may think. Character, destiny, the one leads to the other, and there you have it, nothing more to be said. Ah, but there is, because Heraclitus's dictum doesn't take into account the things about people and stories and language and perception and, yes, moral values that don't stay put, that aren't dependable foundations. James Joyce, that creator of potently destined characters, *agenbitten by inwit*, knew the limitations of the flesh as he knew everything else, was a master of the shifting, the mutable, and near the beginning of *Ulysses* invoked the metamorphic Old Father Ocean, Proteus: 'beware,' as the book warns us, 'of imitations.'

There is, for example, the matter of chance. In the *Mahabharata*, King Yudhisthira, an addictive gambler, loses his wealth, his kingdom, the freedom of his brothers, and even his wife in a series of throws of the dice. So, of course, his character creates his destiny; but the thought remains, what if the dice had fallen differently? Yudhisthira's character didn't account for their random fall, and the suggestion in the *Mahabharata* that his opponent, Shakuni, was a master of the game while Yudhisthira was a novice is unconvincing; there's really no way to be a master of the dice. An explanation of human affairs that omits the influence of the unpredictable, the chaotic, the thing for which there is no reason, will never be a full explanation. For the want of a nail, a battle can be lost. A child falls from a third-floor window and gets up, miraculously unhurt; the same child falling from the same window on another occasion would be killed. We turn right through the crowd at a certain party on a certain night and meet the man or woman who becomes our spouse. If we had turned left we might never have met them. A house is carried away by a whirlwind with a girl inside it and, when it lands, by chance squashes a witch whose magic ruby slippers will eventually take the girl home again. But what if the witch had not been squashed?

The religious writer sees, in chance, the workings of a divine hand. In *The Bridge of San Luis Rey*, Thornton Wilder sets himself the task of understanding the meaning of the deaths of five unconnected individuals who just happened to be crossing the bridge when it collapsed. Why these particular people and not other people? The book rather heroically refuses to accept the answer that there was no reason, that it was just bad luck, and tries to understand the purposes of God. To an extent we all do this, we don't like the idea that our lives can be changed by the vagaries of fortune, by good or bad luck, by things beyond anyone's power to control. Yet chance exists. Paul Auster and Jerzy Kosinski, in their very different ways, are writers who pay a lot of attention to its workings. Auster, like Vyasa, the Homer-figure to whom the *Mahabharata* is ascribed, uses with relish the trope of gambling—the catastrophic poker game played by the central characters, Nashe and Pozzi, against the Pennsylvania recluses Flower and Stone in *The Music of Chance* actually recalls Yudhisthira's disaster—to change his characters' lives, while Kosinski, in his best book, *Being There*, allows his sweet idiot, 'Chauncey Gardiner', whose very name is not his name but given to him by chance, to rise from a rich man's simple-minded menial to become the consort of the grand and the adviser of the mighty. (In the movie of *Being There*, Peter Sellers, in his finest role as Chauncey Gardiner, bears an uncanny resemblance to US Vice-President Dick Cheney, so maybe Kosinski's novel was more prophetic than he knew.)

The Hollywood cinema, of course, would almost cease to exist if film-makers were forbidden to base their work on chance—the accidental spider-bite that turns Peter Parker into Spider-Man, the chance discovery by the hobbit Bilbo Baggins of a mysterious ring of power (to be fair, J. R. R. Tolkien, a member of the Thornton Wilder 'hidden hand' school, would have argued that the ring wanted to be found, and chose Bilbo to find it: its character was its destiny), not to mention the whole movie business of men and women 'meeting cute', to use the technical term. Meg Ryan and Tom Hanks running into one another on the internet, Meg Ryan and Billy Crystal colliding accidentally half a dozen times in the same movie: seems like people in movies are never properly introduced, they prefer to dress up as women to escape a bunch of gangsters and bump into Marilyn Monroe on a train, or to bump into one another on a sinking ship, or to meet by being involved in car accidents or train accidents or aeroplane disasters or by being marooned on islands or forced to marry under the terms of somebody's will so that they can inherit a fortune or forced to marry on account of some fairy-tale law or else give up being Santa Claus.

The significance in human affairs of the unpredictable—the revolution, the avalanche, the sudden illness, the stock market collapse, the accident—obliges us to accept that character isn't the only determinant of our lives. What's more, character isn't what it was two and a half thousand years ago. When Heraclitus made his statement about man's *ethos* being his *daimon*, both those words, *ethos* and *daimon*, expressed concepts that were seen, in his time, as stable. Character was not mutable, but fixed. The spirit that guided one's life did not change. As Popeye the Sailor Man so succinctly put it, 'I yam what I yam and tha's all I yam.' These days, however, we have a slipperier, more fragmented understanding of what character actually is. We argue a good deal about how much of our behaviour is externally determined and how much comes from within. We are by no means certain of the existence of a soul, and we know that we are very different people in different circumstances: we are one way with our families and another way in the workplace. We are more fluid and metamorphic than our forefathers believed they were; we know that within the 'I' there's a bustling crowd of different 'I's jostling for space, coming to the fore, being pushed back again, growing, shrinking, even disappearing entirely, while new 'I's grow. We can change, in the course of a life, so profoundly that we no longer recognize our younger selves. The last Emperor of China, Pu Yi, began life believing himself to be a god and ended it, under Communism, as a gardener, claiming to be happy. Can a man change that much and be content? Was this brainwashing or transformation? It's an open question. But the nature of the self, and the extent to which it determines our actions, are more problematic subjects than they used to be. Character may be destiny, but what is character?

A third answer to Heraclitus is to be found in the political sphere, or at least in the increasing penetration of our private lives by public affairs. The gap between what is private and what is public has diminished to the point at which one can almost say that it has ceased to exist.

In much of the world childhood itself has been abolished, childhood defined as a safe, protected period during which a human being can grow, learn, develop, play and become—in which a human being can be childlike, childish, and be spared the rigours of adulthood. These days global poverty forces children to work in factories and in fields. It turns children into street urchins, criminals and whores. Meanwhile, political instability not only claims children's lives in large numbers—in Sudan, in Rwanda, in India, in Iraq—but turns them into killers, too. See on TV the child soldiers of Africa toting their automatic weapons and speaking with terrifying ease about death. At a time when the external pressures upon us are so great, in Palestine, in Israel, in Afghanistan, in Iran, many artists have felt obliged to take into account the terrible truth that for a great majority of the world's population, their characters, strong or weak, have very little chance of determining their fates. Poverty is destiny, war is destiny, ancient ethnic, tribal and religious hatreds are destiny, a bomb on a bus or in a market square is destiny, and character just has to take its place on the list. A billionaire financial speculator attacks your country's currency, and it collapses, and you lose your job; it doesn't matter who you are or how good a worker you were, you're on the street. Nor is this simply a Third World problem. On September 11, 2001, thousands of people died for reasons unconnected with their characters. On that sad day, their *ethos* was not their *daimon*.

Until the age of fourteen, when I was sent from Bombay to boarding school in faraway England, I was a much more homogeneous self than I am now. I had lived in the same house in the same city all my life, in the bosom of my family, among people whose customs I knew without having to do anything as conscious as 'know' them, speaking the languages that people spoke in that city, in that country, in that time. These are the four roots of the self: language, place, community, custom. But in our age, the great age of migration, many of us have at least one of these roots pulled up. We move away from the place we know, away from the community that knows us, to a place where the customs are different and, perhaps, the most commonly spoken language is one we do not know, or if we speak it, we speak it badly, and cannot express in it the subtleties of what we think and who we are. In my case, I had been brought up multilingually, so my English was fine, it was the one root still planted in the earth, but the others had all gone.

In Norse mythology, the world tree, the great ash Yggdrasil, has three roots. One falls into the Pool of Knowledge near Valhalla, the pool from which Odin drinks, but the others are slowly being destroyed, one gnawed by a monster called the Nidhogg, the other being gradually burned away by the flames of the fire-region,

Muspelheim. When these two roots are destroyed, the tree falls and the *Götterdämmerung* begins. The migrant, too, is at first a tree standing without roots, trying not to fall. Migration is an existential act, stripping us of our defences, mercilessly exposing us to a world that understands us badly, if at all: as if the earth were stripped of its atmosphere and the sun were to bear down upon it in all its pitiless force.

It's an age of migrant writers, voluntary migrants and involuntary exiles and refugees. For such writers instability is a given, instability of abode, of the future, of the family, of the self. For such writers the lack of an automatic subject is a given, too. Some, like the long-time Somali exile Nuruddin Farah, carry Somalia within them just as Joyce carried Dublin within him, and never turn to other places or other themes. Others, like the diaspora Indian writer Bharati Mukherjee, redefine themselves according to their changed circumstances, thinking and writing, in her case, as an American. Others, like myself, fall somewhere in between, sometimes looking east, sometimes west, but always with a sense of the provisionality of all truths, the mutability of all character, the uncertainty of all times and places, no matter how settled things may seem. I can only envy deeply rooted writers like William Faulkner or Eudora Welty, who can take their patch of the earth as a given and mine it for a lifetime. The migrant has no ground to stand on until he invents it. This, too, increases his sense of the precariousness of all things, and leads him towards a literature of precariousness, in which neither destiny nor character can be taken for granted, and nor can their relationship. Borges knew that history is a garden of forking paths, and that although things did go one way they might have gone another and who would we be then, how differently might we have thought or acted? Might not our destinies have shaped our characters rather than the other way around?

American literature, as befits the literature of a land built by migration, knows a good deal about the protean, shape-shifting processes by which migrant selves, and migrant communities, remake themselves and are remade, and it's no accident that so many of its pre-eminent masterpieces, *The Great Gatsby*, for example, deal with the comedy and tragedy of the reinvented self. American literature is entrenched now, it's not arriving across the ocean on boats in quite the way that it used to (although there are always new American stories being added to the crowd—we've already started hearing, for example, from Afghan-Americans: have a look at Khaled Hosseini's novel *The Kite Runner*), but it's good to see that so many of the younger writers, such as those selected as *Granta*'s Best of Young American Novelists in 2007, are embracing America's protean traditions.

At the heart of the novel is and will always be the human figure, and the nature of the novel is to show the human figure in motion through time, space and event. If we don't care about the character, we rarely care about the novel, it's as simple as that; but human beings aren't the whole story, in fact often they aren't even the heroes of the stories they're in, they're bit-part players in their own lives. Even the most potent of fictional characters has to face up at some point to the sheer strangeness of the world.

Character can shape destiny very powerfully, and must be allowed to do so in the novel whenever it can, but the surreal, too, is a part of the real. The surreal is the strangeness of the world made visible: it's a court case that appears to have no end, like Charles Dickens's *Jarndyce and Jarndyce*, it's Dickens's Circumlocution Office that exists in order to do nothing, it's the dust heaps in *Our Mutual Friend*, the refuse piles growing into garbage Alps, garbage Pyrenees, garbage Himalayas, and standing over the city that created them like a metaphor or a judgment. Heraclitus, who taught us that a man's *ethos* is his *daimon*, also wrote:

17
Pythagoras may well have been
the deepest in his learning of all men
And still he claimed to recollect
details of former lives,
being in one a cucumber
and one time a sardine.

I'm with Pythagoras on this. I want the story of the whole Pythagoras, the square on his hypotenuse as well as the sum of the squares on his other two sides, and I wouldn't feel I knew Pythagoras properly if I didn't also know about those secret, earlier lives spent far away from mathematics as a cucumber and a sardine. □

GRANTA

THE WHITE HOLE
OF BOMBAY

Nicholas Shakespeare

Nicholas Shakespeare

Now that I'm no longer living in India, whenever there's a hot day I think of a huge swimming pool in Bombay and Sylvia Billington.

We lay stretched out on canvas chairs—Sylvia, her husband Hugh and I—within splashing distance of the pool, on a strip of lawn facing the Arabian Sea. It was VJ Day, and sounds and perspectives blurred in the mid-morning heat. There was the hum of traffic along Breach Candy Road and a faint sweet-sour smell of garbage. If I half-closed my eyes, the world receded to an oblong of intense blue sky that seemed a projection of the pool.

At the time—the late Sixties—I had only been in India for a few weeks, and as a temporary member of the Breach Candy Swimming Bath Club was new to its hierarchies. Ten yards away, staff from the Russian Consulate had their corner with a net that they strung up, 'when not stringing up dissidents', to use Hugh's words. They didn't talk to anyone much, but thumped a leather volleyball back and forth. I could see a barefoot gardener in khaki shorts squatting as he pulled out weeds. Closer to, a woman even paler than I was squabbled with her teenage son in a needlepoint English accent very similar to Sylvia's. At the glass-topped table where Sylvia had insisted I join them, a waiter in a white jacket unloaded his thousandth tray of the week eyed by several sandwich-hungry crows.

Bogogoingg!

Sylvia squinted up, tensing. Above us, to our left, a muscular young man in tiny crimson swimming trunks bounced from the diving board.

Whoosh. He struck the water.

Seconds later, a blond head broke the surface. He smoothed back his hair in the way a man does who wishes he had a mirror and swam to the steps to do it again.

After another glance at the diver, Sylvia put on her reading glasses and picked up her *Illustrated Weekly*.

The Breach Candy Swimming Bath Club was along the road to the Gymkhana Club. It never opened in the evenings, but on humid days its cold pool drew Bombay's expatriate community to jump in and afterwards enjoy a *nimbu-pani*, a refreshing blend of lime, sugar and water served in tall glasses. Aside from a couple of film stars, no Indians were members. In the circles in which the Billingtons moved, the place was known, good-naturedly, as the 'White Hole of Bombay'.

The Billingtons were among the oldest members in every sense of the word. They were 'part of the furniture' as much as the long planter's chairs that always needed repairing, or the glossy white plates from which we ate our buffalo-steak sandwiches. And rather like the swimming club itself—in pretty good trim but fractionally curling at the edges for being outdoors—they had about them a settled mediocrity. Other members exhibited a pragmatic energy knowing that they would be leaving in eighteen months. The Billingtons in all probability were going to die here.

Even before meeting them, I had formed the image of a couple in late middle age, thrifty, childless, who lived in a modest apartment on Malabar Hill. No one seemed to have visited their home, but the tone in which 'modest' was spoken hinted there were reasons why the Billingtons did their socializing at the club.

This was only our second poolside encounter. Our first had taken place the previous Saturday. I was walking past a chair towards the end of the afternoon when I grew conscious of tight blue eyes investigating me over the top of a magazine.

'You're not, by any chance —.' She said my name.

'That's right.'

The woman took off her glasses and stood at the second attempt. 'Sylvia Billington.'

Her skin was lined beneath her make-up, as if stretched too much and then let go, and her straw-coloured hair, which she later assured me was once 'as long as my elbow and red', had retreated in thin curls close to her scalp. She wore a jade swimming costume that advertised the swell of her breasts.

My initial impression was of a wrinkled, garish, rather sad woman who obtained her leverage by knowing who everyone was— and making sure that they knew her. Much of what she told me I had already gleaned: how she had started coming here after the Second World War, after her husband returned from Burma. How her husband—'Oh, where is he? You two would get on'—used to work for the British Biscuit Company and now was with Makertich & Co, importing textile machinery.

Sylvia Billington didn't think of herself as a transient ex-pat like the rest of us around the pool, but as a local with roots spreading far back. She had been born in India, the daughter of a Protestant Irish cotton merchant. India was where she had met and married Hugh before the war swept him further east.

On this first occasion, she alluded to her husband's 'heroics' and was fishing for me to ask questions. She was even getting quite annoyed that I wasn't playing along, when one of the Russians yelled out and I turned to see a leather ball bouncing in our direction.

It was intercepted by a figure I hadn't really noticed before: a human bulldog, obviously British, in white shorts and a maroon-and-blue bush shirt. He sprang forward and with a surprisingly adroit motion fielded the volleyball, returning it in a hard, accurate throw.

The action had wrecked his cigarette. He paused to heel out the embers before advancing towards us.

'Hugh, come here,' said Sylvia, waving him over.

Hugh Billington struck me then, and in subsequent conversations, as a man of decent instincts, principled, unbegrudging—and disarmingly dull.

'Have I intruded?' He brushed a fly from his fleshy nose.

'I was about to tell him about your time in Burma,' Sylvia said.

The saltiest morsel concerning the Billingtons was how Hugh's 'very good war' was stippled by Sylvia's disappointment that he had not made greater capital of it, as if in some deliberate way he had beggared himself. But her pride in her husband was touching.

'I have to sing his praises,' Sylvia said to me. 'Being brought up in a certain way, Hugh doesn't talk much about anything, do you, darling? But you remember everything.'

I thought I glimpsed in her look the intensity of Sylvia's nostalgia to recapture, beneath the pot belly and strands of white hair, the brave man who had disappeared into the jungle for three long years and made it out.

I also saw a firm resistance on Hugh's part to being recaptured.

He stood there in the afternoon light, shrinking slightly.

'I suppose I do,' he said, already puffing at another of his Indian cigarettes, 'but I don't want to know some of it.'

Then. 'We should be on our way.'

'What are you doing later?' Sylvia turned to me suddenly, and before I could answer asked if I would be their guest at the Lancaster nearby, where they were having dinner.

In the hotel's inexpensive restaurant that night both Billingtons became quite tipsy. I had always enjoyed listening to older people and I must have seemed interested in their story. Besides, I liked them in their different ways. Sylvia, who had changed into an ankle-length dress and switched her lipstick from pink to mulberry, did most of the talking. I tried to bring Hugh into the conversation, asking him about his work, but he was evasive. These days, twenty-three years after Japan's surrender, he was, in his expression, 'a very small biscuit' whom local bigwigs offered up as a friendly, familiar face to British businessmen looking for opportunities in the textile industry. 'A lot of them are scared to invest because, will they get paid? The Indians have a track record of paying eventually, but "eventually" didn't suit my first company.' His indifference to his effect was laudable.

He was more forthright talking about the Russians ('no better than the Japs'). Or cricket (keeping wicket for his regiment). Or—after several beers—the sorry state into which Burma, where he had distinguished himself with General Wingate's Chindits, had disintegrated. The problem was: these days Hugh's bosses at Makertich & Co were less subtle in their demands for him to exploit what they supposed—absurdly—to be his lucrative Burmese contacts.

'Burma's a place not many people know much about, but a lot of people are interested in for the wrong reasons,' he told me, during one of Sylvia's trips to the bathroom. 'Its history is rather more hopeful than its future. I wouldn't rush back. If you like people who hate each other, it's paradise. But give 'em democracy and they use it to fight a civil war. Plus, it's not an easy place to get into. If they don't want you to come, they don't answer.'

Hugh implied that they had not answered.

Our second meeting was the one that took place a week later, on the morning of VJ Day. I had come to the pool to be on my own, but as I crossed the lawn I heard Sylvia say something in an unpleasant tone. Heads turned, and I caught sight of Hugh's harried face. I saw that he wouldn't mind if I came to his rescue.

So instead of walking on to the chair that I'd earmarked, I stopped at the Billingtons' table and interrupted their argument.

'Look who's here,' said Hugh.

'Hello, you...' The effect was a little theatrical since Sylvia had watched me approach.

Whatever ploy I used to dissolve their tension, I can't recall, but soon there was laughter. Once the heads had turned back, I felt I could smile: 'There, what was all that about?'

I was aware of the noon heat and the unresolved domestic humidity in the air and Sylvia telling me how outrageously Hugh had been treated. She was so forward, so un-English, that it crossed my mind she had been drinking.

'Hugh won a Victoria Cross for what he did there,' she said. 'A fat lot of good that is. It means when he applies for a visa they don't even reply!'

'A Victoria Cross?' I was unable to mask my admiration. I'd imagined a DSO, something like that.

'See!' Her irritation was vindicated. 'But if Hugh had his way, he'd forget the whole thing. He won't even attend the annual church service any more.'

'You sure you won't have one of these, dear?' said Hugh.

'No, I'm going for a swim. But he might,' and she beseeched me to pull up a chair and join her husband in a toasted sandwich.

Sylvia grabbed her bathing cap, which was covered with imitation petals, and turned it inside out before stretching it over her head. 'Tell him, Hugh. Don't tell me. It's not all stuff you can't speak about.'

She stood and manoeuvred her toes into a pair of flip-flops.

'My husband can tell you what he did on the night of June 15 1944.'

So over a glass of beer and a buffalo-steak sandwich, which we both agreed was, as always, overcooked, Hugh opened up, without too much prodding from me. I wondered if it was VJ Day that had stirred him. Or whether it was to satisfy his wife. Some sort of concession for which the uneven calculus of marriage had ordained me the receptacle, like a loose volleyball punched in my direction which I had no alternative but to catch. Or maybe he was bored and sick of the heat and being stuck in Bombay.

'My wife wants me to jump up and down and make a fuss. Truth is, I don't want to go back to Burma. Not even for her.' He flicked his eyes to the pool where the orb of her cap stood out like a bullseye.

Then, in the same tone with which he had made his crack about the Russians: 'I wouldn't want to leave Sylvia on her own. She's not very good on her own.'

Maybe the most impressive thing about Hugh Billington was his indifference to his own heroism. After he had told me how he won his Victoria Cross, he lay back. 'I'm going to take a nap.'

I had hoped to steal away before Sylvia returned, but I was still sitting there when a shadow fell across my chest and I jerked up, preparing to bat away a hungry crow.

'Well? Did he reveal all?'

'I think so.'

Sylvia glanced at her husband's prostrate figure, eyes closed, a dribble of gravy at the corner of his mouth. He was a big man who could move when he wanted to. Even so, it was hard to think of those legs and arms crawling back through the mud and darkness to rescue eleven of his men; this was after he had been tortured and interrogated by the Japanese. He had escaped, disguised as a Kachin villager, resolving never to leave Burma without his comrades.

'Hugh?'

He nodded, not stirring nor opening his eyes.

'I'm glad. It's important for people to know.' She turned to me: 'He's so modest it makes one scream. Of course, he's spared me the details, but it was beyond horror.' Imitating what I took to be his voice, she tilted towards me in case he overheard her whisper. 'Think of the worst, most inhumane way you can treat people. Double it. The worst, the worst.'

Hugh made a sound for her to be quiet.

I said in a hushed voice: 'What Hugh did was extraordinary.' I knew lots of war stories, but nothing so brave, or selfless; and not because I had heard it direct.

Sylvia peeled off her bathing cap and shook her hair. 'You wouldn't think so looking at him, would you? I get upset when he leaves it to me to blow his trumpet.' She reached for a towel and patted her glistening cleavage. 'I don't go around asking people to listen to him, you know.' She stared at me in a way to suggest that Hugh, by speaking, had conferred a rare honour on me, and that we were very few, we appreciators of the courage of her husband, this far-from-successful machinery importer who had begun quietly to snore.

'No, he's a real treasure is Hugh,' creaking into her chair.

Sylvia let the towel fall to the grass and loosened her straps. Then she dipped her fingers into a shallow blue tin and started smearing Nivea into her calves and shins.

Like so many of us, Sylvia didn't see herself in the present, but ten years before. She was facing me, to make sure I was attentive, and maybe to intimate that she had been a good-looking woman when she was my age. But I was thirty, she in her mid-fifties. I didn't find her sexually attractive or even poignant—not then, not in that moment.

'You're catching the sun.'

Before I could say anything, Sylvia had leaned forward and was rubbing Nivea into my shoulders. I could tell that my back was red from the tender way her fingers smoothed in the cream; from her breath that she had had a nip of gin.

She lowered her voice: 'In some ways, it was a difficult war for me too,' and looked up.

I waited with dread for her to continue when her face stiffened. She breathed in, holding her breath. She had seen the diver looming above.

One couldn't not look at this great blond idiot. Wherever you happened to be around that pool, if you were talking to someone you saw, out of the corner of your eye, his emphasizing crimson Speedo.

As he walked to the end of the board he straightened his body and gazed down on us.

'Someone please shoot that man,' Sylvia said, but went on watching him.

His chest was like a slab of factory chocolate. He stepped up and somersaulted into the air, entering the water in a perfect dive.

He reminded me in his vanity of a boy I'd been at school with, a restless troublemaker in the classroom, but out on the sports field fluent and focused.

'Do you know him? He must be your age.'

'His name is Jonathan,' I said. 'He's over from Michigan to work in an advertising agency.'

'I know that,' Sylvia replied, in her middle-class voice. She screwed the lid back on. 'Something to drink?' I presumed that she had forgotten what she had been about to say, and our conversation petered out.

I beckoned a waiter, gave him our order, putting it on my tab.

Beside me, Sylvia seemed listless. She was grateful that I recognized her husband's bravery. And, also, she was oddly unsettled by the discovery that Hugh had spoken to me.

She picked up her magazine. But instead of reading it, she was looking at the diver. Thinking of her adventurous youth maybe. Boom. Splash. And it's over.

As he kept bouncing off, I became aware of the movement of his body as a series of outlines, as in a Futurist painting. There was a lot of tidiness, at least, on display. 'He's like a Hockney,' I said. 'He did a splash,' and I mentioned an exhibition I'd seen in London, although immediately I did so, I felt embarrassed: Sylvia wouldn't have any idea about painting.

It was then that she lay down her magazine and removed her glasses and turned to her husband.

'Darling, may I smoke one of your... Oh...darling's nodded off.'

She sneaked an arm under his chair and grabbed the packet, tapping one out.

'I used to know a painter once.'

While Hugh had been 'doing his heroics' in Burma, Sylvia had had an affair in Delhi with an Indian artist and posed nude for him.

I don't know how many people she had told the story to. Not many, I suspect. But some of the spirit had gone out of her and I wondered if she was hoping to retrieve it by confessing a hazardous experience of her own.

'His name was Bhero Sethi. He wasn't well known. We loved each other very much.'

She found an ashtray and struck a match. Her cheekbones became evident as she sucked in.

'He had this Indian nickname for me, the only nickname I've ever had. He called me—oh, it's gone. Infuriating at this age how a word goes. Just wait. It'll come to me.' But it didn't.

I was curious that she should be telling me this story so close to her sleeping husband, and I kept glancing at Hugh. How could she be certain that he wasn't awake? But Sylvia took it in her stride, although she quite often looked towards him in a peremptory way, checking that he was asleep, then swivelling back to reveal more about Bhero.

'I loved his energy. That's what you miss as you get older. I won't explain the why of it. I hadn't heard from Hugh in a year. Bhero could see that I wanted intimacy. He'd say: "Where do your smiles go when you're not laughing?"'

Smoke streamed from her nostrils. I had a sense of the lines on her face melting. She looked younger.

'First time we met, know what he said? "Do you have a portrait in the attic?" Oh, he could never hide his attraction could Bhero. Nor could I. Once, I had on a pleated skirt and he compared my waist to a Christmas cracker. Imagine!' She rested a hand on my wrist.

Again she inhaled, hollowing her cheeks. In memory she saw him. 'Not fat, not thin—what Mother called "neat".' Slightly bloodshot eyes. Greying. A bit of black hair on his chest, a mole on his hip. He'd had polio as a child and wore leg-irons when young which left him with one very slightly withered leg, but he made sure he didn't limp when I was around.'

She had been seeing him for six months before he asked her to pose. 'He couldn't get a model who wasn't a prostitute, so I said okay. I had a body then. It was no problem taking my clothes off. Never was. Funnily enough, it was when my glasses came off I felt naked. You hide behind them if you're a shy child, which I was. But I was determined not to be what Mother wanted me to be.'

'What did she want you to be?'

'Oh, nice. Nice girls keep their clothes on. When I met Hugh, I thought: *Eighteen—get rid of my cherry now.*'

Her voice was light, but there was a seriousness in her gaze. Next thing I knew, her description was guiding me up uncarpeted steps into an artist's studio in west Delhi. She conjured a little veranda. A dividing curtain of yellow shot silk. I looked over at Hugh.

'I loved the smell of gesso in the curtain. Just loved it.'

He had done a few preliminary sketches, with pencil and crayon—and in different poses. 'Some standing, some lying, some sitting in the middle of the room, on this chair, his bed, whatever he said. Do this or that... Oh, what did he call me?' A worm of hot ash dropped to the grass when her hand tried to summon it.

'Names, names, they come back at three in the morning.'

Her small blue eyes had ignited and widened. She was catching one after the other the images that her past was eager to toss at her. And one image she held fast to with a passionate ache. Of herself—propped up on her elbow on a ramshackle divan.

The sketches were for a single voluptuous oil painting.

'Bhero had this ambition for it to be his "magnum opus"—the work by which everyone was bound to remember him. He struggled with it for over a year. This one painting! He kept telling me it was his chance to "break through". I suppose all artists say the same.'

Sylvia smiled, animated, before her seriousness returned. She needed an accomplice, to escort her, without stumbling, beneath that gesso-scented curtain, into the small back room where she had posed for him.

'I felt very special,' she said moistly. 'He wanted me to pose like that woman, you know, with her back to you, in London.'

'The Rokeby Venus.' I nodded.

She half smiled, but without a smidgen of humour. 'Only, I was to lie facing the artist...'

Two yards away, Hugh fidgeted in his sleep.

She leaned further forward, her chin almost to her knees. 'Like I said, we loved each other very much—well above a passion.' Her voice was growing softer and softer. I moved my head closer. We were breathing the same air in front of her face. 'It wasn't anything to do with sex. Oh, it was in a way, but also not part of it at all. When you pose for people, you're sharing with them. Bhero never talked while he worked, but afterwards he'd say: "When I'm painting you, I feel I'm touching you. I know what the texture of your skin is like. I know the texture of your hair in the way your husband does. I feel the bone under your forehead, I'm running my fingers over it..."' Her hand mimicked the motion. 'He taught me that turning someone into art is one of the most intimate things you can do.'

'How did it end?'

'Horribly.' Her arm fell back slowly. 'Hugh came home and it was only with great difficulty that I returned to him. But he had been in the war...'

'Did you see Bhero again?'

She shook her head. Her face had taken on a painful, obscure look. She stared down at her gleaming shins, then at her husband— before hoisting her eyes up to me. 'But I saw his painting.'

Some years after the war, the Billingtons had been guests at a military club in Delhi. After dinner, they went into the officers' bar.

'It's totally Indian now; at the same time, more British than the British—wood panelling, regimental colours and the rest of it. Hugh was offered a whisky, I had one too. Conversation normal. The CO was pretending to speak to Hugh—the smallest of small talk—but I could see from his eyes that his mind was on me, doubtless hoping for some luck if my husband was away on a long business trip. Then he said: "I've got much better stuff. Black Label! I keep it in my bachelor quarters over the yard."'

'I was slightly reluctant to go to with this whiskeyish man to his 'bachelor quarters'—we knew perfectly well he had a wife in Poona— but couldn't see a way out of it.'

Sylvia's voice had grown bleak. I sensed that everything she had told me was a prelude to this journey across the courtyard.

'We went through a room and into a locked room tacked on to it. He said, opening the door, "This is my den where I prepare military campaigns." Eyes glowing, he added in a mildly lascivious way for my benefit: "What secrets it could tell!"'

'We walked in. Everywhere the usual swords and daggers on the walls and an inlaid Afghan rifle. There was a sofa with a blanket tossed over it. And in pride of place, on the wall at the end, this quite large painting in an ornate frame. I looked up and to my horror— there I was. Horizontal. Me with my red hair.'

She held my gaze, to see if I would understand.

'I kept walking, but in fact I froze. My heart pounding, my face on fire, this chill spreading through me…

'Our host pointed at the painting with the bottle he'd opened, eager to know our opinion: "Well, what do you think? I bought it in Nangloi—off a decrepit sort of a fellow with a limp," and he laughed. "He didn't want to sell it, but he had to."'

'I saw Hugh looking at the painting and with every cell in my body braced myself for his response.

'He looked at it and remarked in that jocular way he has: "I'm not the one to ask about modern art."'

I imagined Sylvia's relief—and said something to this effect. But her smile was very slight.

'By then, I was fifteen years older,' she said eventually. 'That can be quite a long time sometimes.'

I looked at her, puzzled.

Her voice had gone ragged and she had tears in her eyes.

Sylvia's expectation that I would understand lasted no more than a few seconds. She spoke in a fierce whisper. The heat of her breath was on my face. She no longer seemed tipsy. 'It's hard to explain... but it went through me like a dose of salts to feel that nothing in my pose connected us. Not a hint.' Her mouth was trembling.

I reached out, touched her arm. I was able, now, to picture the scene: her terror that Hugh would recognize her in the naked figure, and then, almost instantly, her greater sorrow that he hadn't. And behind the fear and sadness, her concern for Bhero Sethi and the circumstances that had forced him to part with his magnum opus.

'I'm sorry,' she said, covering my hand with hers, squeezing it. 'I don't know why I'm upset. I get this decent, good man, my treasure...' She picked up her towel and wiped her eyes, doing it quickly so that she could put her hand back.

I shot a look at the slumbering hero. 'You're positive he didn't see you in the model?'

'I didn't think so at the time—you have to realize how out of context it was. Then as the years passed, I decided he had recognized me and was being protective. Now? To be honest, I have no idea. I've lived so long with the uncertainty, I've come to accept it.'

Bogogogogoinnnngggg!

We both tightened. To our left, the diving board reverberated with a terrific judder, like a ruler twanged in the flap of a school desk. Afterwards, I couldn't help feeling that he had bounced higher to regain our attention. Sandwiched between distinct sounds, the silence was intensified by being prolonged. I remember my hand incongruously beneath her hand, and Sylvia looking sharply up. But not at the diver.

'Neelam!' she exclaimed. 'That was it.'

Whooooshhh.

He smashed through the surface of the water at a loose, untidy angle, jetting spray on to the lawn, on to us.

Behind her, Hugh started. He rose into a sitting position and looked around, blinking.

'It's nothing, dear,' said Sylvia, and moved away.

'Blasted Americans.'

'Don't panic. All is well.' She towelled the drops from her forehead, her swollen blue eyes. 'Our nice young friend has ordered you a *nimbu-pani.*'

Hugh relaxed. He turned in my direction. 'Has she forgiven me?' But he had seen her face.

'Syl?'

'It's nothing, Hugh,' she said in her cross voice. 'He was telling a silly story that made me cry.'   □

The perfect gift

THE MAGAZINE OF NEW WRITING

'In its blend of memoir, photojournalism and reportage, and in its championing of contemporary realist fiction, *Granta* has its face pressed firmly against the window, determined to witness the world.' *Observer*

You can give four issues of GRANTA for only $39.95* and receive this special edition GRANTA Moleskine® notebook with our compliments.

'Top-notch journalism, memoir, fiction, essay and photography'
Chicago Tribune

GRANTA

* US delivery rate, see overleaf for overseas delivery details

CALL TODAY TO PLACE YOUR ORDER 1-866-438-6150
or www.granta.com/subscriptions
(please quote promotion code BUSP100M when placing your order)

Yes, I'd like to give GRANTA as a gift:

Number of subscriptions	Delivery region	Price per subscription	Discount
☐	UK/USA	$39.95	**33%**
☐	Europe/S. America	$40.00	**33%**
☐	Canada & rest of world	$43.25	**28%**

All prices include delivery!

BILLING DETAILS

Title: Initial: Surname: _____

Address: _____

_____ Zip: _____

Telephone: _____ Email: _____

GIFT ONE DELIVERY DETAILS

Title: Initial: Surname: _____

Address: _____

_____

_____ Zip: _____

Telephone: _____

Email: _____

Please start with ☐ this issue ☐ next issue

GIFT TWO DELIVERY DETAILS

Title: Initial: Surname: _____

Address: _____

_____

_____ Zip: _____

Telephone: _____

Email: _____

Please start with ☐ this issue ☐ next issue

PAYMENT

[1] I enclose a check payable to 'Granta' for $_____ for _____ gift subscriptions to GRANTA

[2] Please debit my ☐ Mastercard ☐ Visa ☐ Amex   for $_____ for _____ gift subscriptions

Card number: ☐☐☐☐ ☐☐☐☐ ☐☐☐☐ ☐☐☐☐ ☐☐☐

Expiry date: ☐☐☐☐   Signed _____ Date _____

GRANTA

Please return this form to Granta Subscriptions at:
P.O. Box 359, Congers, NY 10920-0359

Burma cries for help

Today, I received a letter from the Thai/Burma border.

It told me of how much the 'brave men, women and monks' of Burma need our support.

I need your help to send the money that will provide food, shelter, maybe an escape from certain death for these courageous people.

Behind the images in the news, people have lost their careers, homes, lives, everything. It may be unsafe to see their families, or to be seen at all. By calling for freedom, they risk torture, years of imprisonment, isolation, perhaps execution.

All Prisoners of Conscience grants go to named individuals, genuine victims of a vicious regime. Not a penny is wasted.

Even before the latest government crackdown, I had far more names than we could possibly help. Please send what you can.

We must do more than look on in horror. Thank you.

Lynn Carter, Director

To make a donation, please visit **www.prisonersofconscience.org/burma**

Prisoners of Conscience Appeal Fund

PO Box 61044, London SE1 1UP. www.prisonersofconscience.org
Tel: 020 7407 6644 Fax: 020 7407 6655 Emai: info@prisonersofconscience.org

Richard Ford

'Richard Ford, do you know what's important to you?'

'No, but I can make it up.'

The Joy of Difficulty

Lavinia Greenlaw

A withdrawal from form
like the lock of hair found sewn
inside your uncle's waistcoat pocket,
the inherited made strange
by its unheard-of colour.
Did you slip the suit on?
And if so did you breathe differently
as if equipped with an aqualung,
ladder or canister of oxygen? Better
to move freely, to come back early
to sail onto land continuous and bound
to pitch camp on a shingle spit
and to sleep through the coming loose
as it all accumulates to one end
while unmaking itself at the other
as if it were possible to do this
without drawing on old for new.

"So this is how it should be done."*

William Maxwell
Early Novels and Stories

Christopher Carduff, editor

On the centennial of Maxwell's birth, this first volume in an unprecedented two-volume edition gathers *They Came Like Swallows*, the story of two boys, their father, and the unbearable loss they suffer; *The Folded Leaf*, a powerful evocation of an obsessive adolescent friendship that ends in near-tragedy; and *Time Will Darken It*, a portrait of a small, straitlaced community where gossip can ruin even its most blameless member. These major novels are here complemented by the youthful, comic *Bright Center of Heaven*—out of print for nearly 70 years—and nine masterly short stories.

997 pages • $35.00

"I went back and reread the novels I had read before, together with Time Will Darken It *and all the short stories I could find. And I thought: So this is how it should be done. I thought: If only I could go back and write again every single thing I have written."*

—Alice Munro*

THE LIBRARY *of* AMERICA
Celebrating 25 Years of American Classics

Distributed by Penguin Group (USA), Inc.

www.loa.org

GRANTA

ESTONIA, OUT IN THE COUNTRY

Ingo Schulze

TRANSLATED BY JOHN E. WOODS

Ingo Schulze

During that week of September 2000 that Tanya and I spent in
Tallinn and Tartu, I was called upon several times to write
something about Estonia. Each time I explained that while I was
honoured by the request, writing a short story isn't just a matter of
choosing a country and a topic and taking off from there. I knew
nothing about Estonia, and our own experiences of regime change
were scarcely comparable. But I was talking to a brick wall. After
all, I'd written thirty-three stories about St Petersburg, so surely I
could come up with one about Estonia.

For a story set in a foreign country, I said, one needs to have a
certain affinity, a kinship of soul with how things have developed
there. But the more emphatic my arguments, the more I rubbed my
hosts up the wrong way. They were just too polite to tell me straight-
out that they thought my arguments were mere evasion.

I was a guest of the Estonian Writers' Union and had been invited
to Käsmu, where the union has a guest house on the Baltic. Käsmu,
as my hosts never tired of telling me, was a very special place. Not
only was it an ideal spot for total relaxation, but it also inspired one
to work as never before. What we needed was a trip to Käsmu.

I don't want to give the impression that we were treated
inhospitably. On the contrary, ours was a royal reception. Never
before has one of my readings been moderated by the chairman of
a writers' union. He greeted us like old friends and invited us to a
café where we could make plans for the reading. On our way there,
our path was blocked every few steps by someone wanting to shake
the chairman's hand, and once we were sitting down, a steady stream
of people rapped on the café window or stood inside, until we could
hardly exchange two connected sentences. When I inquired about the
profession of a tall, handsome man who shook my hand warmly and
apologized for having to miss the reading that evening, the chairman
said, that was the Minister of Culture. The minister's wife—beautiful,
young, clever, amiable—interviewed me for television. It was just that
they had all studied in Tartu, she said, and were now all working in
Tallinn. They couldn't help knowing one another, right?

Tanya and I took our lunch and dinner in restaurants that were
both upscale and empty, and despite a good number of beers the bill
rarely came to more than twenty marks. So when our small group
went looking for a restaurant after the reading, it was Tanya and I

who could offer suggestions. My translator, on the other hand—who told us how she and the people of Tallinn, of the entire Baltic, had for so many years sung anthems in hope of independence—couldn't remember the last time she'd been in a restaurant. She couldn't imagine buying a book as expensive as mine—which at the time converted at just short of seventeen German marks.

Before describing our days in Käsmu I want to mention another episode that has nothing to do with my story, really. Between a reading for students in the German department of Tartu University and the public reading that evening of the translated version of my book, some students invited Tanya and me for a walk through town. Towards the end of our little tour we passed a kiosk selling soft drinks similar to the kind we have at home. There were two wooden benches out front, and we invited the students to join us.

Tanya said she was amazed at how everyone here cursed the Russians, but almost revered the Germans. Was that simply a matter of hospitality?

It had nothing to do with hospitality, they said. It was simply how they felt. After all, they were German majors. I was about to ask a question myself when the youngest and loveliest of the female students, who until this point had only been listening, said, 'Why are you amazed? Germans have never harmed Estonians.'

'Well, maybe not Estonians...' Tanya said.

The student interrupted her. 'I know what you're getting at. But surely you know that we Estonians had our own SS, and you only have to remember how many Estonians, how many people from the Baltic in general, the Russians killed and deported, even after the war. Only bad things have come from Russia, and mostly good things from the Germans—people can't help noticing that.'

Tanya said that one couldn't limit memory to a particular span of years or to a single nationality, and that, after all, it was the Hitler–Stalin pact that had robbed them of their sovereignty.

'That's true, of course it's true,' the student said, 'but why are you amazed?'

'Why *aren't* you amazed!' Tanya blurted out. After that we returned to the university and exchanged addresses.

On the drive to Käsmu in our rented car, Tanya asked if she had come over as self-righteous. No, I said, just the opposite, but unfortunately I hadn't been able to come up with anything better to say. Tanya said she couldn't help being reminded of some of the phrases in the Estonian fairy tales we'd been reading aloud to each other in the evenings. They kept popping into her head, phrases such as 'she adorned herself in beautiful raiment, as if she were the proudest German child', or 'as happy as a pampered German child'.

We were looking forward to Käsmu. We had read in our guidebook that Lahemaa, Land of Bays, where Käsmu is found, lies about twenty-five miles to the east of Tallinn. It is bounded by the Gulf of Finland on one side and the Tallinn–Narva highway on the other, covers 250 square miles, and was declared a national park in 1971. The guidebook also noted several endangered species to be found there: brown bears, lynx, mink, sea eagles, cranes, arctic loons, mute swans, and even black storks.

We reported to Arne, a gangly man with medium-long hair and a beret who runs a kind of marine museum. He greeted us both with a handshake: a signal, he said, to his two dogs—setters—that we now belonged to the village. Before handing over the keys to the guest house he gave us a brief lecture about the especially favourable magnetic field around Käsmu. But on the way there, he fell silent, as if to allow us to take in the view of tidy frame houses and appreciate the peaceful setting to the full. The two setters bounded ahead of us, came back, circled us, and nudged against our knees.

When I think back to that week now, six years later, the first thing that comes to mind—quite apart from the incredible events I am about to recount—is the way the light turned every colour brighter and paler at the same time.

The house had once belonged to Captain Christian Steen, who had been deported to Siberia in 1947 and has since been listed as missing. The entrance opened on to a large, central dining room where, with one exception, we took all our meals alone at a huge table. At opposite ends of this room were the two guest rooms, and a third door led to the kitchen, which adjoined a winter garden. The dining room's high windows looked out directly on to the sauna cabin and a random moss-covered boulder deposited by the last ice age.

The finest quarters, the Epos Room, had been reserved for Tanya and me. The smaller Novel Room was unoccupied at first, while the two Novella Chambers under the eaves were home to a married couple, both lyric poets. We caught sight only of the wife, however, who had no sooner announced, in English, 'Käsmu is good for work and good for holiday,' than she scurried off again, as if not to waste one second of her precious sojourn.

Käsmu has a narrow beach. You walk through the woods and suddenly there is the sea. Or you stroll out on the pier in the little harbour to watch children fishing and let your imagination run wild as you gaze at the derelict cutters scraping against garlands of tyres strung along the sides of the pier. The town is nothing special, but lovely for that very reason. Somewhere there must be a depot for wooden pallets, because pallets lie about everywhere and, once they have been chopped into firewood by the villagers, are stacked along the sides of their houses.

The one thing we were good at in Käsmu was sleeping. Käsmu is worth a trip simply for its silence. As we sat in the winter garden in the evening—sipping tea, eating the wild berry marmalade we'd bought from an old local woman, listening to the sea and the birds— time seemed to stand still.

Käsmu's peace and quiet was only disrupted in the morning by the two or three buses that came lumbering down the village street to deposit school classes at Arne's museum. The children stood staring in amazement at whale bones, sharks' teeth, ships in bottles, fish hooks, and postcards of lighthouses around the world. They would picnic on the lawn in front of the building, run out on the pier, and then be driven away again.

Tanya and I had tried to engage Arne in conversation and intended to invite him to dinner, but Arne resisted all contact with us. Even when we paid a second visit to his museum, he simply greeted us with a brief nod and then shuffled away.

On the third day—it had been drizzling since early morning—we watched from the window of the Epos Room as schoolchildren got out of their buses, jiggled at Arne's front door, circled the building, peered in from the veranda, until finally their teachers, equally perplexed and upset, rounded them up and herded them back on to the buses, where we could see them eating their picnic lunch. That evening, when we returned from our excursion to the high marshy moorland, the note we had left for Arne asking him to heat the sauna was still wedged in his door. The sky was clear and promised a beautiful sunset.

The fourth day was cold and so gusty we could hear the sea even with the windows shut, and we stayed indoors. Tanya made tea and crawled back into bed with Gustaw Herling's *A World Apart*. Resolved at last to make use of Käsmu's favourable aura and do some work, I turned on my laptop and was staring at the file icons on my screen when savage barking called us to the window.

A green Barkas van was standing beside the museum. Arne's setters were going crazy. I don't know where they had suddenly come from, but it didn't sound exactly welcoming. Although the day before yesterday these same dogs had obeyed Arne's every word, now he had to grab each one by the nape of its neck and drag it into the house. But once inside they still didn't calm down and kept leaping up at the windows that looked out on to the veranda, barking their heads off.

Arne, on the other hand, looked somehow younger—his beret cocked back on his head.

'If you can keep a secret,' he called over, 'I have something to show you.' With a wide swing of his arm, he directed us to take our place behind him, inserted the key in the rear door of the Barkas and opened it a crack. He peered into the van and then with a clownish pantomime wave urged us to do the same. I assumed Arne's daily encounters with schoolchildren were to blame for this exaggerated performance.

It was dark inside the van, and I reeled back at the smell. Tanya took it more slowly. Then she glanced at me and said in a voice that sounded as if I had just asked her the time, 'A bear, there's a dead bear lying in there.'

Arne had dragged over one of the wooden pallets. Tanya opened the door until it stayed securely in place, and Arne and I propped up the pallet to make a ramp. Arne took up his post beside it; Tanya and I retreated behind the opened door.

The bear didn't stir.

We watched as Arne pulled a can from his jacket pocket and, after opening it with his fingernails, plunged a stick into it. He pulled out the stick, handed it to me, nodded as if to thank me, or as if we had agreed on some signal, clapped his hands three times, and cried,

'Seryosha! Seryosha!' He clapped three more times, took back the stick and held it out in front of him like a fishing rod.

I'm really not that much of wimp, but when, no more than an arm's length away, the bear's head emerged from the darkness, I knew the meaning of the phrase, 'so scared I shit my pants'.

'Let's get out of here,' Tanya whispered. Arne, however, armed with just a honey-smeared stick, showed no sign of the jitters. He waited in front of the pallet with his legs astraddle, bending further and further forward—given his height it looked like some sort of gymnastics. The bear stretched its head out even further, but still refused to crawl down the pallet. Arne held the stick so close to Seryosha's mouth that he took a lick and bit off a piece. He crunched the stick and growled. From childhood we know that bears growl. But when you actually hear that rumble, without the protection of a moat or a fence, it leaves a lasting impression.

Strangely enough, my confidence was boosted less by Arne's honey-stick gambit than by the bear's behaviour. When you know how this story ends, that seems a facile observation, but from the start I had the impression that this bear had himself under control, that he knew what he was allowed to do and not to do. He stuck out a paw and pushed the pallet away from the van. Measuring the distance between the edge of the van's bed and the pallet lying below it, he shifted his weight from one paw to the other, reached down further with his right paw, then leapt out so quickly that Arne would have been knocked over if he hadn't performed a reverse buckjump. At the same moment the Barkas bounced with a metallic squeak.

Arne made a few quick jabs at the can. The crunching sound resumed. And then it happened. At first I thought the bear was turning towards us. But he kept going, spun around once on the spot, and then a second time, because Arne was applauding him. He turned and turned, swinging the rope around his neck with him. When we joined in the applause, he suddenly stopped, lurched forward and backward as if dizzy, and ended with a somersault that was a little off-kilter, but still counted as a somersault. For his finale, the bear plopped down on his rear end and raised his paws, begging.

Whether the stick was now too short or whether Arne was following instructions, at any rate he pulled out a handkerchief, dipped it in the can of honey, and tossed it to Seryosha, who simultaneously tore it to shreds and stuffed it in his mouth. Smacking his lips and grunting, he lowered himself on to all fours and set off on a stroll across the lawn. Arne had removed a basket of fruit from the passenger seat. He tossed Seryosha a couple of apples and strewed the rest over the bed of the van. Seryosha turned around and jumped back up into the Barkas, which settled noisily on its rear axle.

It wasn't until weeks later, after we had told the story of Seryosha many times, that it struck me just how curious this little interlude outside Arne's house actually was. Why, after all, had Arne enticed the bear out of the van? Had he wanted to play wild-animal trainer for us? Had his vanity got the better of him? Was that the reason he had risked discovery?

Arne invited us to accompany him. And so, for the first time since our hitchhiking days, Tanya and I found ourselves squeezing into a Barkas—but on this occasion Tanya climbed in first.

What I ask myself now is: why didn't I jot down a single note while we were in Käsmu? Here we were, driving through the woods, an Estonian museum curator and a German writer, along with his one and only love, plus a bear in the back of their van, and it never once dawned on me that all I had to do to provide my hosts with the story they wanted was to write down what was happening to me at that moment.

It would, of course, be an improvement if I could reproduce Arne's speech in the original. His German was tinged with the now defunct East Prussian dialect, but I'm simply unable to replicate its odd syntax and broad vowels. Chugging out of the village in second gear, we at first said nothing. Arne was apparently enjoying keeping us in suspense and pretended that his slalom course to avoid potholes demanded his full attention.

'What kind of bear is it?' Tanya finally asked. In her attempt to look Arne in the eye, she bent so far forward that her forehead almost touched the windshield. 'What are you doing with a bear?'

Arne smiled—a pothole sent us lurching forward. Arne cursed.

'Did you hear that?' Tanya exclaimed. 'He growled, he's growling.'

A couple more slalom manoeuvres later, Arne began to speak, but what he had to say had nothing to do with Tanya's question. He explained that the Writers' Union was poor because its writers were poor. Except for one member, not a single writer in Estonia was able to live from his books, although of course the union also got a government subsidy. And for the quartermaster—that was in fact the term he used—for the quartermaster of a writers' retreat there was really not much left over, and he couldn't depend on the standard practice of tipping in their case either. Once in a while he let a few villagers use the sauna, but they paid, if at all, in produce. As far as his museum work went, all he got out of it was what he squeezed out of it himself. Even ten buses a day wouldn't do the job. 'So, *chto delat*?' he asked in Russian. What was Arne to do?

But why was he taking a trained bear for a joyride through the woods?

Arne was looking for a turn-off. We drove at a snail's pace along a rutted path. Arne talked about the revolution, as he called it. They had achieved everything they had wanted: independence, democracy, a market economy, and so on, the European Union. Except that by now all the islands and coastal properties had been sold to Finns and Swedes, some to Russians and Germans, too, plus the finest houses in Tallinn. There was truly nothing left that hadn't been privatized and incorporated into the market economy. So what now?

Whenever we drove over a root or through a deep puddle, we could hear Seryosha's growls.

The only difference from the old days, Arne said, was that from time to time some Westerner might get lost and end up in Käsmu, and now there was nobody to tell him how to run his museum any more.

Arne turned on his headlights because the fir trees had closed in over the path, so that it was like driving through a tunnel. After an eternity of two or three kilometres, a heather-covered clearing opened up before us. Arne stopped, turned off his lights, pulled the key out of the ignition, leaned back with his arms folded and explained everything.

An acquaintance of his in Finland, called Mika, who also ran a museum and to whom he had sold a couple of old German telescopes at a friendly discount, had passed on an enquiry about whether he, Arne, could perhaps act as an agent to locate a house at a good price along the coast. Although he had not agreed to this arrangement, suddenly, one day, there stood Mika, along with his wife, who was a stunning Argentinian, and their three children. Nothing had come of the house deal, but Mika had been wildly enthusiastic about the local forest—which Arne found surprising, since Finland had plenty of forests of its own. It turned out that Mika was a hunter, and he called this forest a Russian forest and suggested that surely there were bears in a Russian forest. He, Arne, had never seen a bear in Laheema, but, since the house deal had fallen through, he didn't want to dash Mika's hopes a second time, and so he had promised to enquire about bears at the local forestry office. There were plenty of bears, he learned, but it was forbidden to shoot animals in the national park. Unless—here Arne raised his right hand and began to rub his thumb against his first two fingers—unless the bear presented a serious threat to the life and limb of locals and tourists.

Arne had come to an agreement with the game warden as to how many Finnish *markkas* it would cost Mika to obtain the ruling. Mika agreed to the sum, half in advance, the rest on the hide of the bear. In March a family of bears actually turned up in Laheema. But to avoid additional difficulties, the game warden had asked that the hunt be postponed until autumn.

The family of bears vanished in May, and there had been no trace of them since. Then, last week, the warden had telephoned Arne and confessed that unfortunately he was no longer in a position to pay back the advance. In lieu of the cash, the warden had given Arne a hot tip: a once-famous circus from Soviet days was eking out a living in a St Petersburg suburb. They were trying to unload their animals, because the upkeep was too expensive. And so yesterday, for a payment of three hundred marks, Arne had taken charge of Seryosha, whom his caretaker—a woman—had smuggled across the border through the forest. And so now they had a bear.

In response to Tanya's question as to whether he had informed Seryosha's caretaker what fate awaited her charge, Arne brusquely asked in return whether she would prefer that Seryosha starve. Thanks to him, the animal would at least die with a full stomach and the pleasure of having enjoyed a couple of hours in the wild.

The plan was to let Seryosha settle in at the edge of this clearing for a day or two. To ease the pain of separation, his caretaker had also given Arne a pair of her old shoes and a jacket. Arne pulled out a well-worn moccasin, like ones I had worn as a child, and got out of the van.

I smiled, unable to suppress my suspicion that what Arne had told us was your basic cock-and-bear story. 'You don't believe me?' he asked. I shrugged. 'Tomorrow,' Arne said, 'Mika will be here. Maybe you'll want to apologize then.' I apologized on the spot, and several times over, but to no avail. Arne had opened the van's rear door and now clapped three times, called Seryosha's name and, with the shoes and jacket bundled under his arm and a sack of food thrown over his shoulder, set out across the heather.

Tanya and I stood beside the van. As he trotted alongside Arne, Seryosha was a beautiful sight. It wasn't just his loping gait—which made it look as if he were dragging his paws behind him. Under that mass of fur moved a body no less supple than a tiger's, except that Seryosha's elegance was less obvious.

When we finally lost sight of them in the trees at the far side of the clearing, Tanya asked what I would do if Arne were to call out for help. 'Certainly not run in his direction,' I said.

On the drive back each of us was lost in our own thoughts. Our goodbyes were brief. Arne had enough to do calming down his setters—and a clutch of teachers and their students, waiting to visit the museum.

Later that evening, Tanya took it upon herself to walk over to Arne's to ask him about the malfunctioning sauna. But either Arne wasn't there or he didn't want to be disturbed.

As we drank our tea in the winter garden, we tried without success to imagine the hunt. Would Arne clap his hands three times and call out 'Seryosha'? Should we or shouldn't we hope that Seryosha would make his getaway? Did a circus bear have any chance at all in Laheema? Wouldn't he seek out the company of people, so that sooner or later he'd be shot as a dangerous animal? Seryosha's future didn't look rosy, and there was nothing we could do about it.

The next day was warm, the sky cloudless, and we made an excursion to Palmse, once the estate of a German baron. Afterwards we visited a forest chapel, which was set in the middle of an old cemetery. (I've rechecked my notebook. There is not a single entry about Estonia, although Tanya did use two pages to record the names on the wooden crosses and gravestones. I now remember how ashamed I felt that it was she who had written down those names and not me.)

On the drive home the weather turned gloomy and it began to rain. But once we got back our mood immediately lifted—smoke was rising from the sauna cabin. Arne had, in fact, heated it and filled the tin basins at the entrance with fresh birch branches.

As we entered the steam room, each of us with no more than a towel over one arm, we found three men already huddled inside. They neither responded to our greeting nor moved closer together to make room for us. Instead they ogled Tanya. Out of the corner of my eye I saw the man sitting behind her trace a female silhouette in the air with his hands. We couldn't understand what they were saying, because they were speaking Finnish, but their stifled giggles didn't need an interpreter. Tanya left the sauna after a few minutes and went back to the house.

I was idiotic enough to believe I shouldn't yield the battleground to the Finns without a fight, so I was the first to stretch out on the upper bench, leaving them to crowd together on the lower one. During the next half hour I watched as two of them paid court to the third guy, with a blond moustache and a back sprinkled with moles. They held the door open for him and closed it behind him, let him be the first under the shower, the first to select a seat—and everything he said was met with a double echo.

Returning to the Epos Room, I immediately realized something was up. I looked at Tanya—she was already in mid-explosion. Our arguments always follow the same pattern. They begin with my failure to notice, or notice too late, what should be the appropriate response. In this case, since I had chosen not to take on those three louts directly, I ought to have at least followed Tanya out of the sauna. But I was a man who could never forgo his pleasures, and by my behaviour I had, intentionally or not, sided with them.

It's amazing. Although I earn my living observing and describing situations and emotions, compared to Tanya I am completely tone-deaf and dull-witted. The situation escalated when, soon afterwards, the guy with the blond moustache sat down at the dining room table and proceeded to disassemble and clean two guns. While he worked, he whistled loudly. I had to do something.

My suggestion that he might, in fact, tend to his weapons in his room was met with a grin. When I insisted, he said, 'Arne! Arne!', as if it was Arne who had assigned him to his task. But when I picked up the barrel of one of the guns, he shouted in English: 'Don't touch it! Don't touch it!' and snatched it away. The upshot was that we spread our evening meal over one half of the table—the lyric poetess from the Novella Chamber was impervious to our request that she join us in defending the dining room. The other half was occupied by the Finn, who was still busy oiling his weapons. For a while he kept up his inane whistling, but much to our relief was the first to leave.

We were already in bed when there was a knock at our door.

After apologizing for the disturbance, Arne begged for our help.

'You're from the East, too, after all,' he said. One of the Finns, he explained, was Mika's boss, and Mika was in some kind of trouble. He didn't know any more than that. But he would be very grateful if, once back in Tallinn, we didn't mention the fact that the boss had been put up in the union's guest house. If everything went well, the three of them would be gone the day after tomorrow, anyway.

'The day after tomorrow?' Tanya said, 'That's when we're leaving, too.'

'But you'll be here tomorrow?' Arne asked.

He needed us because the Finns had come from Tallinn in a taxi. Could we drive two of them to the hunt?

'Only if they sit in the back,' Tanya said.

Arne came closer and extended a hand to each of us. 'Wake-up call at 3.30, breakfast at my place, departure at 4.30,' he said, and hurried off.

It took us a long time to get to sleep. Then, around three o'clock, we were woken by what we first took to be a barking seal—a sound evidently emanating from the boss Finn under the shower.

It's a strange feeling to sit at a table with people you've first come to know in the buff. Their expensive outfits, which brought to mind an imminent polar expedition, looked to me like a crude attempt to conceal their true natures.

They politely offered us hardboiled eggs and pickled herring—I bought something similar in Berlin recently, where it's marketed as 'Swedish Snax'. Arne and the boss rode in the Barkas. Mika and the other fellow came with us. Both of them had little eyes and stringy hair—Mika's was light brown; the other guy was very blond. They both fell asleep immediately. The alcohol on their breath was only tolerable with a window open.

After the turn-off, we rolled the windows all the way down and breathed in the forest air. It was moist and piney and somehow swallowed up the exhaust of the Barkas in front. Any second I expected to see Seryosha pop up in the narrow beam of the headlights. 'Let's hope, let's hope he's taken off!' Tanya whispered.

We stopped just before the clearing and left it to the boss to shake his fellow countrymen awake. Dawn was breaking by now, and fog lay over the ground.

Arne assigned the hunters places every fifty metres. The boss was given a post on a low mound. Mika took a spot very close to us. The blond stood farthest off. Arne passed out blankets. We could drive back home and get some sleep, he said, evidently worried about us. We didn't need to be back here for another four or five hours.

But we didn't do him the favour.

How lovely it would be if I could describe what comes next in the style of a Leskov or Turgenev. But I knew neither the names of the birds striking up their songs, nor of the beetles crawling under our collars or up our sleeves, nor could I make some observation that testifies to my dendrological expertise.

Freezing, we jogged up and down under the firs and dreamed of the sauna, which was surely the least we could expect in reward for our co-operation. But we never moved too far away from the car. Once fired upon, even Seryosha might turn cranky.

Between seven and eight—the sun had now risen above the treetops—I noticed some movement. Evidently the hunters had seen something. Everyone except us had binoculars, which is why I'm dependent here on Arne's account. He would tell us later that it all began well enough, in fact conditions were ideal, since Seryosha had been meandering along the edge of the forest at the opposite side of the clearing. For hunters who are good shots a distance of two hundred to two hundred and fifty meters is no problem, but Seryosha kept vanishing behind tree stumps and bushes. It makes sense that Arne advised the Finns against firing, since he assumed that Seryosha could be lured closer.

In the real world, spectacular events always happen at great speed and usually almost coincidentally. How can you be in the right place at the right time? To give truth its due, I ought to describe the finale with the brevity and speed with which in fact we experienced it.

Seryosha, then, had been spotted and was in the Finns' crosshairs. I'm certain the argument that broke out among the hunters at that point—in which Arne somehow managed to get involved—would have sent any other bear packing. According to what Arne told us later, the issue was who should fire first, the boss or the blond; who was considered the better shot. The blond had apparently implied that his boss wouldn't have much luck at that distance. At any rate what followed was worthy of a soccer pitch—then, suddenly, a shot. Followed at once by another. Silence. Tanya pressed her fists together and whispered, 'Beat it, Seryosha, beat it!'

The next sound we heard was a screeching female voice. Which is to say that at first I took it to be the wailing of an animal so accustomed to the company of humans that it mimics them in its pain. So it was with real relief that we saw a woman in a black headscarf rise up from the heather, throwing her arms into the air and spinning around. She evidently didn't know what direction the shots had come from. We were standing next to Mika on the low mound, the blond and the boss were a few steps to our right, with Arne behind them. They were fixed to the spot, staring through their binoculars. But even with the naked eye it was obvious that the woman, whose screams had now turned to savage yowls, was pointing to the far edge of the forest.

I have never used the following phrase, and probably never will again, but in this case there's no avoiding it: I didn't believe my eyes, not even when I saw what was happening in front of them. It was Seryosha. But he wasn't jumping or dancing or doing somersaults. Seryosha, if not with great skill, was riding a woman's bicycle. It looked as if his paws kept slipping off the pedals, and every few yards I expected him to go flying over the handlebars. But that was more to do with the uneven forest floor. Seryosha was perched on the seat, pedalling away for all he was worth. Unfortunately, given the situation, I was not watching those around me. It wasn't until I heard a shot that I noticed an ashen-faced Arne and saw the boss raise his gun and fire—followed by a second shot from the blond, and finally one from Mika.

Now it was Arne who was screaming as he pushed the barrel of the boss's gun down. Any shot was irresponsible, even though the wailing woman was not in the direct line of fire and had, in the meantime, dived into the heather—she had fainted at the sight of her commandeered bicycle, we would soon learn. I took advantage of the brief skirmish that followed to borrow Mika's binoculars. Which is why I was presumably the last person to see Seryosha. He fled into the forest, soon breaking into an easy trot on all fours, and vanished among the fir trees.

I probably don't need to describe what was going on among the hunters. Their shouting match was fortunately less about the bear's agility than about Arne's interference and their own failure to maintain an established hierarchy. They even forgot about the woman. Only after she re-emerged from the heather, still nervously prepared to duck for cover, did someone come to her aid.

She was younger than I had guessed. At the sight of her bicycle, an old Wanderer model, she raised another howl. The front wheel was a figure-of-eight with extruding spokes. A shot had shattered the bearings in the back wheel. But there was no sign of blood anywhere.

The woman had come to gather blueberries, and while she held open her hand, one bill of Finnish currency after another was thumbed out until she fell silent. Arne carried the heavy bicycle to the Barkas and drove her home. Without sliding her own seat forward so much as an inch, Tanya watched in the reflector of her sun visor as the boss was forced to squeeze into the back seat between Mika and his chief rival, the blond sharpshooter.

By the time we handed over the keys of the Epos Room to Arne the next morning, thanking him and saying our goodbyes, the Finns had already taken two taxis and left; Mika riding with his boss, whereas the blond had to pay for his own taxi. Arne considered this a victory for Mika because, according to Arne, the hostility that had erupted as a result of the hunting rivalry between the boss and his former right-hand man had given Mika a second chance—so the bear hunt had paid off for him after all, if in unexpected ways. The woman gathering berries, Arne hoped, had been given enough hush money. But if she still couldn't keep her mouth shut—which he feared would be the case—then her punishment would be that no one would believe her story.

Arne promised to let us know as soon as he learned anything about Seryosha's fate. Sad to say, I've never heard another word from him.

Of course I ask myself why, after six years, I'm now writing about that extraordinary hunt. I've forgotten so many details in the meantime—from the names of the lyric poets at the writers' retreat, to the make of our rental car, from exact prices, to the route we took, and so on and so on. Besides which, it's quite possible that things have changed drastically in Estonia in the last few years, so that my story has in some sense become past history. In any case, the fact is that not only has my own life changed, all our lives have taken a different course over those years. And that is perhaps—perhaps— the reason I finally found myself in a position to risk writing a story about Estonia. □

Gao Xingjian

'Gao Xingjian, what have you never done that you would like to do?'

'Music. Inside of me there is a rhythm. But it's very complicated to make it real.'

17 Melbourne Road

Oliver Reynolds

A room at the top of the street
preserving his life in sunlight
square-bottled brilliantine
a comb centre-parting a brush

work-boots on a page of the *Echo*
and the black jacket on its hanger
with the gold-threaded breast badge
of the South Wales Boxing Federation

Mondays my mother cleaned for him
the builder's mate and weekend referee
quiet and dependable as the man
sent ahead to hire a room for our Lord

still there as I close the door on emptiness
then and now looking back at our lodger
Mr Pudge caught in the honest '60s
small blue flowers pressed in a book

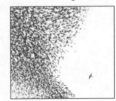

GRANTA

MARRIAGE LINES
Julian Barnes

Julian Barnes

The Twin Otter was only half full as they took off from Glasgow: a few islanders returning from the mainland, plus some early-season weekenders with hiking boots and rucksacks. For almost an hour they flew just above the shifting brainscape of the clouds. Then they descended, and the jigsaw edges of the island appeared below them.

He had always loved this moment. The neck of headland, the long Atlantic beach of Traigh Eais, the large white bungalow they ritually buzzed, then a slow turn over the little humpy island of Orosay, and a final approach to the flat, sheeny expanse of Traigh Mhor. In summer months, you could usually count on some boisterous mainland voice, keen perhaps to impress a girlfriend, shouting over the propeller noise, 'Only commercial beach landing in the world!' But with the years he had grown indulgent even about that. It was part of the folklore of coming here.

They landed hard on the cockle beach, and spray flew up between the wing struts as they raced through shallow puddles. Then the plane slewed side on to the little terminal building, and a minute later they were climbing down the rickety metal steps to the beach. A tractor with a flatbed trailer was standing by to trundle their luggage the dozen yards to a damp concrete slab which served as the carousel. They, their: he knew he must start getting used to the singular pronoun instead. This was going to be the grammar of his life from now on.

Calum was waiting for him, looking past his shoulder, scanning the other passengers. The same slight, grey-haired figure in a green windcheater who met them every year. Being Calum, he didn't ask; he waited. They had known one another, with a kind of intimate formality, for twenty years or so. Now that regularity, that repetition, and all that it contained, was broken.

As the van dawdled along the single-track road, and waited politely in the passing bays, he told Calum the story he was already weary with repeating. The sudden tiredness, the dizzy spells, the blood tests, the scans, hospital, more hospital, the hospice. The speed of it all, the process, the merciless tramp of events. He told it without tears, in a neutral voice, as if it might have happened to someone else. It was the only way, so far, that he knew how.

Outside the dark stone cottage, Calum yanked on the handbrake. 'Rest her soul,' he said quietly, and took charge of the holdall.

The first time they had come to the island, they weren't yet married. She had worn a wedding ring as a concession to...what?—to how they imagined the island morality to be. It made them feel both superior and hypocritical at the same time. Their room at Calum and Flora's B&B had whitewashed walls, rain drying on the window, and a view across the machair to the sharp rise of Beinn Mhartainn. On their first night, they had discovered a bed whose joints wailed against any activity grosser than the minimum required for the sober conception of children. They found themselves comically restricted. Island sex, they had called it, giggling quietly into one another's bodies.

He had bought new binoculars especially for that trip. Inland, there were larks and twites, wheatears and wagtails. On the shoreline, ringed plovers and pipits. But it was the seabirds he loved best, the cormorants and gannets, the shags and fulmars. He spent many a docile, wet-bottomed hour on the clifftops, thumb and middle finger bringing into focus their whirling dives, and their soaring independence. The fulmars were his favourites. Birds which spent their whole lives at sea, coming to land only to nest. Then they laid a single egg, raised the chick, and took to the sea again, skimming the waves, rising on the air currents, being themselves.

She had preferred flowers to birds. Sea pinks, yellow rattle, purple vetch, flag iris. There was something, he remembered, called self-heal. That was as far as his knowledge, and memory, went. She had never picked a single flower here, or anywhere else. To cut a flower was to speed its death, she used to say. She hated the sight of a vase. In the hospital, other patients, seeing the empty metal trolley at the foot of her bed, had thought her friends neglectful, and tried to pass on their excess bouquets. This went on until she was moved to her own room, and then the problem ceased.

That first year, Calum had shown them the island. One afternoon, on a beach where he liked to dig for razor clams, he had looked away from them, and said, almost as if he was addressing the sea, 'My grandparents were married by declaration, you know. That was all you needed in the old days. Approval and declaration. You were married when the moon was waxing and the tide running—to bring you luck. And after the wedding there'd be a rough mattress on the floor of an outbuilding. For the first night. The idea was that you begin marriage in a state of humility.'

'Oh, that's wonderful, Calum,' she had said. But he felt it was a rebuke—to their English manners, their presumption, their silent lie.

The second year, they had returned a few weeks after getting married. They wanted to tell everyone they met; but here was one place they couldn't. Perhaps this had been good for them—to be silly with happiness and obliged into silence. Perhaps it had been their own way of beginning marriage in a state of humility.

He sensed, nevertheless, that Calum and Flora had guessed. No doubt it wasn't difficult, given their new clothes and their daft smiles. On the first night Calum gave them whisky from a bottle without a label. He had many such bottles. There was a lot more whisky drunk than sold on this island, that was for sure.

Flora had taken out of a drawer an old sweater which had belonged to her grandfather. She laid it on the kitchen table, ironing it with her palms. In the old days, she explained, the women of these islands used to tell stories with their knitting. The pattern of this jersey showed that her grandfather had come from Eriksay, while its details, its decorations, told of fishing and faith, of the sea and the sand. And this series of zigzags across one shoulder—these here, look—represented the ups and downs of marriage. They were, quite literally, marriage lines.

Zigzags. Like any newly married couple, they had exchanged a glance of sly confidence, sure that for them there would be no downs—or at least, not downs like those of their parents, or those of friends who were already making the usual stupid, predictable mistakes. They would be different, they would be different from everyone who had ever got married before.

'Tell them about the buttons, Flora,' said Calum.

The pattern of the jersey told you which island its owner came from; the buttons at the neck told you precisely which family they belonged to. It must have been like walking around dressed in your own postcode, he thought.

A day or two later, he had said to Calum, 'I wish everyone was still wearing those sweaters.' Having no sense of tradition himself, he liked other people to display one.

'They had great use,' replied Calum. 'There was many a drowning you could only recognize by the jersey. And then by the buttons. Who the man was.'

'I hadn't thought of that.'

'Well, no reason for it. For you to know. For you to think.'

There were moments when he felt that this was the most distant place he had ever come to. The islanders happened to speak the same language as him, but that was just some strange, geographical coincidence.

This time, Calum and Flora treated him as he knew they would: with a tact and modesty he had once, stupidly, Englishly, mistaken for deference. They didn't press themselves upon him, or make a show of their sympathy. There was a touch on the shoulder, a plate laid before him, a remark about the weather.

Each morning, Flora would give him a sandwich wrapped in greaseproof paper, a piece of cheese and an apple. He would set off across the machair and up Beinn Mhartainn. He made himself climb to the top, from where he could see the island and its jigsaw edges, where he could feel himself alone. Then, binoculars in hand, he would head for the cliffs and the seabirds. Calum had once told him that on some of the islands, generations back, they used to make oil for their lamps from the fulmars. Odd how he had always kept this detail from her, for twenty years and more. The rest of the year round, he never thought of it. Then they would come to the island, and he would say to himself, I mustn't tell her what they did with the fulmars.

That summer she had nearly left him—or had he nearly left her?— at this distance, it was hard to tell—he had gone clam-digging with Calum. She had left them to pursue their sport, preferring to walk the damp, wavy line of the beach from which the sea had just retreated. Here, where the pebbles were barely bigger than sand grains, she liked to search for pieces of coloured glass—tiny shards of broken bottle, worn soft and smooth by water and time. For years he had watched the stooped walk, the inquisitive crouch, the picking, the discarding, the hoarding in the cupped left palm.

Calum explained how you looked for a small declivity in the sand, poured a little salt into it, then waited for the razor clam to shoot up a few inches out of its sandy lair. He wore an oven glove on his left hand, against the sharpness of the rising shell. You had to pull quickly, he said, seizing the clam before it disappeared again.

Mostly, despite Calum's expertise, nothing stirred, and they moved on to the next hollow in the sand. Out of the corner of his eye, he saw her wandering further along the beach, her back turned to him, self-sufficient, content with what she was doing, not giving him a thought.

As he handed Calum more salt, and saw the oven glove poised in anticipation, he found himself saying, man to man, 'Bit like marriage, isn't it?'

Calum frowned slightly. 'What's your meaning?'

'Oh, waiting for something to pop out of the sand. Then it turns out either there's nothing there, or something that cuts your hand open if you aren't bloody careful.'

It had been a stupid thing to say. Stupid because he hadn't really meant it, more stupid because it was presumptuous. Silence told him that Calum found such talk offensive, to himself, to Flora, to the islanders generally.

Each day he walked, and each day soft rain soaked into him. He ate a sodden sandwich, and watched the fulmars skimming the sea. He walked to Greian Head and looked down over the flat rocks where the seals liked to congregate. One year, they had watched a dog swim all the way out from the beach, chase the seals off, and then parade up and down the rock like a new landowner. This year there was no dog.

On the vertiginous side of Greian was part of an unlikely golf course where, year after year, they had never seen a single golfer. There was a small circular green surrounded by a picket fence to keep the cows off. Once, close by, a herd of bullocks had rushed at them, frightening her silly. He had stood his ground, waved his arms wildly, and instinctively shouted the names of the political leaders he most despised. He had somehow not been surprised that it had calmed them down. This year, there were no bullocks to be seen, and he missed them. He supposed they must have long gone to slaughter.

He remembered a crofter on Vatersay telling them about lazy beds. You cut a slice of turf, placed your potatoes on the open soil, relaid the turf upside down on top of them—and that was it. Time and rain and the warmth of the sun did the rest. Lazy beds—he saw her laughing at him, reading his mind, saying afterwards that this would be his idea of gardening, wouldn't it? He remembered her eyes shining like the damp glass jewellery she used to fill her palm with.

On the last morning, Calum drove him back to Traigh Mhor in the van. Politicians had been promising a new airstrip so that modern planes could land. There was talk of tourist development and island regeneration, mixed with warnings about the current cost of subsidy. Calum wanted none of it, and nor did he. He knew that he would need the island to stay as still and unchanging as possible in his memory. He wouldn't come back if jets started landing on tarmac.

He checked in his holdall at the counter, and they went outside. Hanging over a low wall, Calum lit a cigarette. They looked out over the damp and bumpy sand of the cockle beach. The cloud was low, the windsock inert.

'These are for you,' said Calum, handing him half a dozen postcards. He must have bought them at the cafe just now. Views of the island, the beach, the machair; one of the very plane waiting to take him away.

'But...'

'You will be needing the memory.'

A few minutes later, the Twin Otter took off straight out across Orosay and the open sea. There was no last view of the island before that world below was shut out. In the enveloping cloud, he thought about marriage lines and buttons; about razor clams and island sex; about missing bullocks and fulmars being turned into oil; and then, finally, the tears came. Calum had known he would not be coming back. But the tears were not for that, or for himself, or even for her, for their memories. They were tears for his own stupidity. His presumption too.

He had thought he could recapture, and begin to say farewell. He had thought that grief might be assuaged, or if not assuaged, at least speeded up, hurried on its way a little, by going back to a place where they had been happy. But he was not in charge of grief. Grief was in charge of him. And in the months and years ahead, he expected grief to teach him many other things as well. This was just the first of them.

□

Horizons Touched

The Music of ECM

edited by

Steve Lake and Paul Griffiths

GRANTA

GRANTA

MAY WE
BE FORGIVEN

A. M. Homes

A. M. Homes

Was there ever a time you thought—I am doing this on purpose, I am fucking up and I don't know why?

The warning sign. Two years ago, Thanksgiving at their house. Twenty or thirty people at tables spreading from the dining room into the living room and stopping abruptly at the piano bench. He was at the head, picking turkey out of his teeth. I kept watching him as I went back and forth carrying plates into the kitchen—the edges of my fingers dipping into repulsive goo—cranberry sauce, sweet potatoes, a cold pearl onion, gristle. With every trip back and forth from the dining room to the kitchen, I hated him more. Every sin of our childhood came back. He was born eleven months after me, he was at first sickly, not enough oxygen along the way, and got too much attention and then, despite what I tried to tell him about how horrible he was, always acted as though he believed he was a gift of the gods. They named him George. Geo he liked to be called, like that was something cool, something scientific, mathematical, analytical. Geode I called him—like a sedimentary rock. Despite the fact that he was perpetually oblivious to everyone but himself, his preternatural confidence, his divinely arrogant head dappled with blond threads of hair lifted high, drew the attention of others, gave the impression that he knew something. People solicited his opinions, his participation, while I never saw the charm. As much as he and I plotted against each other and blamed the other for our misdeeds, we were surprisingly similar under the surface, which was all the more annoying. By the time we were ten and eleven, he was taller than me, broader, stronger. 'You sure he's not the butcher's boy?' my father would ask jokingly. No one laughed.

I was bringing in plates and platters, casseroles caked with the debris of dinner, and no one, not George, not my wife, Claire, and all the kids, not his awful friends, seemed to notice that help was needed. His wife, Jane, had been at it all day: cooking, cleaning and serving, and now scraping bones and slop into a giant trash bin.

Jane scraped the plates, piling dirty dishes one atop the other and dropping the slimy silver into a sink of steamy soapy water. Glancing at me, she brushed her hair away with the back of her hand and smiled. I went back for more.

The turkey platter was in the centre of the table. I reached over my wife's shoulder and lifted; despite the meat being down to the bone the tray was heavy and wobbled. I willed myself to stay strong, and was able to carry out the mission while balancing a casserole of Brussels sprouts and bacon in the crook of my other arm.

I stood in their kitchen picking at the carcass while Jane did the dishes, bright blue gloves on, up to her elbows in suds. My fingers were deep in the bird, the hollow body still warm, the best bits of stuffing packed in. I dug with my fingers and brought stuffing to my lips. She looked at me—my mouth moist, greasy, my fingers curled into what would have been the turkey's g-spot if they had such things—lifted her hands out of the water and came towards me, planting one on me. Not friendly. The kiss was serious, wet, full of desire. It was terrifying and unexpected. She did it, then snapped off her gloves and walked out of the room. I was holding the counter, gripping it with greasy fingers. Hard.

From Thanksgiving through Christmas and on into the New Year, I thought of George fucking Jane. George on top of her, or, for a special occasion, George on the bottom, and once, fantastically, George having her from the back. I couldn't stop thinking about it. I was convinced that despite his charms George wasn't very good, and that all he knew about sex he learned from the pages of a magazine read furtively while shitting. I thought of my brother fucking his wife—constantly. And whenever I saw her—the nephew's birthday, Christmas Eve, New Year's—I was hard. I wore baggy, pleated pants and double pairs of jockey shorts to contain my treasonous enthusiasm. The effort created bulk, and I worried that it gave me the appearance of having gained weight.

It is almost nine when Jane calls. Claire is still at her office—one or two nights a week she works late, 'preparing, rehearsing, reviewing, strategizing'. Another man would think his wife was having an affair—I think Claire is just smart. 'I need your help,' Jane says.

'Don't worry,' I say, before I even know what the worry is. I imagine her calling me from the kitchen phone. The long curly cord wrapping around her body.

'He's at the police station.'

'Did he do something wrong?' I ask.

'Apparently. And now I'm supposed to go and get him.'

I glance at the New York skyline. From the outside our building is ugly, post-war white brick, dull. But we're up high, the windows are broad and there's a small terrace where we used to sit and have our morning toast. Now the table is rusting and we've got the cat's litter box under it and a bin where we keep recyclables.

'Can you pick him up?' she asks.

Within minutes I'm on the street. When we bought the apartment, the idea of an extra $20,000 for a parking spot seemed outrageous, but over time it's felt like the deal of the century. I call Claire from the car. 'I'm in the car,' I say, 'on my way to George's. There's some kind of problem and I've got to pick him up. I had my dinner—there's some for you in the fridge. Call later.'

A fight. On the way to the police station that's what I'm thinking. George has it in him: a kind of atomic reactivity that stays under the surface until some small something triggers him and he erupts, throwing over a table, smashing his fist through a wall or into something. More than once I've been the recipient of his frustrations: a baseball hurled at my back, striking me at kidney level and dropping me to my knees; in my grandmother's kitchen, a shove hurling me backwards, through a full-length pane of glass, as George blocks me from getting the last of the brownies. I imagined that he'd gone out or had a drink after work and gotten on the wrong side of something.

Thirty-three minutes later, inside the suburban police station, I announce myself to the two cops, 'I'm the brother of the man you called his wife about,' which gets me nowhere. 'I'm here on behalf of Geo Stone. Has a crime been committed?'

'We wanted to take him to the hospital but he wouldn't go; just kept repeating that he was a dangerous man and we should take him downtown, lock him up and be done with it. He's in the back, sitting in the cell. Personally, I think the man needs a doctor—you don't walk away from something like that unscathed.'

'So he got into a fight?'

'Car accident, bad one. Doesn't appear he was under the influence, passed a breath test, and consented the blood and urine, but really he should see a doctor.'

'Was it his fault?'

'He ran a red light, ploughed into a minivan, husband and daughter were killed on impact, the wife was alive at the scene in the back seat next to the surviving boy. Rescue crew used the Jaws of Life to free the wife, upon release she lost consciousness and expired at the scene.'

'Her legs fell out of the car,' someone adds in the background.

'The boy is in a fair condition. He'll survive,' the younger cop says, going into the back to get George.

'Is my brother being charged with a crime?'

'Not at the moment. He was going pretty fast, just ploughed right into them. Officers noted that he appeared disoriented at the scene. Take him home, get him a doctor and a lawyer—these things can get ugly.'

'He won't come out,' the younger cop says.

'Tell him we don't have room for him,' the older one says. 'Tell him that the real criminals are coming soon and if he doesn't come out now he's staying in and they'll butt-fuck him in the middle of the night.'

George comes out. 'How come you're here?' he asks me.

'Jane called, and besides you only had the one car.'

'She could have taken a taxi.'

'It's late.'

I lead George through the small parking lot and into the night, feeling compelled to take his arm, to guide him by his elbow—not sure if I'm preventing him from escaping or just steadying him. George doesn't pull away—he lets himself be led.

'Where's Jane?'

'At the house.'

'Does she know?'

I shake my head—no.

'It was awful. There was a light.'

'Did you see the light?'

'I think I may have seen it but it was like it didn't make sense.'

'Like it didn't apply to you?'

'Like I just didn't know.' He gets into the car. 'Where's Jane?' he asks again.

'At the house,' I repeat.

Pulling into the driveway, the headlights cut through the house and catch Jane in the kitchen, holding a pot of coffee.

'Are you all right?' she asks when we are inside.

'How could I be?' he says. George empties his pockets on to the kitchen counter. He takes off his shoes, socks, pants, boxers, jacket, shirt, undershirt, and stuffs all of it into the kitchen trash can.

'Would you like some coffee?' Jane asks.

Naked, George stands with his head tilted as if he's hearing something.

'Coffee?' she asks again, gesturing with the pot.

He doesn't answer. He walks from the kitchen through the dining room and into the living room, and sits in the dark—naked in a chair.

'Did he get into a fight?' Jane asks.

'Car accident. You'd better call your insurance company and your lawyer. Do you have a lawyer?'

'George, do we have a lawyer?'

'Do I need one?' he asks.

'Something is wrong with him,' Jane says.

'He killed people.'

There is a pause.

She pours George a cup of coffee and brings it into the living room along with a dish towel that she drapes over his genitals like putting a napkin in his lap.

The phone rings.

'Don't answer it,' George says.

'Hello,' she says. 'I'm sorry he's not home right now. May I take a message?' Jane listens. 'Yes, I hear you, perfectly clear,' she says and then hangs up. 'Do you want a drink?' She asks no one in particular and then pours one for herself.

'Who was it?' I ask.

'Friend of the family,' she says, and in a moment I realize that she means a friend of the family that was killed.

For a long time he sits in the chair, the dish towel shielding his privates, the cup of coffee daintily on his lap. Beneath him a puddle forms.

'George,' Jane implores when she hears what sounds like water running, 'you're having an accident.'

Tessie, the old dog, gets up from her bed, comes over and sniffs it.

Jane hurries into the kitchen and comes back with a wad of paper towels. 'It will eat the finish right off the floor,' she says.

Through it all George looks blank, empty, like a husk left by a reptile who has shed his skin.

Jane takes the coffee cup from George and hands it to me. She takes the wet dish towel from his lap, helps him to stand and then wipes the back of his legs and his ass with paper towels. 'Let me help you upstairs.'

I watch as they climb the steps. I see my brother's body, slack, his stomach sagging slightly, the bones of his hips, his pelvis, his flat ass, all so white they appear to glow in the dark. As they climb I see below his ass and tucked between his legs, his low, pinkish purple nut sac swaying like an old lion.

I sit on their couch. Where is my wife? Isn't she curious to know what happened? Why hasn't she called?

The room smells of urine. The wet paper towels are on the floor. Jane doesn't come back to clean up the pee. I do it and then sit back down on the sofa.

I want to go home. I hate this living room. I hate this house. I remember helping them find the house. I remember when they bought it. I remember helping them do things to fix it up. Why do they still live here? Their children are grown, the place is empty, the dog is old.

In the morning there are hurried phone calls and hushed conversations. We will take him to the hospital and they will look for something, some invisible explanation that will relieve him of responsibility.

'Am I going deaf or what the fuck is going on around here?' George wants to know.

'George,' she says clearly, 'we have to go to the hospital, pack your bag.'

And he does.

I drive them. He sits next to me wearing clothes from the wrong season, well-worn corduroy pants, a flannel shirt he's had for fifteen years. He's unevenly shaven.

I drive self-consciously, worried that his complacent mood might shift, that he might flash back, erupt and try to grab the wheel. The seat belts are good; they discourage sudden movements.

'Simple Simon met a pieman going to the fair; Said Simple Simon to the pieman "Let me taste your ware,"' George intones. 'Simple Simon went a-fishing for to catch a whale; All the water he had got was in his mother's pail. Watch out,' he says to me, 'or you'll get what you asked for.'

In the emergency room Jane goes to the counter with their insurance information, with the description from the police that her husband was involved in a fatal car accident the afternoon before and appeared disoriented at the scene.

'That's not what happened,' George bellows. 'The fucking SUV was like a big white cloud in front of me, I couldn't see over it, couldn't see around it, I couldn't help but punch through it like a cheap piece of aluminum, like a fat fucking pillow. The airbag punched me back, slammed me, knocked the wind right outta me, and when I finally got out there were people pushed together like lasagne. The boy in the back doesn't stop crying. I wanted to just punch him but his mother was looking at me, her eyes popping out of her head.'

As George is talking, two large men make their way towards him from the rear. He doesn't see it coming. They grab him. He fights back. He's strong. They're strong. In the end they win. And I wonder, was it necessary?

The next time we see George, he's in a cubical in the back of the emergency room, arms and legs tied to a gurney

'Do you know why you're here?' a doctor asks him.

'I've got bad aim,' George says.

'Can you remember what happened?'

'It's more like I'll never forget. I left work at about eight, drove towards home, decided to stop for a bite, which is not something I normally do, but I was tired, I can admit that. I didn't see her. As soon as I realized I'd hit something I stopped. I stayed with her. I held on to her. She was slipping out from under herself, fluid was leaking out, like a broken engine. I felt sick. And I hated her. I hated her for how stunned she looked, how grey, the pool forming beneath her—I didn't even know where exactly it was coming from. It started to rain. There were people with blankets—where did the blankets come from? I heard sirens. People in cars drove around us, I saw them staring.'

'What is he talking about?' I insist. 'That's not what happened. That's not this accident. Perhaps it's another one, but it's not his.'

'George,' Jane says. 'I read the police report, that's not the right story. Are you thinking of something else? Something you dreamed or something you saw on television?'

'Any history of mental or neurological symptoms?' the doctor asks. We all shake our heads. 'What line of work are you in?'

'Law,' George says. 'I studied law.'

'Why don't you leave him with us for now? We'll order some tests,' the doctor says, 'and then we'll talk further.'

The next morning we go to see him. 'Is this the right place for him, a psych ward?' I ask.

'It's the suburbs,' she says. 'How dangerous could a suburban psych ward be?'

He is alone in his room.

'Good morning,' Jane says.

'Is it—I wouldn't know.'

'Did you have your breakfast?' she asks, seeing the tray in front of him.

'It's dog food,' he says. 'Take it home to Tessie.'

'Your breath stinks—did you brush your teeth?' I ask.

'Don't they do it for you?' George asks. 'I've never been in a mental hospital before.'

'It's not a mental hospital,' Jane says. 'You just happen to be in the mental unit.'

'I can't go into the bathroom,' he says. 'I can't look at myself in the mirror—I can't.' He begins to sound hysterical.

'Do you need me to help you? I can help you clean up.' Jane opens the toilet kit they have left for him.

'Don't make her do this,' I say. 'You're not an infant. Snap out of it—stop acting like a zombie.'

He begins to cry. I walk out of the room. As I leave, Jane is running water on a washcloth.

In the evening after work, Claire comes to the hospital bringing Chinese food from the city for the four of us. We reheat it in the microwave marked FOR PATIENT USE—NO MEDICAL PRODUCTS. We clean our hands with the bottles of foaming cleanser that are on every wall of every room. I worry about putting anything down, touching any surfaces—suddenly I fear I could be eating deadly germs.

'You have a big trip coming up,' Jane says, making conversation with Claire.

'I'm going to China for a few days,' Claire says.

'No one goes to China for a couple of days,' George growls.

Refusing to eat, he will only allow himself to suck the hot mustard directly from the plastic packets—self-punishment. No one stops him.

'When are you leaving?' Jane asks.

'Friday.'

I pass another packet of mustard to George.

Later, in private, Claire tells me not to leave Jane alone—it's all too strange. 'I wouldn't be surprised if she comes home one night and the family of the family is camped out on her lawn, or worse, inside her house. George destroyed them—he took their lives and they're going to want something back. Do Jane and George have a gun? If not they should get one.'

'What are you saying? You sound so paranoid. And even if it were true, you'd want me to be there to do what—scare them away or shoot them?'

'She's very vulnerable. Imagine if it were you: if you went nuts wouldn't you want someone to stay home with me and keep an eye on the house?'

'We live in an apartment with a doorman. If I went crazy, you'd be fine.'

'That's true, but Jane is not me. She needs someone. Also you should visit the surviving boy. The lawyer is going to tell you not to but just do it. There is a reason I'm a lawyer,' Claire says. 'I'm always thinking.'

And so without telling anyone I do it. I go and visit the boy.

'Are you from the insurance company?' someone asks.

I nod—is a nod the same as a lie?

'Do you have everything you need?' I ask, and I'm not sure why. They don't answer.

It's funny how quickly something becomes a routine, a way of doing business. I stay with Jane and it is as though we are playing house. At night I take out the trash, lock the door, she makes a snack, we watch a little television and read. I read whatever it was that George had been reading; his newspapers and magazines and a big history of Thomas Jefferson that sits beside the bed.

The accident happened and then it happened. It didn't happen the night of the accident or the night we all visited. It happened the night after that, the night after Claire told me not to leave Jane alone, the night after Claire left for China. Claire went on her trip, George went downhill and then it happened. It was the thing that was never meant to happen.

The evening visit to the hospital went badly. For reasons that were not clear, George was locked in a padded room, his arms bound to his body. We took turns peering through the small window. He looked horrible. Jane asked to go in and see him. The nurse cautioned her against it, but she insisted. Jane went to him, called his name. He looked at her; she swept his hair out of his face, wiped his furrowed brow, and he turned on her, he pinned her with his body and bit her again and again, breaking the skin in several places. The aides rushed in and pulled him off of her. She was taken downstairs and treated in the emergency room, the wounds cleaned and dressed. She was given some kind of a shot, like a rabies vaccination.

We came back to the house, had our tea and went about our business. I changed out of my clothes, the same clothes I'd been wearing for days and washing every night. I put on a pair of his pyjamas and went upstairs.

I hugged her. I wanted to be comforting. I was in his pyjamas, she was still dressed and I didn't think anything would happen. 'I apologize,' I said, without knowing what I was saying. And she was against me; she put her hands on the sides of her skirt and slid it down. Jane pulled me towards her.

There was one time that I almost told Claire about Thanksgiving— in fact I tried to tell her. It was one night just after sex when I was feeling particularly close to her. As I started to tell the story, Claire sat up straight; she pulled the sheet tight against her body and I backed away from what I was about to say. I changed it. I left out the kiss. And I just mentioned something about Jane brushing against me.

'You were in her way and she was trying to get past you and not get to you,' Claire said.

I didn't mention that I felt the head of my cock pressing against my sister-in-law's tight skirt, her hips, her thighs pressed together.

'Only you would think she was making a pass,' Claire said, disgusted.

'Only me,' I repeated.

She pulled me to her; her hips were narrow. My hand slid down into her panties. It was a new jungle, new wildlife. She sighed.

The feel of her, this private softness, was incredible. I remember thinking, This is not really going to happen—is it?

Her mouth was on me. She reached for something, some kind of cream; it started cold and then went warm. She stroked me, looking me straight in the eye. And then again her mouth was on me and there was no way of saying no. She pulled my trousers out from under, quickly had me down and was upon me, riding me. It was like nervous heaven. I exploded.

Drenched in her scent, but too shaken to shower or to fall asleep in their bed, I waited until she was asleep and then went downstairs into the kitchen and washed myself with dish soap. I was in my brother's kitchen at three in the morning, soaping my cock at his sink, drying myself with a dish towel that said 'Home Sweet Home'.

It happened again in the morning when she found me on the sofa, and then again in the afternoon after we visited him.

'What happened to your hand?' George asked her. He was back in his room with no memory of the night before.

Jane began to cry.

'You look like hell,' he said. 'Get some rest.'

'It's been a difficult time,' I said.

That evening we opened a bottle of wine and did it again, more slowly, deliberately, intentionally.

Somehow the hospital let him out, or perhaps he just decided to leave. Inexplicably, he was able to walk out unnoticed in the middle of the night. He comes home in a taxi, using money that he's found wrinkled at the bottom of his pocket. He can't find his keys so he rings the bell and the dog barks.

I think I remember that part—the dog barking.

Or maybe he didn't ring the bell and the dog didn't bark. Maybe he took the spare key from under the mat, or from inside the fake rock in the garden by the door, and like an intruder he came silently into his own house.

He comes upstairs thinking he'll crawl into his bed, but his spot is taken. I don't know how long he stood there. I don't know how long he waited before he lifted the lamp from her side of the bed and smashed it onto her head.

That's when I woke up.

She was screaming. The one blow wasn't enough. She tried to get up; the lamp wasn't even broken. George looked at me and then picked the lamp up again and swung it at her, a big blow like a baseball bat. The porcelain vase that was the base, exploded against her head. By then I was out of bed. He dropped what remained of the lamp—blood streaming down his fingers—picked up the telephone and tossed it to me.

'Call it in,' he said.

I stood facing him. We were the same. We have the same gestures, the same faces, the family chin, my father's brow, the same mismatched selves. I was staring at him, not knowing how this was going to work out. An awful gurgling sound prompted me to dial the phone.

Accidentally, I drop the phone. I bend to pick it up and my brother's foot catches me under the chin, kicking me hard. My head snaps back. I am down as he leaves the room. I see his hospital gown under his clothes, hanging out like some kind of tail. She is making a horrible noise. I can't get up. I dial 0. I dial 0 like it is a hotel, like I expect someone to answer. There is a long recording, a kind of spoken-word essay about what the 0 button can do for you, and I realize it will be forever before a real person comes on. I hang up and after several shaky starts am able to call the police.

'A woman has been beaten. Hurry,' I say, and give them the address.

I go into the bathroom and get a washcloth as though that will help, as though I can just wipe the blood away. I couldn't even find the spot, her head was a mash, blood and hair and bone and lamp, and I just held the washcloth there and waited.

And it took forever.

Later when I went downstairs George was in the kitchen drinking a cup of coffee. There was blood on his hands and flecks of something on his face—pieces of the lamp, I realized later, shards.

'May I have some clothing?' George asked.

'Escort him,' one of the cops said. 'Take the clothes he's wearing as evidence and search what he wants to put on.'

When George comes back he's wearing my clothes, the ones I've been wearing for days. The ones I washed and had folded and draped over a chair.

'Those are my clothes,' I say.

'And those are my pyjamas,' he says, looking at me. 'Now you've gone and done it.'

'I'm not going to be able to help you this time,' I tell him.

'Have I committed a crime?'

'It's hard to know, isn't it?' one of the cops says.

I dress. The cops take George, the ambulance takes Jane, and an extra cop waits for me. I take the house key and her purse; it has her cellphone, it has whatever information will be needed.

'Are we going to the hospital or the police station?'

'Station,' he says.

Before we go I call Claire in China. 'There's been an accident. Jane has been injured.'

'Should I come there?' Claire asks.

'No,' I say. I am hating her for how willing she was to let me go. Why did she send me into Jane's arms: was she testing me? Did she really trust me that much?

A t the police station, I am told that I am not a suspect, that they just need to ask a couple of questions to fill in the story.

'Did you have sex with her?'

'I'm going to decline to answer that.'

'Were you having sex with her when your brother came home?'

'No.'

'Had you been having a relationship with your brother's wife?'

'No. I was there because my brother has been in the hospital.'

'And your wife?'

'She's in China. It was her suggestion that I stay with my brother's wife.'

'How would you describe your relationship with your brother?'

'Close but competitive. I remember when they bought the house. I remember helping them to pick things out—the kitchen tiles. After the accident I comforted her.'

The cop drives me to the hospital. The doctors tell me that if Jane survives she will never be the same. 'Even in the short time she's been with us, there has been a decline. She is retreating as if folding into herself. We have taken her into the operating room to clean the wound;

we'll drill holes to accommodate the swelling. The prognosis is poor.'

I have to call the children and say, Your mother is in a coma and your father is in jail.

I dial the oldest one first. 'I comforted her—after the accident. I was asleep in your parents' bed when he came home.'

'Did he walk in on you?' the boy asks.

'He came home unexpectedly. He saw us sleeping. Your father has gone insane—they're not even going to be able to hold him responsible. Maybe you should come home or maybe you don't want to come home. Maybe you never want to come home again. Whatever it is we all understand. I remember when your parents bought the house, I remember picking out things.'

The boy tells me that he will call his sister—I am grateful for that, for not having to go through this again.

When Jane comes out of surgery I see her. They bring her down the hall attached to a huge mechanical ventilator—her head wrapped like a mummy, her eyes black and blue, broken nose. Her face looks like a meatball. There is a hose coming out from under the blanket, urine back at the end of the bed.

I kissed her there last night—she said no one had ever done that before—and then I kissed her again, deeply. I made out with her down there. I used my tongue—no one will ever know that.

I am telling myself that I did what I was told. Claire told me to stay. Jane wanted me—she pulled me towards her. Why am I being so weak? Why am I blaming the victim? I ask myself, did you ever think you should stop yourself or someone else but in the moment you couldn't or didn't? Now I understand the meaning of—it just happened. Or—it was an accident.

A police officer comes to find me in the waiting room. 'Does your brother have a history of violence?'

'Not really,' I say. 'Why?'

'We found these in his pocket.' He hands me a wad of newspaper clippings: LOVE TRIANGLE GONE WRONG. TRYST AWRY. CUCKOLDED HUSBAND PLUNGES 20 FLOORS. THE BEST DUMPLINGS IN HONK KONG. WESTCHESTER LOVE NEST RANSACKED. Scribbled on the clips are little notations: 'I would have done it differently,' 'Good job,' 'Next time don't forget Grandma.' The handwriting looks familiar.

'Someone has been in a library looking things up. Someone has been doing a lot of thinking.'

'Where did you find these?' I ask.

'In the pocket of the pants he wore to the station. What were you thinking?'

I shrug. 'I suppose we all try to make sense of things.'

I visit George on Tuesdays. They bring him to the visiting area in shackles; we speak through holes drilled in thick Plexiglas, holes filled with the spittle of every criminal's family that has come before us.

'How are you?' I ask.

'How could I be?'

'It was an accident,' I say.

'I am not asking for your opinion,' George says.

'How are my roses?' he asks.

'They have black spot. I'll spray again tonight if it doesn't rain.' □

GRANTA

PIE-KAH

Helen Oyeyemi

Helen Oyeyemi

when miranda

finally discharged herself from the clinic, Eliot and Luc came to pick
her up. They looked at her strangely. She didn't know what it could
be: she was more normal than she had been in months. She sat in
the back of the car and looked very seriously at her suitcase while
her twin brother and father looked at her, looked away, looked at
her again. She passed a hand over her hair, which lay meek and wispy
against her neck. Her hair had been bobbed out of necessity at first:
she'd been admitted to the clinic because one morning Eliot had
found her wordless and thoughtful. It had been a long night, a perfect
full moon tugging the sky around it into clumsy wrinkles. Miranda
had been bleeding slightly from the scalp, and her wrists were bound
together with extreme dexterity and thin braids of her own hair. It
had been six months since then, but her hair had been kept short.
She didn't know why, she couldn't remember having expressed a
preference. There was much that she was unable to remember.

It was in the clinic that Miranda lost her inner 'I'. She was no
longer able to take herself seriously enough to be associated with any
action. Miranda Silver, she thought shamefacedly, is a complete joke
and is not deserving of a personality. After her mother's death, her
brother and father had held themselves up and had tried to heal with
their eyes open, while Miranda had gone another way and completely
wimped out. Especially unclear were the days immediately after she
and Eliot had heard the news about Lily. She remembered going into
school and everyone being very sorry for her loss, but Eliot said that
he had gone to school and she had stayed at home. The incident with
the hair was completely lost: it seemed that when she'd left herself
she'd left completely. It was not worth trying to fetch the images back,
pointless trying to identify what exactly it was that had made her
snap. The two doctors who had been 'working with' her at the clinic
had mistaken her resignation for stubbornness, and constantly
hovered on the edge of pressing her to remember. She objected mildly,
with a sense of wasting her father's money. The clinic was a private
one; her room had its own phone line and plush curtains, and in the
common room people checked their email and played snooker. She had
agreed to be admitted to an adolescent psychiatric unit because no one
at home knew how to help her feel comfortable. She had had such a
strong feeling that she needed to talk to someone who would tell her

some secret that would make everything all right. She had been unable to think who it was. She had sat awake long hours downstairs, looking into the empty white arch of the fireplace, her hands on her ribcage. Who was it that needed to talk to her, that she needed to talk to? She had gone through lists of people it could be. She could only think of people that it couldn't be. It wasn't Lily, it wasn't her father, it wasn't Eliot, it wasn't any of the poets whose words stuck spikes in her. It wasn't God. She did not think it was someone who was alive. She did not think it was anyone who existed, this messenger. So she went with her father to see the doctor. She had signed a form, her name near her father's, and admitted herself to the clinic.

When she got home, she went to her bedroom. She rattled down some pills without water and lay back and didn't want to shut her eyes. With the curtains drawn it could almost be night. But she heard someone talking to Luc downstairs, she heard the clatter of cutlery, she heard the whir of

the lift

broke down in the night. No one knew what time. The timing became important when Azwer, the gardener, and Ezma, the housekeeper, couldn't find their oldest daughter in the morning. Luc had got the attic converted into two large, low rooms. Azwer and Ezma slept in one, while Deme and her little sister, Suryaz, slept in a double bed in the second room. Deme was ten and Suryaz was seven. The two of them went about with their hands joined, smiling and full of secrets so simple that they were given up if asked after. Deme and Suryaz hopped more than they walked; it was always as if they had just left the site of some mirth particular to them. They babbled in prettily accented voices. The combination of their near-identical manes of curly hair and their mother's tendency to dress them in similarly patterned dresses meant that Suryaz had an air of having been formed without detail. The effect was of a two-part Russian doll set: Deme was the outer case, and it had been the doll-maker's intention that you would only see Suryaz if you opened up Deme for inspection.

Both girls admitted that they had spent the day before playing around with the lift, pressing buttons for three floors all at once, holding the DOOR OPEN button until the lift zinged with confusion. That was reason enough for the lift to later get confused and try to travel unbidden from first floor to second, grinding to a halt between the two. But why was Deme standing in the corner of the lift when Luc, Azwer and the technician prised the doors open? She was standing, not sitting or kneeling. They found her in the back left corner, where there had once been a hole in the floor, and she was standing on tiptoe, so close to the alarm button, looking at it in fact, her eyes wide as if all night she had been sinking and all night a stubborn thing in her had kept her on her feet. 'I tucked her into bed with Suryaz,' Ezma kept repeating. 'I did, didn't I?' she said to Suryaz, who looked and looked and then shrugged. Ezma hissed at her, but Suryaz would say nothing. At first Deme wouldn't talk either, then when Ezma shouted at her, she spat a large piece of Suryaz's Lego out into her hand and tried her best to answer the questions that everyone levelled at her, even Eliot, who tugged her ponytail and teased her about her 'midnight journey'.

The only reply Deme ventured was that she didn't know.

'Why did you get into the lift so late, when everyone was sleeping?'

'I don't know.'

'Deme, where is your sense? Why didn't you just ring the alarm?'

'I don't know.'

Miranda asked, 'Deme, are you all right?'

Deme and Suryaz leaned on each other and Suryaz said, 'Thank you, she is all right.'

Miranda, Luc and Eliot slept on the third floor; above the guests but below the housekeepers. Miranda told Eliot, 'I heard someone crying last night. But I thought I was just remembering the clinic.'

Or herself, she had thought she was hearing herself.

Azwer gave his notice the day of Eliot and Miranda's Cambridge University interviews. He stopped Luc as he was on his way out to meet the twins by the car. Azwer said, 'My wife and daughters are afraid. If we stay they will only become more afraid, and then something bad will happen.' His heavy eyebrows lowered and he made some small, involuntary hand gesture that was recognizably superstitious, as if the words 'God forbid' had flowed into his body.

Luc said, 'Two weeks is too short notice for me to find replacements for you and Ezma. And we've had the lift looked at.'

Azwer said quickly, heatedly, 'It's not just the lift—'

Luc put his car keys down on the hall table, and tension pulled him taller. 'Then what?'

Azwer kept his eyes fixed on Luc.

Luc looked at Miranda, then lowered his voice and said to Azwer, 'Do you need more pay?'

Azwer spread his hands. 'We cannot stay.'

Azwer and Ezma, who had come to Britain from Armenia, didn't have papers; as far as the government was concerned, Luc was running the bed and breakfast alone. Luc said, 'Azwer, listen, Think about it. Where will you work? Where will you go?'

Azwer shrugged. 'To London.'

Since Azwer and Ezma were leaving, Miranda felt she should give their daughters something. Suryaz and Deme would each need a talisman, an object that smelled lovely, or that felt kind to the hand; such things are little suitcases to put sad feelings in so that they can go away by themselves. Miranda didn't have to go back to school until after the Christmas holidays, so for Suryaz she spent five nights under her bedroom lamp, making a cloth doll with a seed-pearl smile and rose petals for eyes. She slept sparingly and unwillingly. Rest seized her and kept her until she twitched awake two or three hours later. When Suryaz and Deme came home in the afternoons and sat down in the kitchen for their after-school snack, Miranda mustered the energy to shuffle downstairs. She poked her head around the kitchen door for a brief but fond sighting of Suryaz, who was invariably a creature of jam, all sticky mouth and gooey ringlets. She thought, soon I will have something to give you, and you don't know it yet. Each night Miranda worked on the doll, and then she spent the day in bed, half dreaming of her needle in a circle of white. On the night that Suryaz's doll was finished, she took her big bottle of attar of roses, unplugged its glass stopper and filled a bowl, then swam Suryaz's doll in it. When the doll was slack and fat with liquid, she removed it and dropped it on the floor, where it lay beside her with arms and legs spread until the morning, by which time it had dried out.

Deme was harder to think of a gift for—Deme who'd stood on tiptoe in a box in the night, looking at the alarm button. Deme wouldn't want a thing that flopped charmingly and had nothing to tell her. When Azwer and Ezma began loading things into Luc's car,

Miranda went to find Deme. 'Please come and choose a going-away present for yourself. Anything I have that you like,' she said, feeling shy now under the younger girl's glossy stare. The girls had become steely since the lift broke down; they seemed full of resolutions not to smile any more. Deme wouldn't come without Suryaz, so the three of them stood in Miranda's room, peering around in the gloom. Miranda covered the face of Lily's watch with her hand and thought to herself, Be giving. She watched Deme's eyes move from her books to the sticks of chalk that she kept in a Marlboro cigarette box.

'Never smoke,' she told Deme firmly.

Deme put her hand out and pointed at a hairbrush that Lily had given Miranda. It was bone-backed, with tiny skulls carved into it. Some of the skulls faced each other and were blended together at the jaw. Miranda had only recently realized that these were the skulls that were kissing. Deme chose that hairbrush, and Miranda wrapped it up in a silk scarf and gave it to her gladly. Suryaz stood by, rocking her new doll in the big pocket of her dress.

Suryaz bowed her head and her curls swung before her closed eyes, her face scrunched as if she was about to describe something and was trying to remember it with exactness and close attention. But she only seemed able to say, 'Oh, Miranda. Be careful.'

And Deme urged, 'It is true. You're nice, and you haven't been well. Do be careful.'

Ezma called her daughters' names from a floor down. Suryaz said something to Deme in Azeri. Deme replied to her, then turned a sweet smile on Miranda and dropped a square of lined writing paper on to Miranda's pillow.

Miranda shook hands with Suryaz. Deme shook hands with Miranda. Each said goodbye.

Miranda stretched, then sat for a while after the noise of their departure had died in their ears. She was feeling fragile and had missed her morning dose, so she took more pills than was customary for her and washed them down with vinegar. She poured attar of roses on to her tongue to mask the sourness her drink brought. She knelt down with her neck bowed, as though for an axe, and ran her perfume-wettened fingers through her hair.

Then she opened Suryaz and Deme's letter. It was written in a round and extra-neat hand that was unmarred by the splotches the fountain pen nib had made in several places.

The letter read:

Dear Miranda Silver,

<u>Very important warning!!! This house is bigger than you know!</u>
<u>This house is hiding stuff from you!</u>
We have been longing to talk to you about this before but you
would probably not believe us and now it is our last chance
because we are leaving. The looking people don't want us here;
they are angry about something and are trying to take it out on us.
Our mother knows, even though she pretends she doesn't because it
is easier that way.
We first saw the looking people about a year and a half ago, give
or take a few days. We do not know why we did not see them for
half a year. We heard noises and people walking but there are
always other people in this house, so how are we supposed to
know when there are extra people? Besides where is the room for
them, you may wonder (as we did)?
<u>Very important!!! On the extra floors of this house, that is where.</u>
There are two extra floors, maybe more than that, but we have
only been on two; after your floor there is a fourth and then there
is a fifth floor before the attic. When was the last time you went up
to the attic? We bet it was before us and our parents moved in,
wasn't it?
There are lots of people on the fourth and fifth floors. The lift
takes you to the fourth and fifth floors and you never know when
it will. So far we have always been able to leave by taking the
staircase, though we have never reached the fourth and fifth floors
by using the staircase, only by using the lift.
Things about the people on the fourth and fifth floors:
They are looking people. They look at you in a way that is very
unpleasant.
They are very tall people. They are the tallest people we have ever
seen. Actually they are not tall, they are something else. We do not
like the way these people look. They look very strange and it
makes us uncomfortable.
They move around and talk as if it is a big party, and they are

347

saying weird things and not answering each other's questions but just talking and saying what they feel like saying. It only *looks* as if they are talking to each other. They are not really talking to each other.

We have tried really hard and done a lot of spying but we have not been able to find out why.

And when me and Suryaz go into one of the rooms with all the people, they freeze and it is as if they never moved or talked at all, except that they keep looking in that horrible way, as if they would like to grab you and might do it. They never do, though. It is only that they all look in the same direction, at us. At first it was sort of scary fun to run in between them and stick our tongues out at them and stuff, but then we became more and more sure that the looking people would grab us, or that we would not be able to leave the fourth and fifth floors. We have discussed it and we don't know why we began to believe this.

We are not joking about here. We are trying to give you as much information as possible, to help you in the fight, since there has probably got to be a fight.

The night the lift broke down was the worst night.

I, Deme Kosarzadeh, solemnly declare that if I did not have a sister who had seen these things with me I would have <u>died of fright!</u>

I, Suryaz Kosarzadeh, solemnly declare that if I did not have a sister who had seen these things with me I would have <u>died of fright!</u>

This is the end of our letter.

Miranda folded the letter several times and put it in her pocket. She tried to smile, and managed, but not for long. She took the letter out and read it again. She was thinking things, but she couldn't understand her thoughts. It wasn't necessarily about Suryaz and Deme. It was more about the exhaustion of having finished Suryaz's doll, of having worked her eyes and her nerves for someone different and distant, someone who had lived in a different house from her when she'd thought they were all living in the same house.

On the ground floor, Miranda went down through a trapdoor and curled up in a corner of the indoor bomb shelter. She cried with her face turned to the wall. Lily had told her and Eliot that this house, with their great-grandmother inside it, had escaped the effects of a bomb in 1942, that the houses a short distance away had been torn apart, their roofs whirling away to reveal cakes of brick with savage bites taken out of them. The house was lucky. Or storing its collapse.

To live here without her mother... Miranda found that the sadness was far, far bigger than her, and it was forcing her back. The wall she leaned against had a damp, high temperature to it, like tears on skin.

☐

Somewhere the Wave

Derek Mahon

Once more the window and a furious fly
shifting position, niftier on the pane
than the slow liner or the tiny plane.
Dazzled by the sun, dazed by the rain,
today this frantic speck against the sky,
so desperate to get out in the open air
and cruise among the roses, starts to know
not all transparency is come and go.

But the window opens like an opened door
so the wild fly escapes to the airstream,
the raw crescendo of the crashing shore
and 'a radical astonishment at existence' –
a voice, not quite a voice, in the sea distance
listening to its own thin cetaceous whistle,
sea music gasp and sigh, slow wash and rustle.
Somewhere the wave is forming which in time...